SCHOOLS MAKING A DIFFERENCE: DIFFERENCE: LET'S BE REALISTIC!

SCHOOLS MAKING A DIFFERENCE: DIFFERENCE: LET'S BE REALISTIC!
School mix, school effectiveness
and the social limits of reform

Martin Thrupp

Open University Press
Buckingham · Philadelphia

Open University Press
Celtic Court
22 Ballmoor
Buckingham
MK18 1XW

email: enquiries@openup. co.uk
world wide web: http://www.openup.co.uk

and
325 Chestnut Street
Philadelphia, PA 19106, USA

First Published 1999

A catalogue record of this book is available from the British Library

ISBN   0 335 20212 8 (pb)   0 335 20213 6 (hb)

Library of Congress Cataloging-in-Publication Data
Thrupp. Martin, 1964–
     Schools making a difference – let's be realistic!: school mix, school effectiveness, and the social limits of reform/Martin Thrupp.
          p.   cm.
     Includes bibliographical references and index.
     ISBN 0-335-20213-6 (hb). – ISBN 0-335-20212-8 (pbk.)
     1. Educational evaluation – New Zealand – Case studies. 2. High schools – New Zealand – Sociological aspects – Case studies. 3. High school students – New Zealand – Social conditions – Case studies. 4. School integration – New Zealand – Case studies. 5. Working class – Education (Secondary) – New Zealand – Case studies. 6. Academic achievement – New Zealand – Case studies. 7. Educational change – Social aspects – New Zealand – Case studies. 8. Educational sociology – New Zealand – Case studies.   I. Title.
LB2822.75.T537   1999   98-41547
306.43'2'0993–dc21   CIP

Typeset by Type Study, Scarborough
Printed in Great Britain by St Edmundsbury Press Ltd, Bury St Edmunds, Suffolk

Contents

List of figures and tables

Preface and acknowledgements

This book reflects six years of work on the social limits of educational reform, including my doctoral research on school mix and other work on school markets and school accountability. However its deeper roots are to be found in my experiences as a young secondary (high) school teacher. I taught in a middle class suburban school before moving to a school with a much lower socioeconomic (SES) student intake. I enjoyed working in both schools but was quickly forced to come to terms with the quite different constraints and possibilities they offered to staff and students. It was this experience which created my interest in the question of school mix and its possible effects on school processes and student achievement.

One memory which stands out from my teaching experiences in both schools was the task of organizing 'tramping' (overnight hiking) trips for students in the two schools. At the first, the middle class school, students participated in large numbers, paid the required trip fees, arrived on the day with the necessary backpacks, sleeping bags, warm clothing and other equipment and generally took the experience in their stride, even though for some it was quite new. At the low-SES school almost nothing worked that easily. The idea of heading into the hills was new – and frightening – to many students and their families. Nor did students have easy access to the necessary funds and equipment. In the event I was usually able to work through these problems and run the trips successfully. Nevertheless the effort required of me seemed truly Herculean in comparison with my previous experiences at the middle class school.

Another memory is of a student at the middle class school with a reputation for being difficult and disruptive. Soon after I finished teaching there, I heard that the principal had announced in a staff meeting that the student would be leaving the school. This was apparently greeted with clapping and cheering from teachers, followed by even greater mirth when he announced that the student was to enrol at the lower SES school I had moved to: 'Ha Ha! Now Martin's going to have to deal with her!' Yet I was surprised to note that when she came to my new school she didn't stand out at all. Although her demeanour and actions did not seem to have changed, the school had so many 'problem' students that this student was quite unexceptional.

Experiences such as these, as well as a fortuitous meeting in 1992 with Prof. Hugh Lauder at Victoria University (now at the University of Bath), launched my doctoral investigation into school mix. Shortly afterwards I began work on the Smithfield Project, a major study of the impact of market policies on New Zealand schools (Hughes *et al.* 1999). More recently I have been part of a team which has researched New Zealand's Education Review Office (Robertson *et al.* 1997). These projects have helped me to understand better the implications of school mix, the reasons why policy makers frequently prefer to ignore the social limits of reform, and how they often manage quite successfully to do so.

Like many books, *Schools Making a Difference: Let's be Realistic!* has had to be juggled with other responsibilities, in my case parenting two young children, teaching, editing and research. I have also suffered from the common problem of wanting to say too much. In particular the original thesis included some 400 pages of rich case study material from the Wellington schools. Only some of this has been able to be included here because I have also wanted to offer the bigger research and policy picture. Nevertheless I hope there will be enough to open up the debate around school mix. Also, just as I was completing the book, I received a copy of *School Effectiveness for Whom?* by Slee *et al.* (1998) which contains a fresh round of critiques of the school effectiveness and school improvement movement. I have included some insights from this collection here but would also recommend it to readers.

Thanks are due to those who helped with the preparation of this book. I am particularly grateful to Ian McLaren who edited a draft and also to Hugh Lauder and Cathy Wylie for their constructive criticisms. Diane Bushell, Glenys Fayen, Joan Gibbons, Garth Ritchie, Val Lazenby, Logan Moss, Grant Saxton, Sue Turner-Jones and Mary Wernham also all helped in various ways. I also want to use this opportunity to thank others who have supported my work over the last six years. Apart from good colleagues at Victoria University of Wellington and the University of Waikato too numerous to mention, they include Sandie Aikin, Stephen Ball, Phil Brown, John Codd, Bronwyn Cross, Roger Dale, Brian Delany, John Fitz, Bill Firestone, Liz Gordon, Dick Harker, David Hughes, Ben Levin, Ruth Mansell, Lauren Massey, Mark Olssen, Ken Rae, Peter Roberts, Susan Robertson, Richard Smith, Kelvin Smythe, Ivan Snook and Geoff Whitty. To all of these and others I have overlooked, my heartfelt thanks.

I must acknowledge those in the Wellington schools who cannot be named but who made much of this account possible. The matched students and their classmates and friends shared their school lives, dreams and disappointments. The teachers, guidance staff and principals of Tui, Wakefield, Victoria and

Plimmer Colleges also gave very generously of their precious time, as did an independent group of Waikato teachers.

I am also grateful for permission to use material here which has appeared previously as part of the following articles, chapters and reports:

Thrupp, M. (1995) Poor performers or just plain poor? Assumptions in the neo-liberal account of school failure, *Waikato Journal of Education*, 1: 45–60.

Thrupp, M. (1995) The school mix effect: the history of an enduring problem in educational research, policy and practice, *British Journal of Sociology of Education*, 16(3): 183–203.

Robertson, S., Dale, R., Thrupp, M., Vaughan, K. and Jacka, S. (1997) *A Review of ERO – Final Report for the PPTA*. Auckland: University of Auckland.

Thrupp, M. (1997) ERO and South Auckland schools: a case of ideology over analysis? *New Zealand Annual Review of Education*, 6: 51–70.

Thrupp, M. (1997) How school mix shapes school processes: a comparative study of New Zealand schools, *New Zealand Journal of Education Studies*, 32(1): 53–82.

Thrupp, M. (1997) School mix and the outcomes of educational quasi-markets, in M. Olssen and K. Morris Matthews (eds) *New Zealand Education Policy in the 1990s*. Palmerston North: Dunmore Press.

Thrupp, M. (1997) Shaping a crisis: the Education Review Office and South Auckland schools, in M. Olssen and K. Morris Matthews (eds) *New Zealand Education Policy in the 1990s*. Palmerston North: Dunmore Press.

Thrupp, M. (1998) The art of the possible: organizing and managing high and low socioeconomic schools, *Journal of Education Policy*, 13(2): 197–219.

Thrupp, M. (1998) Exploring the politics of blame: school inspection and its contestation in New Zealand and England, *Comparative Education*, 34(2): 195–209.

Finally, I especially want to thank my family, particularly my wife Tracy Buckland. As well as tolerating my distractions, Tracy proofed the final draft of this book.

Martin Thrupp

PART 1

THE PROBLEM OF SCHOOL MIX

1

Introduction: the social limits of reform

While schools located in middle class suburbs present challenges for today's teachers and school leaders, those who work in low-socioeconomic school settings face even greater problems. Often located in areas with high levels of unemployment and crime, as well as poor housing and health conditions, these schools are required to take on a huge caring role in addition to their academic one in order to achieve academic goals. Working class schools also have to cope with many students who bring low levels of prior achievement and who are frequently disaffected. Many of these schools are underfunded and inadequately staffed compared to schools in wealthier areas. They also attract little status or political support. In short, despite the evident humour and dignity of most staff and students, low-socioeconomic (SES) schools face extremely tough problems: they are at the sharp end of what Kozol (1991) has called 'savage inequalities'.

Given all of this, many accounts of the reform of working class schools are remarkably optimistic. Through the use of better management and teaching practices, low-SES schools are seen as capable of 'success against the odds' (National Commission on Education 1996). Others predict 'an end to failure in urban education' (Barber 1995), 'success for all' is on the cards (Slavin 1996), while some are even committed to 'failure free' schooling (Reynolds and Stringfield 1996). A similarly buoyant outlook can often be found among those who write about the reform of teachers and teaching. Skilful and inspirational teachers are regarded as able to overcome huge impediments. The OECD (1994a: 21) notes a common theme of research on teacher quality: 'Gifted teachers create excellence almost regardless of what is going on around them.'

Such upbeat discussions about the possible reform of low-SES schools and teaching practices stem from what might be called the 'effectiveness and improvement' (E&I) fields of educational research: school 'effectiveness', school 'improvement', school 'restructuring', school 'change', school 'leadership', school 'development', school 'management', teacher 'effectiveness' and teacher 'quality'. Writers in these often overlapping areas have an unashamedly practical orientation – the goal of trying to find feasible ways to improve classrooms, schools and school systems. Over the last two decades they have sent a powerful message to policy makers and practitioners alike – that teachers and schools 'can make a difference'. This of course has been a welcome message, especially heartening when the prevailing theme of earlier research was that schools could not compensate for society (Bernstein 1970). Not surprisingly, E&I research has become extremely popular, in many respects the educational research success story of our time.

Nevertheless, the central theme of this book is that the 'schools can make a difference' message has been thoroughly overplayed. At first this may seem a familiar claim. After all, as recent titles such as *No Quick Fixes* (Stoll and Myers 1998) suggest, it has become apparent to many E&I writers themselves that 'failing' schools are proving much harder to 'turn around' than almost anyone expected a decade ago. A. Hargreaves (1997a ix) has cautioned that 'fundamental educational change is even more difficult, complex and controversial than the change literature has acknowledged so far' while Fullan (1997: 216) notes that there are 'many legitimate reasons to be discouraged'. But E&I writers drawing breath to reconsider school and teacher reform usually remain optimistic about its possibilities. For instance Evans (1996) criticizes school improvement literature for its relentless assertiveness but still goes on to argue that '[school] culture change can occur' (p. 49). In a similar vein Stringfield (1997:143) suggests that while the USA is 'perpetually awash in "new" and self-proclaimed "highly effective" programmes for improving students' academic achievement', schools can still become 'High Reliability Organizations' (HROs).

However I shall suggest that even some of the revised level of confidence now apparent among E&I researchers is likely to be misplaced. This is because the emerging E&I discourse of constraints on reform, while emphasizing instructional, organizational and policy/systems problems, remains insufficently critical. In Dale's (1992: 206) terms it is too often 'problem solving' research which 'takes the world as it finds it' rather than 'standing back from the existing social order and asking how that social order comes about'. In contrast, in this book I want to work within the more searching traditions of what Grace (1995) calls 'policy scholarship' (as a critical alternative to a technicist 'policy science') and of what Moore (1996) calls 'sociology *of* education' (rather than 'sociology *for* education'). While not eschewing the solving of school problems I therefore want to consider a wider social and political context than E&I research typically does, and by doing so highlight some problems which plague this research literature and its often questionable claims. I also want to join Whitty *et al.* (1998) in the important task of attempting to bridge the 'conceptual gulf' between empirical studies of schools and the 'bigger picture' of national and global restructuring.

Similar goals have also been expressed by many of the authors in Slee *et al.* (1998). What is also offered here, however, is perhaps the first worked through example of an alternative approach. *Schools Making a Difference: Let's Be Realistic!* focuses on the likely impact on school processes and student achievement of what I call *school mix* – the social class composition of a school's student intake. I shall suggest that many school processes which have been identified as contributing to student achievement may be less independent of school mix than researchers have typically allowed. Instead, aspects of schooling such as student relations, classroom instruction and school organization and management may be powerfully influenced by school mix. The likely effect of this will be to lift mean levels of student achievement in middle class settings and reduce mean levels of achievement in low-SES settings.

This view that school mix may have a significant influence on school processes poses important challenges to current thinking in the E&I fields. First, it raises questions about the 'value added' by schools. It suggests that much of the so-called 'school effect' which has been found by school effectiveness studies may not reflect a school's effectiveness at all, but continue to be indirectly related to student body characteristics by way of school processes that are influenced by school mix. Second, it suggests that many effectiveness factors identified as contributing to student achievement will be hard to replicate. This is because while they may be *school-based*, they may nevertheless not be *school-caused*. They will relate to students' class backgrounds and therefore be difficult to modify. Third, the argument for school mix also critiques the notions of school 'ethos', 'climate' and 'culture', as they are used in the E&I literature. Whereas this literature tends to view these as organizational features of schools created mostly by their staff, especially principals or headteachers, I shall argue that they often reflect school mix. Finally, investigation into school mix emphasizes the negotiated order of schools. It treats teaching and learning as a two-way process, rather than something imposed by teachers and principals on passive pupils, as the E&I literature frequently seems to assume.

These may seem to be new challenges to the findings of E&I researchers, however the issues involved have a long history. Ever since the seminal Coleman report (Coleman *et al.* 1966) there has been continuing debate within quantitative school effectiveness research (SER) about whether the effectiveness of schools is primarily due to their student characteristics or to their policies and practices independent of intake. Although Coleman and other early researchers did point to the importance of school mix, in a polemic attempt to prove that 'schools *can* make a difference', SER over the last two decades has tended to ignore or downplay the impact of school mix. Thus the effect of school mix on achievement (often known in this literature as a 'contextual' or 'compositional' effect of SES) is usually only regarded as small or negligible. This reflects what Mac An Ghaill (1996) has referred to as the 'decentring of social class' in SER. Yet among E&I proponents, SER is often seen as well founded, indeed sometimes as the most rigorous E&I field of all (Hopkins *et al.* 1994). This perception helps to highlight the fact that other kinds of E&I research have always lacked a focus on social class. Here social class has been not so much 'decentred' as never present anyway.

The politics of polarization and blame

My motive for raising these issues is not simply to rain on the E&I parade. This body of literature has given teachers and principals/headteachers a sense of direction in difficult times. Sarason (1995: 22) points out that although hope is 'no universal solvent', it is certainly a necessary prerequisite to bring about any change. What's more, as my two-year-old daughter Grace recently reminded me one summer night when she solemnly asked to go outside to 'touch the moon', excessive hope in some contexts can be rather delightful!

Nevertheless the E&I message that 'schools can make a difference' entirely fails to question the longstanding provision of schooling via a social hierarchy of schools (what I refer to here as the *social class segregation* of schooling). Essentially the E&I literature tends to put social class segregation in the 'too hard' basket and therefore helps to naturalize this phenomenon. For instance, Scheerens (1992: 93) argues that 'High numbers of disadvantaged pupils and ethnic minorities push down the performance of the entire pupil population [of a school]' but adds, 'Because the central concern [here] is with the "construction" of effective schools no further attention is given to these contextual characteristics'. Yet this sort of approach could hold out false hope to teachers and principals who are asked to put energy into activities which have comparatively limited effect because of the effects of school mix. As Whitty *et al.* (1998: 113) put it, 'lack of contextualisation can lead to a false optimism, exaggerating the extent to which local agency can challenge structural inequalities'. The E&I approach also fails to critique the likely unequal impact of segregation on children's life chances. In contrast we shall see that the idea that school mix does have a significant impact on achievement reinforces the importance of viewing attendance at high-SES schools as a class strategy.

Social class segregation has been an enduring problem in educational provision but Scheeren's account also ignores the way that contemporary educational policies are able to have some ameliorating effect upon levels of social class segregation and/or take account of it to a greater or lesser extent. This kind of perspective highlights the problem that E&I literature may have provided direct or indirect support for the often inequitable effects of the restructuring of education systems around the globe over the last two decades.[1] This restructuring has both managerial and market or 'quasi-market' dimensions which vary from country to country but are generally marked by the withdrawal of the state from direct responsibility for educational provision in the name of 'self-management' or increased 'autonomy' while retaining control from a distance, through 'accountability' and 'target-setting'. There is also the development of market competition between schools under the rubric of choice. Cutting across all of these reforms in a way that suggests that they will be very damaging for low-SES schools and their students are important issues related to social class and school mix. I refer to these as the *politics of polarization and blame.*

By the politics of polarization I mean the increasing social class differentiation of school intakes as a result of parental choice in education, as well as the growing disparities in educational resources and educational quality which result from this within the context of school self-management. As we shall see, evidence from a number of countries suggests that market-led 'choice' policies not only fail to counter existing levels of segregation between schools but also have a polarizing effect on school intakes as middle class parents 'exit' schools with predominantly working class intakes whenever this becomes possible. To many E&I writers the growing gap between rich and poor schools is of no great moment because they believe that schools can still be effective, irrespective of their intake. But what if school effectiveness *is* linked to school mix? This suggests reduced levels of achievement in (increasingly) working class schools, and enhanced levels of achievement in (increasingly) middle class schools as a result of educational markets. This possibility has been hinted at by critics of educational markets but not previously examined in any depth. In this respect the present study can be seen as part of a 'second wave' of studies of choice concerned with the impact of commodifying education on children's experiences of schooling (Dale 1997).

Another aspect of the polarization argument has to do with school autonomy or self-management. By suggesting that schools are capable of being largely self-managing, self-evaluating and self-improving, E&I research may have underpinned decentralizing reforms which have removed important forms of administrative support and funding in the name of more autonomy for schools. The problem here is that although self-management may work for schools in middle class settings, E&I researchers are likely to have underestimated the intense intake-related pressures which accrue to teachers and school leaders in working class settings and the effects of unequal resourcing and so assumed that these schools can do more than they really can. Despite claims of the existence of exemplary low-SES schools, the school mix thesis suggests that decentralization could be expected to be much less successful in low-SES settings because of insufficient time, energy and material resources to implement demands from central agencies or to undertake school improvements.

If the politics of polarization have to do with the way in which between-school social class disparities in education are actually intensified by recent reforms, the politics of blame refer to the way in which these disparities are explained away as a technical rather than social or political matter by those who place their faith in market forces. A neo-liberal strand of the politics of blame links the popularity of schools to their performance rather than their intakes. Schools which 'lose' in educational markets are seen as those whose teachers and principals have not been able to improve enough to boost their reputation and hence the size of their student intakes. The running down and eventual failure of such schools can therefore be justified by neo-liberals as simply the price to be paid for a quality education system. Again E&I research tends to provide at least tacit support for this view because of its insistence that schools can dramatically improve. Yet given that most schools in decline in the marketplace have low-SES intakes, the idea of a school mix effect challenges the neo-liberal account of the failure of schools since it suggests that teachers and principals at (low-SES) declining schools may often be overwhelmed rather than ineffective, as they are typically painted.

The managerialist 'evaluative state' (Neave 1988) also frequently employs the politics of blame. The introduction of common yardsticks of school accountability through central inspection agencies such as England's Office for Standards in Education (Ofsted) and New Zealand's Education Review Office (ERO) and through league tables of performance indicators has been supported by the general claim of E&I researchers that substantial reform of low-SES schools is feasible, along with the attempts by some school effectiveness researchers to provide these agencies with value-added data on student performance. However as Tyack and Cuban (1995) note, schools can easily shift from panacea to scapegoat. Governments have often used E&I arguments to construct school failure as the responsibility of schools alone with any reference to the broader socio-political context, such as the impact of poverty, ruled out as an excuse for poor performance. Nevertheless if school mix does have a significant effect, even when students' individual background characteristics are taken into account, schools can not be expected to perform at the same level unless the impact of their group characteristics is also carefully taken into account. (Of course this is still only a means of better considering inequalities between schools rather than actually addressing them.)

A further problem with the E&I literature is that it may have acted as a kind of Trojan horse for the neo-liberal agenda by encouraging school staff to accept the politics of blame. This is because E&I literature uncritically fosters the belief that teachers and principals largely control, and are therefore responsible for, student achievement.

On the face of it then, school mix cannot be ignored. It appears to go to the heart of enduring questions about the impact of unequal access and provision of education as well as to current debates over choice, self-management, accountability, standards and the role of the state in education. At the same time, whether or not school mix does have an important impact on school processes and student achievement is a complex and contested issue, and one which is considered here in some detail.

The approach of this book

In order to examine the question of school mix and its implications, my account analyses several kinds of research literature and discusses the findings of an empirical study of students and schools I completed recently in Wellington, New Zealand (Thrupp 1996). Chapter 2 illustrates how the effect of school mix on student achievement is an issue which has often been overlooked because researchers have assumed or wished it resolved. This chapter reviews SER literature since the 1960s to show how political, ideological and methodological considerations have coloured it to make the question of the impact of school mix very difficult to answer. Given the limitations of this work, I argue that a case can be made for school mix having a significant effect on student achievement, and that the most rewarding direction for further research is to explore likely causal mechanisms through detailed qualitative research.

Chapter 3 then draws on a range of research literature to hypothesize causal mechanisms and describes how the Wellington study was designed to explore them. It is suggested that three mechanisms, or some combination of them, is likely to be involved – reference group processes, instructional processes, and organizational and management processes. The Wellington study set about investigating these possibilities by focussing on the experiences of 13 matched working class students attending four secondary schools with varying social mix and organizational characteristics. A nested approach to data collection, analysis and presentation and the use of multiple data sources created a particularly rich and wide-ranging comparative picture of school processes.

Chapter 4 aims to familarize readers with the four Wellington schools studied and to give an overview of their major features as found by the study. Chapters 5, 6 and 7 summarize the main findings of the Wellington study in relation to each of the sets of processes thought to cause the impact of school mix. Collectively they point to numerous reference group, instructional and organizational/management advantages which accrued to the matched students at the middle class schools. The matched students at these schools learnt alongside students with a wider range of curriculum-relevant experiences/ social capital, higher academic goals, higher SES occupational aspirations/ expectations and less involvement in 'alienated' student subcultures than those at the less advantaged school. The middle class schools were able to support more academic school programmes and their teachers taught classes which were more compliant and more able to cope with difficult work. The classes used more demanding texts and other teaching resources and their teachers were more qualified and more motivated. The middle class schools also had more efficient and easily accomplished daily routines and less pressured guidance and discipline systems. Their senior management teams had fewer student, staff, marketing and fundraising problems and more time to devote to planning and monitoring performance.

Chapter 8 pulls these findings together to argue for a 'whole school' effect, based cumulatively on the numerous factors discussed in Chapters 5, 6, and 7. I draw on Bourdieu's well-known theories of relations between home and school to suggest a theoretical framework for understanding a school mix effect. This chapter also looks at the study's most immediate implications for school practice by revisiting the characteristics of 'effective' or 'successful' schools and considering how much the staff of working class schools can really do to promote such characteristics.

Chapter 9 discusses social class segregation between schools and the politics of polarization and blame. I suggest that the intuitive preference of many parents for high-SES schools may have some tangible basis because of the advantageous effects of their school mix. The difficulty however is that what may be good for some individuals will be damaging for the education of others. Related to this I consider how recent policies and practices related to school markets and self-management are likely to have the effect of polarizing school quality. I also examine how the impact of school mix on school and teacher performance is typically ignored or played down in ways which unfairly attribute blame to the staff of low-SES schools. I look particularly at New Zealand's ERO, Ofsted and 'special measures' legislation in England, school performance indicators and the use of generic criteria for evaluating teachers.

Chapter 10 returns to the E&I literature, but this time to review critically recent work in areas such as school improvement, school development and teacher quality. It is important to see whether writers in these generally less quantitative but increasingly popular 'improvement' fields are questioning of the SER assertion of policy and practice over mix, or whether this perspective is simply carried over into improvement writing. This chapter also considers evidence of the support of improvement research for the politics of polarization and blame.

Chapter 11 concludes by looking to the future. Although not convinced about the possibility of greatly improving academic achievement in low-SES settings through better management and teaching alone, this book is not an invitation to give up attempts to improve working class schools. Arguments for and against various interventions are discussed in relation to the current political climate. It is argued that any sustained reform of low-SES schools will require reducing SES segregation between schools, although providing substantial amounts of additional resources to low-SES schools would also help. These are unpopular suggestions at present but I maintain that they are more promising than many of those which are currently fashionable. However, since the current political climate makes such intervention unlikely, I also consider a range of counter-ideological and practical steps which could more feasibly be taken by researchers, teacher educators and those in and around schools.

Schooling for life chances

A central assumption underlying this book is that improving working class academic attainment within existing school systems should be an important goal for educationalists, researchers and policy makers. Most E&I researchers will have little difficulty with this, but it could be disputed from a number of more critical perspectives. One is the view that since there are more fundamental class inequalities outside the school than within it (Anyon 1995), the failure of working class students in schools will not be addressed without measures to reduce poverty and powerlessness outside schools. Another view is that the present school curriculum is so disempowering that, instead of asking working class students to 'jump through the hoop' of current schooling systems, wholesale curriculum reform is required (Connell 1994). Perhaps most significantly (especially where discourses of ethnicity have come to marginalize those of social class), emphasizing the importance of school mix may be seen to run counter to moves towards greater ethnic self-determination because of its possibly assimilatory effects (Foster 1993).

These are important visions for a fairer education system and all are matters to which we will return. For instance, the tension between teaching for relevance and teaching an academic curriculum was problematic in many of the classrooms examined in the Wellington study. Nevertheless, at present anyway, it is only through academic success in schools and tertiary institutions that most students can gain entry to higher socioeconomic occupations and improved life chances. For this reason alone, improving the academic (examination) success of working class students in existing school systems remains a legitimate goal of those concerned with social inequalities in education, alongside the more far-reaching agendas signalled above. It is this understanding which informs this book.

Intended audience

Schools Making a Difference: Let's be Realistic! has been written as a wake-up call to those involved in E&I research, especially those who are most assertive about the possibilities of change, to take more account of the social limits of reform. It should also be read by policy makers and the staff of school evaluation agencies who often use E&I literature. Teachers, school leaders, teacher education students and teacher educators may find the book useful to understand the limits of practice in various school settings as well as a warning (if it is needed) to take the E&I literature with a pinch of salt. Finally, it may also be illuminating for parents as it will confirm what educators have often denied – that attending high-socioeconomic schools does have its advantages. On the other hand, it is clear that school choice does not occur in a moral or ethical vacuum – the choice of school we make for our own children has very real consequences for the education of others.

I have also written with an international audience in mind, with a particular focus on the UK and the USA where much E&I thinking has originated. There are, of course, numerous differences between the context of education in these countries and New Zealand – their considerably larger urban centres being one obvious point of contrast. Nevertheless, no similar study has been done on either side of the Atlantic – in this situation the Wellington study fills an important gap. The New Zealand schooling system also originated in Britain and at times has borrowed heavily from the USA. Furthermore, in New Zealand since 1984 when a Labour government first launched 'Rogernomics', an Antipodean variant of 'Thatcherism' and

'Reaganism', New Zealand has become something of a social laboratory for a market-driven society – what is often referred to as the 'New Zealand Experiment' (Kelsey 1995). Indeed Gordon and Whitty (1997: 454) argue of New Zealand and England that 'there are few places where reform has proceeded with such similarity of pace, approach, rhetoric and policy patterns'. All of these are good reasons to suggest that, with due caution, many of the lessons to be learned from the Wellington study will be useful elsewhere.

Some notes on terminology

While it is accepted that there are important theoretical and practical problems involved in defining social class,[2] both 'social class' and 'socioeconomic status' (SES) are used here in a general way to indicate differences in family wealth, occupational status, levels of education and cultural capital. SES is sometimes also used specifically to refer to a rating on a socioeconomic scale, the Elley–Irving Index (see p. 45)

It is in deference to the USA roots of some of the hypotheses presented in this book that I often use the term 'instruction' to refer to teaching matters and 'reference groups' to talk about student peer group processes.

The large amount of USA literature on the effects of 'tracking' has also often made it easiest to use this term for within-school differentiation of students in general, including banding, streaming, setting and other variants on the theme. Readers should be mindful however of the possible implications of differences between these forms of allocation to teaching classes.

The whole notion of student 'resistance' is very problematic. I shall use the term here to indicate disaffection and non-compliance but do not wish to imply that this results from insights into the nature of capitalism. See Walker 1988, Furlong 1991 and Abraham 1995 for useful discussions of resistance theory and its limitations.

Finally, I use 'able' and 'ability' in quotation marks here to indicate perceived or demonstrated competence in a narrow, schooling sense. Following Bourdieu and others, I regard 'ability' as primarily socially constructed. No judgement about the actual or potential capabilities of any individual or group should therefore be implied.

2

School effectiveness research and the enduring problem of school mix

The story of SER and of research into the effect of school mix within this field provides a fascinating example of the way research is never 'neutral' but is coloured by the political, ideological and methodological concerns of its time. In the case of school mix this has meant:

- considerable interest during the 1960s when matters of equality of opportunity were to the fore;
- disinterest during the 1970s when it was considered that schools had little effect of any kind on life chances;
- abandonment during the 1980s with the rise of the Right and as issues of social class were marginalized by SER's claims that school policies and practices were independent of social class;
- the partial re-emergence of school mix in recent years as several studies have again pointed to its importance and as limitations of the SER paradigm have become apparent.

In order to open the way to a better approach for investigating the question of school mix, I now examine the research of each of these periods in turn.

The 1960s: Coleman *et al.* and liberal educational intervention

It was the release of the influential Coleman report in the USA (Coleman *et al.* 1966) that first drew widespread attention to the possible effects of school mix on student achievement. *Equality of Educational Opportunity* was a report on the extent and causes of educational inequality in the USA, commissioned by Congress in response to Section 402 of the 1964 Civil Rights Act. Coleman and his colleagues wrote at a time when ethnic conflict in inner city ghettos appeared to threaten seriously the cohesion of American life. As part of President Johnson's 'Great Society' programme, the liberal reforms of the 'War on Poverty' attempted to meet public expectations set up by the preceding Kennedy administration for a more egalitarian society. From its conception the Coleman report was destined to be an influential document because the congressmen who commissioned Coleman hoped that he would find glaring inequalities in the resources received by schools in different communities which would justify massive Federal intervention in ghetto schools.

They were to be disappointed. Coleman's conclusion was that there was little inequity in the allocation of material resources to schools. Coleman also found that most school variables made little difference to school outcomes over and above the influence of student background characteristics. Nonetheless he did find that minority achievement was highest in ethnically integrated schools. This became a trumpeted finding because, in contrast to the rest of the report, it appeared to offer some solution to ethnic inequality. Coleman argued that the apparent positive effects of a largely white student body came not from racial composition as such but from the better educational background and higher aspirations that were on the average found among white students (1966: 307). He suggested, 'The effects of the student body environment upon a student's achievement appear to lie in the educational proficiency possessed by that student body, whatever its racial or ethnic composition' (*ibid.*).

Therefore although Coleman's brief was to explore ethnic inequalities, he argued that it was the social class/prior achievement mix of schools which made the difference. Indeed, Coleman found that school mix was the only school variable that had a significant impact on academic outcomes. He regarded the unique contributions of school and teacher as 'vanishingly small' but considered the unique contribution of student body characteristics 'very large' (p. 304).

Coleman's findings had two important consequences for the way school mix was later perceived by most educational researchers and policy makers. First, the Coleman report led to the development of bussing policies in the USA during the 1960s and 1970s. When bussing was discounted in later, more conservative times as a failed liberal reform, the notion of balancing school mix became politically untenable. This in turn probably influenced the demise of research into school mix. Yet the evidence on the apparent failure of bussing does not in itself substantiate the view that balancing school mix could not provide a potentially powerful educational intervention. Rather it points to deficiencies in the way bussing policies have often been implemented. For example, desegregation schemes, generally applied only to inner city areas rather than bigger metropolitan regions, easily allowed white, middle class families to move beyond their reach (Orfield *et al.* 1996).

A second consequence stems from the report's seemingly ambiguous findings concerning school mix. Coleman's conclusion that minority achievement was highest in ethnically integrated schools appears inconsistent with another of his findings – that minority students had lower academic self-concept in high-SES schools. Coleman found that 'school integration has conflicting effects on attitudes of minority group children: it increases their sense of control of the environment or their sense of opportunity, but decreases their self concept' (1966: 324).

This ambiguity helped researchers in the 1970s[1] to theorize an oppositional, counterbalancing explanation of their lack of success at discovering a significant overall school mix effect. Typically these researchers argued that while school SES mix did have a positive normative effect on status aspirations, it also created a negative effect as a result of status comparison. In high-SES schools, students were seen to have higher aspirations from interacting with others likely to attend university, but suffered comparatively by having to compete with them. The latter influence was often known as the 'frogpond' effect from the maxim that 'It is better to be a big frog in a small pond than a small frog in a big pond' (Davis 1966). The 'ability' mix of the school was therefore thought to work against the SES mix in a counterbalancing way such that while these 'different' mix effects might be considerable, overall mix effects would be small. Coleman's findings were sometimes seen to have supported this hypothesis.

In fact, Coleman never did regard the apparently conflicting findings concerning school mix to be of the same magnitude – he clearly held that integrating schools would boost minority achievement (1966: 324). The reinterpretation of Coleman's findings implicit in the counterbalancing hypothesis can in part be attributed to later doubts about his methodology.[2] More fundamental, however, was that in the 1970s the dominant educational ideology among researchers came to preclude the notion that school mix, or indeed any school variable, could have a significant impact on school outcomes.

The 1970s: Jencks *et al.* and the impasse in school performance research

The post-war liberal belief that schools could equalize students' life chances came under attack in the 1970s. The view that schools could not compensate for society (Bernstein 1970) had its roots in the failure of liberal educational policies designed to equalize life chances. The view was that compensatory educational programmes and bussing in the USA had failed while in the UK research showed that comprehensive schools did not necessarily improve life chances (Ford 1969). This gave the opportunity for both Right and Left to claim schools could not promote equality of opportunity in the strong sense of equalizing life chances. For the Right the reason lay in the genetically determined nature of intelligence (Jensen 1969); for the Marxist Left, schools could not promote equality of opportunity because they were effectively agents of the ruling class (Bowles and Gintis 1976); while for Left liberals like Jencks *et al.* (1972) the route to greater equality of opportunity lay not in education, but in other social and economic policies.

In *Inequality* (1972) Jencks *et al.* attempted to show the inadequacy of a reform strategy based on education by providing an analysis which drew upon what Coleman (1973: 1524) described as a 'skilful but highly motivated use of statistics'. Jencks introduced his discussion of school mix by noting that methodological considerations surrounding the issue – the importance of various correlated variables, their specification and measurement – had become the subject of a 'minor sociological industry during the 1960s' (1972: 151). He argued that, while numerous early studies did find strong positive school mix effects, with better data and more sophisticated use of statistics 'the best recent studies have concluded that the socioeconomic composition of a high school has virtually no effect on students' aspirations' (p. 152).

These 'best recent studies' numbered only two however (Sewell and Armer 1966; Hauser 1970), both of which were widely regarded at the time as methodologically and theoretically unsound.[3] Moreover Jencks dismissed studies which indicated positive mix effects at elementary level arguing that 'the evidence [was] not very weighty' (1972: 103). On balance the same would have to be said for Jencks's refutation of the effects of school mix.

Supporting the political orientation of researchers like Jencks was a particular approach to research methodology known as methodological empiricism. This research approach, epitomized by the work of Coleman and Jencks, used a quantitative methodology and emphasized neutrality in a way which left *ends* in the hands of policy makers and concentrated the efforts of the researcher on the *means* by which these ends could be attained (Gouldner 1971). It was an approach directed towards establishing the existence of school effects rather than the problem of explaining them. The statistical measures used were incapable of unravelling the actual processes occurring within schools because as Karabel and Halsey (1977: 18) noted, they 'neglected those problems that did not readily lend themselves to quantification'.

The extent to which researchers ignored the limitations of methodological empiricism or were simply unaware of them is difficult to assess. By 1972 Jencks was certainly becoming aware of the limitations of this approach but used it nonetheless:

> We have ignored . . . the internal life of schools. We have been preoccupied with the *effects* [Jencks's emphasis] of schooling . . . This has led us to adopt a 'factory' metaphor . . . Our research has convinced us that this is the wrong way to think about schools. The long-term effects of schooling seem much less significant to us than they did when we began our work, and the internal life of the schools seems correspondingly more important. But we will not explore the implications of this alternative view in much detail. Instead we will be content to document our scepticism about the importance of school outputs.
>
> (Jencks *et al.* 1972: 13)

On the other hand there is little evidence of widespread doubt about the validity of methodological empiricism among school performance researchers until the late 1970s. Overall it appears that during this period researchers were preoccupied by debates over the measurement and validity of a narrow set of empirical findings, precluding fresh examination of the problem from different methodological and theoretical perspectives.

By the late 1970s the view that schools were powerless to address social inequalities was widely accepted. It appeared that any school mix effect which did exist would not make any difference to school outcomes and could be ignored. Many researchers agreed with Hauser and his colleagues when they argued that 'research on the schooling process could profitably be turned to issues other than the explanation of school to school variations in aspirations and achievements' (1976: 341).

Research into school performance was at an impasse. In political terms it had discounted the impact of schooling in redressing inequalities of educational opportunity, while in methodological terms it was incapable of investigating possible key school processes, such as school mix. However, the political climate was also changing as Right-wing governments took over in the UK and the USA. The priority accorded to equality of opportunity was superseded by questions concerning efficiency and value for money.

The 1980s: the school effectiveness movement and the 'decentring' of social class

After the pessimism that characterized the research of the 1970s, the popular appeal of SER rested largely on the ability of its central message – 'schools *can* make a difference' – to speak in an optimistic and 'commonsense' way to the needs of educators and policy makers.[4] SER soon became an international success story with its own 'congress' membership, journal (*School Effectiveness and School Improvement*) and annual conference circuit. It rapidly took on the trappings of a movement, complete with almost religious overtones: 'For just a second or two Professor Peter Mortimore looked and sounded like an evangelist bringing tidings of great joy. His arms were outstretched and his smile was blissful. "In many ways I think our time is rapidly coming" he told his brethren' (Budge cited in Brown 1994: 55).

There can be little doubt that SER did represent a methodological advance over previous macro-level studies in that it, to some extent, examined the internal workings of schools. Beyond this, however, it constitutes a highly problematic body of research much criticized over the last decade. The most common complaint is that SER is an essentially technicist literature which lacks a critical perspective on the relationship between schools and their social and political context. This is a concern we should examine in more detail before returning to look at how SER has treated the question of school mix.

Contextual criticisms of SER

SER lacks a socially critical perspective primarily because it eschews many of the central questions raised by earlier studies about the relationship of students' social origins to their school achievement and adult life chances. While these difficult questions have continued to absorb many researchers, early SER researchers maintained, first, that 'exemplary' schools exist which achieve considerable academic success regardless of student background, and second, that specific, identifiable and reproducible characteristics could be identified to explain the success of these schools. As Angus (1993: 335) has put it in an often-cited critique of this literature, the school effectiveness response to the pessimism of the 1970s 'was simply to deny it, assume that schools do make a difference to student outcomes, and search for indicators of this difference'.

At the outset the approach was probably well intended if naive. It was a polemic directed against what proponents saw as the overdeterministic concerns of researchers such as Coleman and Jencks who emphasized the influence of students' background characteristics. This position was taken to focus more attention on the potential for positive reform of low-SES schools. For instance, Edmonds, the 'founding father' of the effective schools move-ment in the USA, argued that 'repudiation of the social science notion that family background is the principal cause of pupil acquisition of basic school skills is probably prerequisite to successful reform of public schools for the children of the poor' (1979: 23).

Ralph and Fennessey, in an all-too-rare response, countered, 'To repudiate an established relationship between family background and schooling simply because it conflicts with one's goals is neither pragmatically productive nor intellectually respectable behaviour' (1983: 689). Nevertheless it was not long before an emphasis on the ability of schools to 'make a difference' became popular in educational discourse and the broader agendas signalled by the research of the 1960s and 1970s began to disappear. This is not to say that SER researchers completely rejected the idea that social class backgrounds have a powerful effect on student achievement. Rather they saw social class as a factor which is 'containable' through value-added analyses and which should not be examined in any case because it lies outside the control of schools. In short, as Angus again points out, social class was regarded as a 'given'. 'Family background, social class, any notion of context, are typically regarded as "noise" – as outside background factors which must be controlled and then stripped away so that the researcher can concentrate on the important domain of school factors' (1993: 341).

Part of the reason SER was able to adopt a socially decontextualized approach was because those who might have challenged it were otherwise engaged. While SER proponents were abandoning class, so too were many in the sociology of education who had carried the concerns of the 1960s and '70s. Mac an Ghaill (1996) points to the 'decentring' of social class in SER being related to the more general problem of the 'erasure' of social class in sociology which has accompanied the rise of post-modern forms of theorizing that emphasized social complexity and difference. The net effect was surprisingly little critique during the 1980s of the socially decontextualized approach which SER was developing.

Further related to the decentring of social class, SER is also often seen by critics to have provided support for neo-liberal or managerial politics in education. This is because in the conservative climate of the 1980s, the kind of position taken by Edmonds and others in the interests of equity was easily turned to the cause of efficiency and accountability. With respect to 'efficiency' Angus writes:

> School effectiveness research indicates that resources don't matter . . . it is simply a matter of incorporating effectiveness factors into school practice. This pragmatic orientation suits conservative governments that are interested as much in cost cutting as conservative restoration . . . Not that school effectiveness researchers necessarily see themselves as being of the Right . . . However this does not prevent the school effectiveness project sitting quite comfortably with the conservative educational project.
>
> (Angus 1993: 342–3)

In a similar vein Whitty *et al.* suggest:

> While those working in the areas of school improvement and school effectiveness would probably distance themselves from the values of neo-liberalism, there is more common ground than appears at first sight. Both the New Right and the school effectiveness lobby take the discursive repositioning of schools as autonomous self-improving agencies at face value, rather than recognising that, in practice, the atomization of schooling too often merely allows advantaged schools to maximize their advantages.
>
> (Whitty *et al.* 1998: 113)

SER has also helped the Right to argue that schools could be held directly accountable for their outcomes as Lauder *et al.* point out:

> For teachers effective school research has been a two edged sword. It has raised the possibility that they can make a difference to educational outcomes [but] . . . in the post-Reagan and Thatcher eras it has also saddled them with responsibilities over which they would claim to have little control . . . At the height of the implementation of the New Right agenda the claim that schools could make a difference was used ideologically to deny any suggestions that schools were limited in their performance by their socioeconomic intake or context.
>
> (Lauder *et al.* 1997: 1)

Tomlinson further argues:

> By the 1990s school effectiveness research had become a political tool and

the basis for the denigration of particular schools . . . The intention of the [early studies] was not to pillory or deride schools that did not appear to be as successful as others . . . however by the 1990s the school effectiveness research had been hijacked by politicans who used evidence which indicated that some schools with similar intakes of students appeared to be doing better in GCSE league tables, or at key stages, to castigate less effective schools.

(Tomlinson 1997: 13–14)

There are many other ways that concerns over the politics of SER have been expressed over the last decade. Ball (1988: 146) has argued that SER is 'thoroughly implicated' in the growth of a management culture in education which 'reduces the autonomy of teachers and attempts to minimise their influence over policymaking: it is also couched in an ideology of neutrality'. It also 'provides a technology for the possibility of "blaming" the school' (Ball 1990: 161). Dale (1992: 215) believes that SER 'demonstrates very well the intrinsic shortcomings of the problem solving approach which it has implicitly adopted'. Hatcher argues that SER writers have 'nothing to say about . . . the interaction between pupil cultures and the official culture of the school, at the centre of which is the curriculum' (1996: 37). Mac an Ghaill (1996) suggests that SER underplays the central role of the state in policy making and that it is ahistorical in its emphasis on educational change. To Marginson, SER is 'functional in policy terms because it separate[s] school improvement from social background and other external factors that might underwrite a case for resource increases' (1997: 128).

A recent set of criticisms of SER has been provided by Slee *et al.* (1998). The writers in this collection are often very critical of the way SER 'bleaches context from its analytic frame' (Slee and Weiner 1998). Amongst other things, SER is regarded as

- 'educationally and politically dangerous', 'politically promiscuous and malleable', a 'juggernaut' which 'rides roughshod over educational policy-making and research' (Slee and Weiner 1998);
- 'an ethnocentric psuedo-science', 'peddling "feel good" fictions' (Hamilton 1998);
- the 'antithesis of . . . empowerment', a literature which pathologizes and renders invisible the lived experiences of those studying and teaching in poorer areas (Rea and Weiner 1998);
- containing 'deep tensions', systematically omitting key variables and concepts (Lauder *et al.* 1998);
- a case of 'policy entrepreneurship', which articulates with the commodification of education and which 'fit[s] perfectly . . . into the discourses of derision' (Ball 1998b); and
- a 'hurried', 'abstracted' and decontextualized literature, which replaces political questions with technical ones and which provides a means of the 'hollowed out' state 'steering from a distance' at the lowest cost (Lingard *et al.* 1998).

Although we will return to many of these themes, the key point to note here is that SER proponents rarely acknowledge that anything is much astray with their work despite all these criticisms. There are occasional circumspect moments but for the most part the 'juggernaut' continues unabated. For instance in response to criticism from Elliott (1996), Sammons and Reynolds (1997) give their whole-hearted approval to Edmonds's agenda and argue that since value-added approaches demonstrate the limitations of league tables of raw exam results, these approaches have been 'far from music to the ears of politicians' (p. 124). On the other hand Myers and Goldstein query the latter claim, and point out that 'Ironically, contextualising performance, by using adjusted league tables of test scores, for example, may actually strengthen the belief that blame resides in the school by encouraging the view that *all* other factors have been accounted for, and that any residual variation must reside in the school' (1998: 184).

This interchange supports Angus's contention that the SER field contains 'a great deal of internal debate and criticism, an awareness of many past limitations and a strong desire to remedy methodological weaknesses and build a theoretical base' (1993: 340). However, the concerns of SER researchers rarely run as deep or as wide as those of external critics. A good example is provided by Sammons and Reynolds when they propose the following agenda for future SER research:

> The need for better theoretical underpinnings is recognised and receiving increasing attention (e.g. Creemers 1994; Scheerens, 1992; Sammons *et al.* 1996a). The links with the school improvement field, though expanding, require further development. Little is known about so-called 'ineffective' schools in contrast to the work on effectiveness. Moreover much less is known about how to effect change in schools. More research is needed on the context specificity and generalisability of results. And of course the controversial topic on what can be learnt from international comparisons remains a little explored although increasingly important theme (Reynolds and Farrell 1996).
> (Sammons and Reynolds 1997: 134, their references)

At first glance this may seem a fair and balanced mission but on closer inspection illustrates several ways in which SER remains blinkered. The kind of 'theoretical' work being cited is hardly strongly insightful (see Lauder *et al.* 1998). Nor should we be fooled by the reference to context – we shall see shortly that this also has only a limited meaning in SER. What is missing as well is any sense of the politics of Reynolds and Farrell's (1996) cited work. Tomlinson (1997: 14) reports that this was commissioned by Ofsted and used to 'denigrate the state of UK schools generally'. In short, the most important problems are being ignored.

How SER cancelled out school mix

The SER argument that schools have considerable control over student outcomes has required the use of theoretical constructs which could, on the one hand, explain the causal processes which give schools their power to determine outcomes while, by implication, minimizing the causal contribution of school intake characteristics. While most, although not all, early school effectiveness studies acknowledged some impact of individual social class background on achievement, the notion of school 'climate' or 'ethos' was frequently used to explain away processes which might alternatively be seen as the result of school mix.[5] It was typically maintained that school ethos impacted upon students (and teachers) by raising expectations and aspirations and by improving motivation and morale.

The privileged explanatory role accorded to school ethos in the development of school effectiveness literature deserves closer attention here, for it might reasonably be asked how a school could create an ethos independent of social class mix which was so powerful that it could play a major role in overcoming the social disadvantage encountered by many working class and ethnic minority students. I shall begin by looking at the research of Rutter and his associates. Their work achieved a high profile and constitutes a good example of early SER with respect to these two strategies. In *Fifteen Thousand Hours* Rutter grasped the central causal issue: 'The question is whether schools were as they were because of the children they admitted or rather whether children behaved in the way they did because of school influences' (Rutter *et al.* 1979: 181).

But did he answer the question adequately? Rutter found that school 'ethos' – the style and quality of school life, patterns of student and teacher behaviour, management and treatment of students and care of school buildings and grounds – explained many between-school differences in academic attainment. He hypothesized that the mean intake characteristics of a school, 'balance of intake', could be one important variable determining ethos.

> The presence of a relatively high concentration of pupils in the upper ability groups may work to the advantage not only of the pupils themselves but also to their peers. In a similar way, a largely disadvantaged intake might depress outcomes in some cumulative way over and above the effects of a disadvantaged background on the individual pupil.
>
> (Rutter *et al.* 1979: 154)

Rutter found that both 'ability' and SES mix were weakly but significantly correlated with academic attainment. He then investigated whether the mix effects identified were direct or mediated through school processes by examining the relationship between the 'balance of intake' measures and the school process variables used by the study. These included the academic emphasis of schools, teacher actions in lessons, rewards and punishments, pupil conditions, children's responsibilities and participation in the school, stability of teaching and friendship groups, and staff planning and management. As he found no correlation between any of these process variables and 'balance of intake', he concluded:

however the balance in the intake to a school may be associated with the pupils' outcomes, it does not have its impact . . . on school functioning in terms of the process variables we measured. Instead it presumably has some kind of impact on the children themselves, probably through its influence on the composition and thereby on the attitudes and behaviour of the peer group.

(Rutter *et al.* 1979: 159)

There are three interesting points here. First, Rutter formulated the problem in terms of 'ability' mix rather than social class mix. Second, although Rutter acknowledged a relationship between ability/SES mix and the academic outcome measure, he could not explain how this relationship works. These are both points to which I shall return. Third, and more important in this discussion, the argument about mix takes second place to those about ethos in Rutter's work, for his conclusion was that

variations in outcomes were systematically and strongly associated with the characteristics of schools as social institutions. The patterns of findings suggested . . . a causal relationship . . . not only were pupils influenced by the way they were dealt with as individuals, but also there was a group influence resulting from the ethos of the school as a social institution.

(Rutter *et al.* 1979: 205)

This conclusion was inadequate, however, because the main body of Rutter's analysis suggests that a more balanced treatment of ethos and 'balance of intake' was warranted. Indeed, as both Acton (1980) and Purkey and Smith (1983) observed, the 'balance of intake' variable came to assume such importance in Rutter's analysis that it was plausible that it, rather than school ethos, was influencing school outcomes.

Rutter's is only one study and since I am claiming that the privileging of school climate or ethos over social class mix was a general feature of the development of SER during this period, we should look at other influential research. Brookover (Brookover *et al.* 1979) examined two pairs of low-SES schools in the USA – one predominantly white, the other largely black. Each pair shared a similar SES mix but differed considerably in their mean levels of achievement. Following fieldwork in each school, observers concluded that there were predictable differences in school climate variables between the low- and high-achieving schools in each pair. Brookover attributed the differences in achievement between each pair of schools to these school climate variables.

The key question to be asked here is the difference climate variables, stemming from school policies and practices, can make *independent* of school mix. What really underpinned this kind of claim was the central tenet of the school effectiveness literature that there were verifiable examples of exemplary schools that achieve high academic standards with poor urban minority children. Brookover argued for example:

The fact that some low SES white and black schools do demonstrate a high level of academic achievement suggests that the socioeconomic and racial variables are not directly causal forces in the school social system. We therefore conclude that the school social climate and the instructional behaviour associated with it are more direct causal links in the production of achievement.

(Brookover *et al.* 1979: 142)

Central to this type of claim was the issue of whether in fact schools in studies like this were truly similar in terms of SES composition yet very different in terms of achievement in the first place. It did not take critics long to realize that 'exemplary' was at best a relative term – the mean score of the exemplary black school in Brookover's study was considerably less than that of the exemplary white school and the state as a whole. Purkey and Smith (1983: 436) pointed out that 'while the black school may have narrowed the gap, the gap remains'. They argued that an 'unusually effective' school serving predominantly low-income and minority students may in fact have considerably lower levels of attainment than a white middle class suburban school because of the pervasive influences of social class on achievement and the possibility that even the 'typical' suburban school has some important advantages over the relatively effective inner-city school.[6]

A further kind of argument for the primacy of school policy over school mix was cited by Maughan *et al.* (1980) who used the presence of an increased correlation between school process measures and pupil measures at the end of secondary schooling compared to the beginning, to infer the direction of causality. As school process measures were found to correlate more strongly with pupil characteristics at the end of school than at intake, they argued that teacher behaviour and school climate shape pupil characteristics, rather than the other way around. This argument did not, however, take into account the possibility that pupils' orientations towards schooling might change over time because of processes that have little to do with school policies and practices but rather relate to the influence of wider social structures within and beyond the school – such as awareness of the labour market or the absence of early school leavers. For instance Brown (1987) and Lauder *et al.* (1992) have both shown the likely importance of students' views of local labour markets in determining their attitudes towards their work and towards school authority in their last years of schooling.

Finally, school mix has also frequently been sidelined by using the notion of 'ability' mix. For instance, Maughan and Rutter conclude vaguely that while 'an unfavourable [ability] balance was no *necessary* [their emphasis] bar to attainments', nonetheless

in *general*, [their emphasis] the ability balance in the intakes to . . . schools showed an association with the intakes of their more able pupils: the smaller the proportion of able children, the more difficult it was for schools to promote high levels of attainment.

(Maughan and Rutter 1987: 67)

Mortimore (1995) uses the same approach to argue for the benefits of an 'academic balance' in school intakes. We might ask what agenda is served by such bald discussion of 'ability' or 'academic' balance without reference to the effects of social class, particularly in the face of the large body of evidence for a powerful relationship, at a general level, between school performance and social class (Halsey *et al.* 1980; Lauder and Hughes 1990a). Such analyses fail to acknowledge the advantage gained by various groups in society at the expense of others by taking political dimensions out of the question of school mix, once again rendering it a merely technical problem.

The 1990s: the partial re-emergence of school mix

Although SER literature has shown little sign of disappearing during the 1990s, it has begun to reach its limits. In part, this is because it remains tightly tied to large-scale methodologies which have not allowed it to move beyond the rather narrow set of findings already developed. Even a recent review by British proponents notes that 'ongoing work . . . remains partially situated within the same intellectual traditions and at the same intellectual cutting edges as in the 1980s' (Reynolds *et al.* 1996: 136). Despite attempts to remain relevant so that the 'performative characteristics of the "effective school" . . . be seen to underpin and inform the "improving school" ' (Rea and Weiner 1998: 26), the SER movement has been losing its place in the sun to the more 'relevant' school improvement literature discussed in Chapter 10. In this literature SER is generally seen to have laid a foundation of reliable findings which can support the notion of schools being improvable but not actually show the way.

But in any case the ideological work of SER may now be largely complete. The view that 'schools can make a difference' has become widely accepted among policy makers and is also accepted by many, if not all, practitioners. Perhaps because they feel the battle won, SER proponents in recent times have become more relaxed about the idea that school mix could have some influence on school effectiveness.

In the USA this possibility has been raised through 'sensitivity to context' research which has highlighted the limitations of a comprehensive 'recipe' approach to effectiveness in schools with different intake characteristics. Hallinger and Murphy (1986: 347), for instance, found that for the most part, schools of different SES have quite different effectiveness correlates. 'High and low SES effective schools [are] characterised by different patterns of curricular breadth, time allocation, goal emphasis, instructional leadership, opportunities for student reward, expectations for student achievement and home–school relations.' Similar conclusions were reached by Teddlie *et al.* (1989) and Teddlie and Stringfield (1993). These findings have limited depth and are rarely given much emphasis in SER, especially when other quantitative US studies also continue to find little impact of school mix.[7] They are important nevertheless because they contradict the assumption that effectiveness correlates can be generalized across all schools. While generic correlates remain popular (Sammons *et al*. 1995), the 'sensitivity to context' findings do begin to render problematic the notion that school effectiveness can be theorized independently of school mix. As Wimpleberg *et al*. note:

> Although many practitioners and academics continue to cling to the classic handful of correlates of effective schools research, extensions of that research persist in exposing context conditions that challenge the more literal readings of the earlier findings.
>
> (Wimpleberg *et al*. 1989: 87)

Within the SER literature 'sensitivity to context' findings are generally regarded as a fresh development. Scheerens (1991: 385) suggests that 'including contextual variables like student body composition . . . can be seen as a relatively new and very interesting development in school effectiveness research' while Reynolds (1992: 16) describes 'sensitivity to context' findings as 'cutting edge'. In a sense both are correct – an overt concern with contextual variables is new in the SER literature. Yet the findings can also be seen to relate to the older tradition established by Coleman which viewed school mix as a key theoretical construct.

An undercurrent of that tradition has continued to exist in the sociology of education[8] and has been given some prominence over the last decade by the findings of McPherson and Willms (1987). Their longitudinal study examined the effects of creating a system of comprehensive schooling in Scotland between 1970 and 1984. It found that comprehensivization significantly reduced social class inequalities of attainment and improved average levels of attainment when measured against the inequitable pattern established in the preceding six decades. McPherson and Willms attributed the decline of SES inequality in attainment to a school mix effect. They found that comprehensivization resulted in the abolition of selection at 12 years, the closure of many short-course schools, and the redefinition of school catchments which, they argued,

> led to a reduction in between-school segregation in many communities. This reduction, allied to the rise in the SES level of the school population, distributed the benefits of a favourable school context more widely, though it must be added that these benefits are not well understood.
>
> (McPherson and Willms 1987: 23)

More recently Willms has suggested that 'the composition of a school's intake can have a substantial effect on pupils' outcomes over and above the effects associated with pupils' individual ability and social class' (1992: 41). There is support for this view among some British researchers (Paterson 1991; Heath and Blakey 1992), but other British researchers have found little or no evidence of a school mix effect. For instance, Thomas and Mortimore (1994) claim that when 'rich and wide-ranging data' on prior achievement is available at the pupil level, contextual effects disappear. Sammons *et al.* (1996) review research on both sides of the debate. Mortimore *et al.* (1994) argue that recent British findings contradict each other and describe the effects of school context as one of a number of 'unresolved issues' in SER.

Part of the problem may be the tendency of British SER researchers to study homogeneous, socially disadvantaged schools rather than more wide-ranging samples which could highlight contextual issues as in the USA (Reynolds 1992; Reynolds *et al.* 1996). Perhaps here we can find at least some of the explanation for the privileging of 'ability' mix over social class mix noted earlier. Narrow sampling was a limitation for instance in *School Matters* (Mortimore *et al.* 1988), one of the most influential British SER studies of recent times. This study found only weak effects of school mix (p. 223) but it is doubtful whether the sample had sufficient distribution, range or size to address the issue properly. First, most of the students in the study were from working class homes. Second, the authors only used two broad social class categories for their analysis – manual and non-manual. Third, although they argued that this crude classification was necessary because of the small numbers that would result from a more detailed analysis, they nevertheless based their findings with respect to the contextual influence of school intakes on as few as five students in any school in either of these two crude categories (p. 207).

Yet it may also be that the debate will never be satisfactorily resolved through large-scale quantitative studies alone, no matter how well conducted. For instance, two recent New Zealand studies, both using hierarchical linear modelling (HLM) techniques, have developed quite different findings with respect to the impact of school mix. The Progress at School Project (Harker and Nash 1996) provides little support for the idea of a school mix effect – indeed school-level contextual variables are seen to account, at best, for only about 1 or 2 per cent of between-school variance in student achievement. On the other hand, the Smithfield Project (Hughes *et al.* 1997, 1999) gives substantially more weight to the impact of contextual effects. Hughes and his colleagues suggest that the 'marked contrast' between the two projects might reflect their different samples, different variables or different outcome measures (Hughes *et al.* 1997). Whatever the case, with little other evidence to go on, we are back to the familiar problem of trying to decide which finding to accept on this issue or whether to accept any of them at all.

There is an important parallel here to the diffident findings of quantitative literature on 'ability' grouping or tracking *within* schools. Most statistical analyses of tracking suggest there is not a lot of difference in measured achievement between schools which group/track and those which do not (Slavin 1987, 1990). Elmore *et al.* comment:

> Most reformers regard these results, when they choose to acknowledge them at all, as puzzling . . . regardless of where they stand on the tracking issue, most teachers and principals would say that grouping and tracking practices *must* matter. How could a structure that apparently has so direct

a relationship to teaching and learning have such a seemingly ambiguous and weak effect on what students actually learn?

(Elmore *et al.* 1996: 10)

Elmore and colleagues suggest a range of possibilities to explain this. First, that the statistical studies may not adequately measure student learning or be sensitive enough to pick up the effects of 'ability' grouping or tracking; second that grouping or tracking practices may be more flexible in implementation than often assumed; or finally, that teaching practices may not vary much by track or group. Whichever is the case, the quantitative claim that grouping/tracking does not matter remains counter-intuitive for many educators. What helps to further problematize it is that analyses which draw on more qualitative forms of evidence such as school ethnographies invariably argue that tracking or grouping is important (Oakes *et al.* 1992).

The relevant point here for school mix is that a qualitative literature on the impact of school mix which might similarly unsettle the quantitative SER account has been largely absent. There are probably many reasons for this including the different political, theoretical and empirical concerns of those typically using different methodological approaches to school research, as well as the complexity of doing detailed qualitative research across several school sites – most ethnographies have only looked at individual schools. Nevertheless the effect of this oversight has been to allow the conclusion that school mix is not important to become widely accepted when another research approach might challenge this view.

Towards a qualitative account

In this situation, it may be helpful to examine a recent SER study which has taken a more qualitative approach and which does, to some extent, argue for the importance of school mix. The research agenda of Brown and her colleagues is summed up in the wordy title 'Possibilities and problems of small-scale studies to unpack the findings of large-scale studies of school effectiveness' (Brown *et al.* 1996a).[9] Their study was associated with the quantitative work of McPherson and Willms (1987) noted earlier and shares its emphasis on social class. Four contrasting schools of high and low SES and effectiveness were selected using a quantitative dataset. Within these schools the study focussed on the progress of, and support for, 'below average' pupils. It used a range of data collection methods including the analysis of policy documents, interviews with school managers, teachers and pupils. A major emphasis was on classroom observation and follow-up interviews with teachers as a means of trying to make sense of 'what, in teachers' eyes, constitutes "progress" for low achieving pupils and how they make sense of the "support" they provide for such pupils' (Brown *et al.* 1996a: 103).

Three main findings are reported from this study. First, teachers in the schools had richly complex constructs about their pupils and the kinds of support they provided to them. Second, only two factors seemed to be common to the 'highly effective' schools – namely the history of the schools and their efforts to involve pupils in the running of the school. Third, there were some 'striking contrasts' between the schools related to SES. Brown *et al.* (1996a: 114–15) highlight three:

- the impact of the schools' achievement profiles. Since high-SES schools could take for granted the exam success of most students, they were able to give special attention to those with learning difficulties. In the low-SES schools learning support was more thinly spread because there were many more students in need;
- the impact of different levels of motivation across the schools. At the low-SES schools much greater efforts were needed to improve teacher morale, to encourage students to learn and to raise the level of parental involvement;
- the differential impact of marketing on the schools. Marketing was a source of anxiety at the less popular low-SES schools who could not advertise their emphasis on supporting low achievers in the prevailing national 'culture of achievement'. Again this was not an issue at the high-SES schools where much higher exam results were the norm even though one of these schools was judged not to be effective.

What stands out about these findings is the depth of information about school processes which is provided compared with what is available through quantitative SER. As Brown *et al.* note, the latter 'has a very "bare bones" appearance in comparison with the richness of the portraits that are painted by those within the schools' (1996a: 112). Undoubtedly related to this, the findings also provide some of the clearest support in the SER literature for the idea that it is school mix rather than school policies and practices which may be most important in determining school effectiveness. Gray *et al.* (1996: x) comment: 'If these conclusions hold in other settings, then they offer some additional purchase on why many school improvement efforts may have stumbled – they have failed to disengage causes from correlations.'

A case for school mix? Questions worth asking and a way forward

The preceding review has illustrated that the relationship between school mix and school achievement is an enduring problem in the school effectiveness field. While some research suggests that school mix has no significant effect, both the general and specific limitations of that research cannot be ignored. On balance, taking into account the dispositions of researchers in this area in the past, there does seem to be at least a *prima facie* case for the existence of a significant relationship between school mix and school achievement.

If this argument is accepted, it raises a number of obvious research questions.

First, does a genuine school mix effect really exist or is it just a proxy for some other variable? The statistical correlations found between school mix and successful school processes do not prove the existence of a genuine school mix effect because we cannot be sure of the direction of causal influence. The correlation could theoretically come about because of measurement error (Gray *et al.* 1990) or because (a) successful school processes cause school mix, (b) school mix causes successful school processes, or (c) some third variable causes both.[10] The difficulty with this question is that the problem of causal direction is a particularly stubborn one that is likely to continue to resist any kind of conclusive answer.

Second, if a school mix effect does exist, how significant is it? We have seen that much of the quantitative literature suggests that a school mix effect, if it does exist, is very small while other research attributes a much greater degree of influence. The importance of any school mix effect will clearly depend on its size in relation to other variables.

Third, if a school mix effect does exist, how is it caused? For instance, would a school mix effect be caused directly in some way by students from different social classes being in contact with each other at school, or by the impact of teaching practices that are possible in relatively mixed schools but not in more working class schools, or both of the above?

This last question of causal mechanisms underlying a school mix effect is likely to be the most critical in further developing the case for or against school mix. For so long as the impact of school mix continues to be seen as a largely technical problem which merely requires a more rigorous, precise and well-controlled version of the same 'value-added' approach, the question of school mix is likely to remain unanswered. This is because the multilevel modelling methods such as Hierarchical Linear Modelling currently favoured by SER researchers may, despite their increasingly sophisticated nature, fail to capture the subtle processes represented by the concept of a school mix effect.

Given the problems inherent in more of the same, investigation of possible causal mechanisms appears likely to be a more rewarding direction for further research. In effect this approach would attempt to answer questions about the existence and significance of a school mix effect by demonstrating how it could work. But if we are to advance our understanding of school mix, it is also clear that we need to open up the methodological approaches used for research. There has been some support within quantitative SER literature for a more detailed approach to the problem of school mix (see Thrupp 1995). For instance, Rutter *et al.* conclude with respect to 'balance of intake' that 'our analysis can only represent the beginnings of attempts to unravel the network of interacting influences' (1979: 155).

S. Brown and her colleagues have also argued that the methodologies traditionally employed by SER researchers have simply not allowed them to get sufficiently close to the fine grain of school life to illuminate complex processes. But does their own study go far enough? They based it on a sample of outliers provided by a quantitative SER study. This means they started from the understanding that some of the schools were substantially more effective than others, even if their own findings threw doubt on this. This is likely to have coloured how they saw the schools and their processes in a way which would arguably not have occurred had they approached a set of high- and low-SES schools without any such assumptions.

This concern is really an extension of Brown *et al.*'s own criticism of school effectiveness studies which purport to combine quantitative and qualitative work but which really only use semi-structured interviews to extend the quantitative paradigm. They complain that 'the framework within which these data are collected . . . is for the most part that of the *researchers*' construct and is based on earlier findings of school effectiveness studies' (Brown *et al.* 1996a: 97). They argue that their own approach, based on interviews with teachers, was more open-ended. This is partly correct but given the methodological problems which continue to haunt quantitative SER studies, their approach may still give too much weight to the findings of this work.

Overall a better approach for a study of school mix will be to build a qualitative case which is less reliant on the findings of the quantitative SER literature. Such an approach would certainly take into account what quantitative researchers have speculated are the likely causes of a school mix effect. However it would also draw heavily on relevant qualitative studies and use detailed ethnographic methods to come to its own conclusions about the relationships between school mix, school processes and student achievement. Although the resulting analysis would be unlikely to provide generalizable answers to the stubborn causal questions at the heart of the concept of a school mix effect, it should nonetheless serve to illuminate the causal mechanisms working in particular contexts. Chapter 3 discusses how the Wellington study was designed to explore possible causal mechanisms in four New Zealand schools.

3

Possible mechanisms and a research strategy

When I first began to think about researching the impact of school mix through a detailed study of possible causal mechanisms, research advice from Delamont and Hamilton (1984: 24) seemed particularly attractive. They suggest that 'instead of looking for one solution to all problems . . . more consideration be given to the nature of the specific problems faced and, hence, to choosing a particular research strategy appropriate for the problem'.

In this spirit the Wellington study came to represent a response to what I thought might cause a school mix effect, based on a wide reading of previous research, and to a range of other theoretical and practical considerations, particularly those related to causality and the sample of students and schools available for the study. This chapter explains why the study was designed as it was and how it was carried out.[1]

Pointers to causal mechanisms from previous research

The quantitative and qualitative literature on schools and school processes suggests four possible causes of a school mix effect:

- reference group processes;
- instructional processes;
- organizational and management processes, and
- a 'whole school effect' caused by all of these.

Reference group processes

It is possible that student attainment is somehow raised by informal contact with higher SES school peers in middle class schools. Early quantitative studies argued that a higher SES school composition may increase the chances of a working class student having higher SES friendships (Wilson 1959; Davis 1966). If this is the case, there are a variety of ways middle class students could share their success with working class students. First, values and attitudes to schooling typical of students from middle class families may influence working class friends, raising their level of achievement. Second, the cultural resources of middle class students – gained from events attended by their families, workplaces of parents and family friends, family holidays, family reading material and so on – may also be passed on to working class students. Third, curriculum knowledge may be directly shared through working together on assignments and homework. Last, there may be some process of 'ability' formation occurring where working class students change their perception of their capabilities through interaction with middle class peers (Rosenholtz and Simpson 1984).

The problem with all of this however is that several ethnographic studies from the UK and USA have suggested there is little voluntary contact between working class and higher SES students in schools.[2] Brantlinger found:

> In spite of being present in the same secondary schools, low and high-income adolescents experienced almost complete separation. Students rode different buses arriving at school at different times, areas of the school were the traditional territories of specific groups . . . and were off limits to members of other groups.
>
> (Brantlinger 1992: 17)

Brantlinger (1993: 32) also suggests that the likelihood of cross-class friendships does not vary across schools with different social class compositions: 'social class isolation existed regardless of whether the students attended schools of homogeneous or heterogeneous social class makeup'. However findings like this are rare because most studies have investigated friendships in only one school while others have studied schools with quite similar compositions. While Brantlinger's claim should not be ignored, there are good reasons to expect that attendance at a school with a large proportion of middle class students *would* make it more likely that a working class student's friends are middle class.

To begin with, since there will be a greater proportion of middle class students in the school overall, working class students are more likely to be forced to rub shoulders with them. Greater contact at least provides the possibility that cross-class friendships may develop. Middle and working class students may also have more in common in higher SES schools because there will be less likelihood of alienated subcultures developing which working class students may be drawn to. Furthermore there are likely to be more shared experiences through which friendships may develop. In the classrooms of higher SES schools, as we shall see shortly, instructional processes are likely to stress more co-operative work and more oral discussion. Outside of lessons, schools with higher SES compositions, by virtue of having more resources and less harassed teachers, may also offer a greater number and range of voluntary sporting and cultural activities through which cross-class friendships may develop.

Instructional processes

A second possibility is that student attainment is somehow raised by higher quality instruction in middle class schools. In quantitative research on school mix this idea has grown out of the work on tracking and curriculum placement pioneered by Parsons (1959) in which allocation to different tracks is seen to lead to variation in the kinds and amounts of learning for the individuals exposed to them, such that, even after levels of prior attainment have been taken into account, those exposed to academic tracks will achieve at a higher level.[3] While this perspective on tracking is by no means generally accepted, the same approach has also been used on occasion to explain between-school differences related to school mix.[4] Alexander *et al.*, for instance, made the connection between some of the literature on the effects of track placement and studies which showed that the proportion of students placed in academic courses varied systematically according to school composition. They argued:

> The higher educational goals evidenced in high SES schools may be a function not only of school-wide normative climates and of the distribution of interpersonal relations but also of the greater likelihood of enrolling in a college preparatory course in such settings.
>
> (Alexander *et al.* 1979: 224)

Yet Gamoran (1987) has pointed out there has been little research on how learning opportunities vary between schools with different compositions, as most studies have examined within-school differences in instruction in classes or tracks with different compositions. He explains this is because instructional theorists do not give any particular significance to school-level composition over the composition of other within-school levels such as the class or learning group. The rationale, as argued by Dreeban and Barr, lies in a nested perspective of schools:

> Since school systems comprise nested layers of organisation, among them, schools, tracks, grades, classes, and instructional groups, all of which have compositional qualities, there is no special justification for singling out schools as the proper locus of compositional effects.
>
> (Dreeban and Barr 1988: 132)

From this perspective, as schools attempt to 'provide appropriate instruction to a large and diverse clientele in aggregations of workable size and composition' (*ibid.*), each layer of the school has a different composition from those up- or downstream. The problem is therefore not how the composition of any single level of the schooling system, in our case the school as a whole, has an impact on instruction, but how the composition of successive levels within the system shapes the arrangement of instructional settings. Thus, while instructional theorists would agree that school-level composition constrains the characteristics of students available to other levels within schools, they have concentrated on within-school processes on the grounds that, because they are closer to the instructional process, learning groups, classes and tracks are more likely to provide an understanding of how compositional effects might work. For instance, after a discussion of compositional effects at the school level, Dreeban and Barr provide their own analysis at the class and learning group level.

The nested argument, if seriously entertained, has important implications for thinking about the impact of school mix. It suggests that there is no particular reason to look for explanations of a school mix effect solely at the school level such as normative school 'climate' or the quality of the principal. Rather the mechanisms which create differences in achievement could lie at the departmental, track, classroom or small group level. This suggests the need to examine how compositional effects occur at different levels within schools to form a cumulative compositional effect at the school level. (Note that while the nested argument has been raised in conjunction with instructional processes, there is nothing logically to preclude the argument applying to other school processes as well.)

Numerous qualitative studies at the track level provide most of the evidence of instruction varying according to SES composition.[5] To begin with, high-track students take more academic courses and more courses overall than low-track students. In a similar way higher SES schools, responding to parent and student pressure, may provide a more demanding range of course offerings to working class students than predominantly working class schools and may insist on working class students taking more courses. Qualitative tracking literature also points to numerous differences in instructional *quality* between high and low tracks. A large number of studies have shown that the pace and complexity of the taught curriculum is much less demanding in lower tracks. Because there is more use of oral recitation and structured writing, students are given a fragmented rather than comprehensive coverage of topics. Questions tend to be answered at a lower level of complexity in lower tracks and tasks often involve rote learning rather than the deeper kinds of analysis more common in higher tracks. Topics may be left out entirely and assessment is less frequent and less demanding.

Why do these differences occur? One reason may be that students in different tracks actively construct differential classroom practice as their actions and responses influence what is taught (Davies 1983; Delamont 1983). It is likely that implicit 'treaties' are negotiated between classes and teachers as to the kind and amount of work done (Powell *et al.* 1985). Jones (1991) also suggests that it may be the social class characteristics of students which largely determine the pace and nature of instruction. In her study, working class girls in '5 Mason' encouraged their teachers to give copying work by working silently and discouraged them from asking substantive questions by failing to co-operate. On the other hand, middle class '5

Simmonds' girls reinforced teachers who gave project work and frequently asked questions of the teachers. Jones argues that both groups of girls were producing classroom practices according to their class cultural conceptions of what it was to 'get the teacher's knowledge' and 'do school work'.

Studies of tracking also point to possible differences in instructional processes which stem from school mix. The patterns are often similar to those found by Connell *et al.* (1982) and Metz (1990) in schools of different SES composition. Similar processes of curriculum differentiation as a result of SES composition could also occur at other levels. Working class schools, gearing themselves towards the kinds of students they mainly teach, may purchase or develop less demanding teaching resources than those in higher SES schools or have fewer resources to teach with anyway. There may be less expectation to cover a curriculum comprehensively and school- or department-based tests and exams may be less frequent and less demanding.

The finding that the low-stream girls in Jones's (1991) study would not co-operate willingly in some activities also points to the likelihood that disciplinary and pastoral aspects of classroom practice will differ by school composition. Teachers in higher SES schools are likely to find it easier to be demanding of students over issues such as classroom behaviour and homework because there will generally be a higher level of compliance. Where teaching is more difficult, discipline issues may be ignored as a survival strategy. Similarly, higher SES school teachers may have more time and attention to give to working class students because, with more students 'coping', they do not have to respond to a mass of learning and social needs as teachers in more working class schools do.

Instructional quality may also be affected by teacher characteristics which vary by track. Experienced teachers and those considered more successful are disproportionately allocated to higher tracks. Teachers put more time and energy into preparing for high-track classes, tend to be more enthusiastic when teaching them and have a higher expectation of being challenged intellectually. By contrast, prolonged exposure to low-track classes is said to worsen teachers' competencies. Teachers are also seen to stereotype and label students differentially according to track, viewing high-track students positively and low-track students negatively. These differences between tracks in teacher motivation and stereotyping may result from the way track composition affects a teacher's sense of self-efficacy (Raudenbush *et al.* 1992). Teachers often prefer high-track classes because students in these classes are orientated towards the academic goals of the school.

All of these findings about teachers and tracking may again be extrapolated to the school level. For a start, higher SES schools are likely to have more experienced teachers, and perhaps more teachers overall, than lower SES schools (Orfield *et al.* 1996: 68–9). This is because the horizontal mobility in the careers of teachers and administrators noted by Becker (1952) probably persists. Teachers may be more likely to move from low- to high-SES schools than the other way around. Metz (1990: 95) found that 'Teachers who worked with high SES children received more intrinsic rewards . . . more status . . . and more logistical and professional support from better funded schools.' Conversely poor teacher motivation and negative stereotyping of pupils may be a common phenomenon at low-SES schools. Teachers and administrators may collectively feel they are 'at the bottom of the heap' relative to other schools and develop, over time, lowered expectations and competencies. Petrie (1984) calls this 'low institutional pride syndrome'.

Although tracking literature is useful, it is unlikely to suggest *all* the instructional mechanisms that contribute to a school mix effect. One evident omission is consideration of lesson content. The work of Bernstein on the classification and framing of educational knowledge suggests that differential framing of knowledge in higher SES and working class schools might provide some further answers. It is likely that, in Bernstein's (1975) terms, there is a tight framing of knowledge in many schools with inflexible boundaries between the uncommonsense knowledge of the school and the commonsense knowledge of the pupils and their families. In high-SES schools the idea that academic knowledge is important, despite being relatively abstract, is likely to be accepted by students because middle class children are socialized from an early age to understand what of the outside world may be brought in to the pedagogical frame. Yet this tight framing of knowledge may be relaxed by teachers in lower SES schools in pursuit of relevancy to the everyday realities of working class students. This is because teachers in working class schools are likely to be faced with a 'Hobson's choice'. They could teach a tightly framed curriculum in order to provide students with credentials and life chances but this approach would probably generate high levels of resistance and alienation from many students and create discipline problems. Therefore a more popular approach may be to teach in a way which, although creating less resistance, also fails to provide the good academic outcomes students might have gained in predominantly middle class schools.

Organizational and management processes

A further possibility is that student attainment is somehow raised by school organizational and management processes which support the instructional work of schools indirectly by keeping them running smoothly and safely. These processes might be seen to include the work schools do when monitoring truancy, addressing the 'social welfare' needs of 'at risk' students, organizing meetings and assemblies, maintaining buildings and resources, raising money, recruiting staff and promoting themselves in the marketplace. These organizational and management factors do not appear to have been seriously considered in the quantitative discussion to date because of its classroom focus. However there is more support in qualitative literature (Metz 1990; Brown *et al.* 1996a).

A 'whole school' effect

It is also important to consider the possibility that a number of processes may underlie the impact of school mix. Dreeban and Barr (1988) argue that instructional processes are likely to be more important than reference group processes, at least in junior classes, but Hallinan argues that both sets of processes may be important. 'Is it not more reasonable to argue', she asks, 'that both reference group and instructional processes are set in motion by school or class composition?' (1988: 144). Hallinan points out these processes are also likely to interact with each other to transmit compositional effects to student achievement. Student relations are likely to assist or hinder particular approaches to instruction, while different kinds of instruction might also foster or preclude various kinds of student relations (Bossert 1979). Hallinan (1988) makes the further point that while both reference group and instructional processes may cause a school mix effect, one or other may predominate according to the school setting.

Others have taken an even broader view of the complexity of schools and the way in which seemingly quite disparate school processes might be linked to one another. Connell (1994) has argued that the best interventions for low-SES schools will be those which use a 'whole school' approach to change. Connell's whole school argument suggests a more holistic view of the possible causes of a school mix effect by incorporating *all* processes occurring within a school including reference group, instructional *and* organizational and management processes. Thus the processes underlying the effect of school mix may be even more multidimensional than Hallinan proposes. Indeed a school mix effect could represent the cumulative effect of numerous smaller effects of school mix on school processes across many dimensions of school life.

Other issues raised by previous research

The above possibilities all needed to be considered in a satisfactory research design but to incorporate them in a single study was difficult. Previous ethnographic studies have rarely had such a broad focus nor tried to examine school processes at a variety of levels. To complicate matters further, at least three other issues raised by previous research need consideration before we turn to the actual design of the Wellington study. These are the problem of within-school differentiation, the issue of individual student orientations, and the difficulty of determining causality in quantitative and qualitative research.

Within-school differentiation

One implication of conceptualizing a school mix effect in a multi-level way is that where practices such as tracking occur, working class students are invariably allocated to lower 'ability' groups (Woods 1990; Hallinan 1994). This could be seen to counteract the beneficial effects of a high-SES school mix because tracking may create compositional conditions at the track level (and therefore at the class and within-class level) that do not reflect those of the school as a whole. As Alexander *et al.* (1978: 65) argue, 'Differential tracking in secondary schools . . . introduces academic inequalities where none previously existed, and in doing so contributes independently to educational and socioeconomic inequalities.'

Shavit and Williams (1985) have suggested that the effects of school mix may be replaced, in part, by the effects of within-school grouping where schools are internally stratified. On the other hand, banding in many of the schools in Lauder and Hughes's (1990b) study appeared to have little effect on the school mix effect they report. This points to the possibility that a school mix effect might occur *despite* tracking for a number of reasons, the most likely being that low tracks in higher SES schools would differ substantially in their student characteristics from low tracks in low-SES schools.

How would we explain this? In higher SES schools greater competition may make entry into high tracks more difficult than in predominantly working class schools. Garet and Delany (1988) found, for instance, that in high-SES schools, students had less chance of getting into academic science courses than similar students in lower SES schools. As a result of this competition for high-track places, many middle class students would be in the lower tracks of higher SES schools; these then, in terms of their instructional and social processes, would be more conducive to academic success than parallel classes in working class schools. The low tracks of middle class schools may therefore resemble the high rather than low tracks of predominantly working class schools.

The argument that tracks in high- and low-SES schools differ in their SES composition not only takes account of the compositional effects of tracking, but suggests a school mix effect might actually work through them. It suggests that working class students are more likely to succeed at middle class schools because they are exposed to advantaged learning conditions through reference group and instructional processes, typically associated with higher tracks, which in turn are related to higher SES school composition. It is also possible that organizational/management processes at the school level influence students irrespective of tracking within schools.

The importance of student orientations

The quantitative account, by treating all students as essentially similar, fails to recognize that even students from common social class backgrounds can have quite different orientations to schooling. In contrast, the issue of student subcultures and their orientations to schooling has been a central concern of qualitative research in education. The ethnographies of Lacey 1970, Willis 1977, Ball 1981, Brown 1987 and Jones 1991 all have important implications for the way in which causal mechanisms are hypothesized.

Underpinning these ethnographies is the theory that school subcultures reflect societies deeply structured by class, gender and ethnic relations. Class-based school subcultures are seen to interact in a variety of ways with the culture of schools to produce different outcomes for different subcultural groups. According to this view schooling primarily reflects dominant or ruling class culture – that of high-SES groups such as those from professional and managerial backgrounds. It follows that students from high-SES backgrounds have an organic class relationship to the school (Bourdieu and Passeron 1977; Connell *et al.* 1982). In Bourdieu's terms, ruling class students find that the school's values, expectations and perspectives are largely consistent with their own world views. These students are amenable towards and accepted by the school such that they are able to convert their cultural capital into high credentials. As they usually perceive the school as working in their interests, they generally take a positive, normative approach to the school's social and academic goals. Working class students on the other hand will usually be instrumental or alienated rather than normative because, as a result of their significantly different class cultural background, they lack the cultural capital needed to identify with and/or be favourably received by the school. Consequently many working class students struggle with their schooling and often fail to achieve academic qualifications.

It might then be argued that in a school with a reasonably balanced mix, the predominant ethos of the school and of the high-SES students with cultural capital would somehow 'rub off' on working class students, lifting their academic performance compared to their counterparts in predominantly working class schools. That is, the normal working class subcultural response to schooling is in some way modified or altered in schools with a higher SES mix. Yet how this might happen depends very much on the manner in which the subcultures themselves are theorized. This issue, a central concern of the ethnographic literature on school subcultures, relates to Rutter's question about causal direction cited earlier – whether children influence schools or schools influence children. It translates in this context as the question of whether subcultures result from the influence of the school; or subcultures have already been determined by children's class cultural backgrounds so that the school makes little difference; or subcultures result from the interaction of both the school and class cultural processes.

The first view is taken in the UK by Lacey (1970) and Ball (1981) who argue that the development of school subcultures stems from the internal sorting and selecting arrangements of schools. Over time, pupils placed in low streams/bands (generally working class) develop anti-school values while those placed in upper streams/bands (generally middle class) exhibit pro-school and pro-academic attitudes. From this perspective, working class students would prefer to take a normative or at least instrumental orientation to school but are constrained from doing so by school influences which cause them to develop negative, anti-school attitudes and values.

It follows that if it is the school that 'cools out' working class pupils then the modification of school processes may in some way allow working class students to improve their achievement in schools with a broad school mix. Most obviously, it might be thought that schools with a heterogeneous mix have less internal selection and therefore are less likely to alienate students. However, we have just seen that school mix effects have often been found even where schools are formally differentiated. This model may also point to direct rather than indirect influences of high-SES peers as the source of a school mix effect. Perhaps *despite* school selection processes alienating working class students, the presence within the school of large numbers of high-SES students is helpful to working class students, influencing their aspirations and lifting academic performance.

Willis (1977) argues for the second view. He believes that working class students fail not so much because school processes work against them but because of their own class cultural characteristics. His now famous position is that the 'lads' prefer to take an alienated orientation to their schooling. Willis's account recognizes that working class pupils might be unwilling to succeed academically rather than being unable to do so. From this point of view a school mix effect would only occur because working class students are less able to form an alienated subculture in schools – greater working class success in socially mixed schools would essentially be imposed.

This might occur because the relative balance of power between the class-based orientations of students in schools and therefore the effectiveness of school processes is modified by school mix. In socially mixed schools, working class students may achieve better academic results because they are forced to meet the more demanding characteristics of the school created by its higher mean SES mix. An alienated orientation would be more difficult to sustain here for several reasons. First, given the large scale of compliance, the general administrative/disciplinary system of the school may be more effective and demanding of resisters. Second, teachers may be able to give more time and energy to 'difficult' pupils given that they are less likely to be swamped by motivational, behavioural and learning difficulties. Resistance would also be more difficult in socially mixed schools because there would simply be fewer students with alienated orientations to provide support to resisters. The situation might be similar to that noted by Willis in the years prior to the 'coming out' of the 'lads':

> Even if there is some form of social division in the junior school, in the first years of the secondary school everyone it seems is an 'ear'ole'. Even the few who come to the school with a developed delinquent eye for the social landscape behave in a conformist way because of the lack of any visible support group.
>
> (Willis 1977: 60)

This model poses difficulties for the concept of a school mix effect because if working class students are inherently alienated it is doubtful whether schools could win them over. In any case, Willis's analysis is problematic. His data do not easily support his argument that the 'lads' were true resisters (Walker 1985, 1986). Moreover, as Brown (1987) points out, Willis dismisses as ideological dupes the great majority of working class students who do not overtly resist their schooling. Furthermore, his work does not explain why school resistance doesn't surface much earlier. Given that it is being viewed as a class cultural attribute, an alienated orientation might be expected to show up in the early school years, but there is no evidence of this.

The third, interactional view is offered by Brown (1987), and in New Zealand by Jones (1991). They discard the dichotomy inherent in the previous approaches where pupils are seen as either accepting, normative and pro-school or rejecting, alienated and anti-school. Instead they view the majority of working class students as fitting neither category. Working class students are seen to comply with school and go along with its processes for instrumental reasons – as a means to working class ends.

Brown (1987) usefully proposes the notion of 'frames of reference' (FOR) to highlight a range of working class responses to schooling. Working class pupils are seen either to accept school (a normative 'getting out' FOR), reject it (an alienated 'getting in' FOR) or, most commonly, just comply with it (an instrumental 'getting on' FOR). FORs, the focal concerns of working class youth, represent different selections from the various class cultural and educational resources available to working class youth. Brown argues that working class academic success depends neither solely on pupils' attitudes to school nor on the evaluations of students by teachers but on the *interplay* between pupils' collective understandings of the purpose of being in school (especially their perceptions of the relationship between schooling and the labour market) and the school's own selection processes.

Brown's approach presents a number of further implications for a school mix effect beyond those posed by the previous models. It suggests that working class students make various types of educational decisions based on the cultural and educational resources available to them and that their school orientations represent some kind of selection from those resources. His model implies, therefore, that a school mix effect could work in different ways and to varying extents for different groups of working class students. For instance, it may be that for working class students with a normative 'out' FOR, school mix is important because it extends the resources available, given that, as Lacey and Ball would have it, they are already disposed towards academic success. For those working class students with an alienated 'in' FOR, school mix might overcome their cultural resistance in imposed ways as described in relation to Willis's work. However, it is for the most numerous working class 'ordinary kids' with an instrumental 'on' FOR that school mix may be particularly significant. According to Brown, these pupils are usually compliant, accepting the school's offerings in a passive, non-decision-making way. In this case the influence of higher SES students may 'rub off' as the exposure to cultural capital *modifies* their cultural attitudes, values, knowledge and world views and leads to greater academic success.

Causality in quantitative and qualitative research

In Chapter 2 it was argued that large quantitative studies are not capable of examining subtle processes such as those that might be causing a school mix effect. Where quantitative researchers have tried, their instruments have often proved inadequate. A pupil questionnaire used by Rutter *et al.* to elicit information on student behaviours provides an example:

> Q27 During this term have you drawn or written anything on any part of the school building? (Do not include desks).
> Q28 Since last September, how many times have you been kept in detention?

(Rutter et al. 1979: 214–216)

Rutter used this kind of data to create a delinquency rate for each of the schools in the study. Yet how accurate or insightful can data gathered in this way be? We have seen from Brown's work that, if anything, resistance is likely to be a resource available to working class students rather than a fixed student attribute. Lauder *et al.* (1992) take this argument further, suggesting that school organization, peer group subcultures, family background and views of the labour market may all influence student responses to schooling to varying extents. For this reason the composition and nature of 'delinquent' student subcultures are likely to be dynamic rather than static. An instrument such as Rutter's pupil questionnaire cannot hope to investigate the changing nature of shared meanings within student cultures or the shifting power relations within and among them.

By comparison, detailed qualitative analyses over time are much more suited to investigating subtle processes such as these. However they in turn are not able to demonstrate the extent of causal relationships. This is because many key causal relationships can only be 'observed' and inferred by qualitative studies. For instance, power relations within a school may be indicated by signs on doors or where teachers sit in staff meetings but they cannot be 'proven'. Nor is there any logical way to relate detailed qualitative findings to highly aggregated quantitative data. Thus quantitative research can find correlations but not investigate the causal processes that underlie them, while qualitative research can investigate those processes in more depth, but not demonstrate causality either. This problem is not unique to this study. The slippage between quantitative and qualitative methodologies is an enduring problem in social science research (Hogan 1992).

There is, then, a hiatus between quantitative and qualitative studies which means that a full causal account of school processes will remain elusive. In an ideal world a study could be developed which would bring the two sufficiently close to create a strong presumption in favour of one particular causal explanation. However, over and above the epistemological difficulties in developing such an account, there were further practical constraints on the research methodology that could be employed for the Wellington study, related both to the sample of students observed and to the sample of schools. The net effect of these constraints was to limit the aim of the Wellington study to that of establishing whether the *conditions* existed to support one or more of the hypotheses articulated earlier.

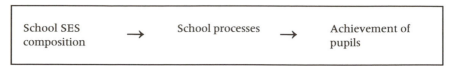

Figure 3.1   General model of the relationship between SES composition, school processes and individual achievement

A research strategy for the Wellington study

A general model of the relationship between the influence of SES composition on various school processes (reference group, instructional, organizational/ management) which in turn influence the achievement of individuals is presented in Figure 3.1.

I decided that one way to approach the study would be to find out whether certain kinds of processes were to be found in schools with particular social class mixes and to investigate whether these processes *created the conditions* which could plausibly lay the foundations for explaining a school mix effect. For instance, it could be investigated whether students in predominantly middle class schools do have higher socioeconomic friends than those in more working class schools. If this turned out to be the case, the feasibility of a reference group explanation for a school mix effect could be confirmed despite the fact that it would not be possible to demonstrate directly the achievement benefits that contact with higher SES students might bring. In a similar way, it would be possible to work through each of the processes described above and ask whether the conditions exist for them to be plausible as a cause of a school mix effect.

The matched students

The Wellington study used matched students partly because it was thought that individual students could be useful 'guides' to the often confusing social landscape of the schools. It was also apparent that the students observed in the Wellington schools should be matched across the schools to be sure of comparing like with like – of studying the experiences of similar sorts of students in the different schools. I chose to focus on 'ordinary kids' (Brown 1987) – the 'invisible majority' of working class students who neither accept nor reject the school but comply with it in order to 'get on' in working class terms. The students selected were chosen from a cohort of approximately 1700 students in Wellington who were entering secondary schools as Year 9 students in 1994 and who were part of the Smithfield Project (Waslander *et al.* 1994). The criteria considered for the selection of the matched students were:

- school attended;
- socioeconomic status;
- prior attainment and orientation.

School attended

The students were all drawn from contributing schools to the four secondary schools selected for the study (to be discussed shortly). The decision to focus on Year 9 students was mostly pragmatic as this was the age level of the Smithfield cohort at the time of this study. However, the junior secondary school may also be a particularly good level at which to view differences in school processes as curricula at that level are not directly tied to national examinations and may therefore be more likely to reflect school-specific processes.

Socioeconomic status

A reasonably sophisticated family-based and longitudinal measure of SES was used to select the matched students. This measure built on the Elley–Irving Index (Elley and Irving 1985), a commonly used New Zealand SES measure based on occupations, but also took account of the occupations of both parents or caregivers where appropriate, as well as both past and present employment. The matched students involved in the study had SES ratings between 4.0 and 5.0 (where 1 is the highest SES and 6 the lowest). A more clearly working class cohort may have been preferable (say 5–6) but this was not possible because there were insufficent working class students in any of the higher SES schools once other criteria were considered.

Prior attainment and orientation

Students close to the mean for their SES groups across the four schools were selected. The students were matched on standardized achievement tests of reading comprehension, reading vocabulary, listening comprehension and maths as well as a number series test specifically developed for the Smithfield Project (Thrupp 1996; Waslander *et al.* 1994). I also checked that the selected students had a similarly positive orientation to schooling by examining their replies to a number of questions drawn from an academic self-concept instrument also developed for the Smithfield Project.

It is important to enter the caveat that the matching process should only be seen as a 'best guess' attempt to find a group of working class students with similar characteristics. It is necessary to be somewhat sceptical about the prior achievement data in particular as there has been debate in New Zealand about the accuracy of the standardized tests used (Beck and St George 1983; Chapman *et al.* 1985). The matched students were, however, briefly visited in their contributing schools the year before going to the four secondary schools selected for the study. This allowed me a chance to confirm, through

Table 3.1   The matched students – gender, ethnic and SES characteristics

Name	Gender	Ethnicity	SES	Mother's occupation/s	Father's occupation/s
Tui College					
Tony	M	European/Pakeha	4.2	Planning manager, sandwich hand	Spray painter
Terry	M	Pacific Islands	5.0	Housewife	Plasterer
Tina	F	European/Pakeha	5.0	Shop assistant, nurse aide, housewife	Absent
Trudy	F	European/Pakeha	4.1	Office clerk, housewife	Electronic installer, bus driver
Teresa	F	European/Pakeha	4.8	Housewife, housemaid, shop assistant	Boilermaker, bus driver, service station attendant
Victoria College					
Vince	M	European/Pakeha	4.0	Hairdresser, clerk	Printer
Vicky	F	European/Pakeha	4.6	Photocopy supervisor	Fitter-welder, tyre fitter
Wakefield College					
Wilma	F	European/Pakeha	4.7	Factory worker, housewife, shop assistant	Cable jointer, overseer, custom liaison officer
Wendy	F	European/Pakeha	5.0	Shoe shop assistant, fashion assistant	Painter and paperhanger
Winona	F	European/Pakeha	4.5	Payroll clerk, costing clerk	Smallgoods person, butcher
Plimmer College					
Penny	F	European/Pakeha	4.1	Receptionist, cashier, salesperson	Car parts manager, sales rep.
Pauline	F	European/Pakeha	4.2	Receptionist, telephonist, night filler	Typewriter mechanic
Polly	F	European/Pakeha	4.5	Clerk, salesperson	Self-employed builder

observation and casual discussion with teachers, that these students did, in fact, have the kinds of characteristics the matching data suggested.

Some characteristics of the 13 students finally selected for the study are shown in Table 3.1 above. (Note that the names given to the matched students start with the same letter of the alphabet as their school.) The mothers of the matched students were likely to work at home or in clerical or sales jobs while their fathers were often skilled tradespeople, clerical workers or small business owners.[6] Although no attempt was made to match the students in terms of ethnicity and gender, 10 of the 13 students turned out to be female and only one, a New Zealand-born Samoan, was non-European/Pakeha.[7] The gender balance was probably a matter of chance but the ethnic bias may have resulted from the decision to choose students of average prior attainment for their SES group. Most Maori and Pacific Islands students were below average within their SES group in the four schools.

A range of schools

A key consideration when choosing schools for this study was the extent to which the relationship between school mix and school policy and practice could be explored. For instance, selecting schools by their different mix characteristics only would leave substantially unanswered the question of whether policy and practice differences between schools were a result of their mix or independent of it. Rather, to investigate better whether the policy and practice features of schools are related to mix or independent of it would require a sample of schools of not only different but also similar composition. The 'ideal' cross-section could not be used, however, because the sheer number of schools required was not feasible when balanced with the need for detailed fieldwork and because the combinations were not available locally. Truly mixed schools could not be found in Wellington because of the effects of residential segregation and school selection.

The Wellington study therefore involved just four schools but some of them had similar as well as different mix characteristics. The schools were all coeducational suburban high schools with roughly equal numbers of boys and girls. Table 3.2 provides their main SES, ethnic and size characteristics.

Tui College is by far the lowest SES school in the sample, Wakefield and Victoria colleges are middle class schools with very similar SES intakes and Plimmer College has a slightly higher mean SES again. Similar and different proportions of students from different SES groups are presented in the selected schools. Wakefield and Victoria colleges, with similar compositional features, are particularly useful in terms of the mix versus independent policies and

Table 3.2   Features of the Wellington schools: SES, ethnicity, size[8]

School	School SES				Ethnicity (%)			
	%Low	%Mid	%High	Mean	Pakeha	Maori	Pacific Islands	No. of students
Tui	44	51	5	4.62	40	39	20	550
Wakefield	11	68	21	2.92	76	12	3	600
Victoria	11	66	23	2.97	81	7	5	950
Plimmer	6	57	37	2.63	85	9	1	700

practices debate. The schools by no means represent the full mean SES range that exists in Wellington. The mean SES of the 11 Wellington secondary schools involved in the Smithfield Project, for instance, ranged from a low of 5.31 to a high of 2.14.[9] However, those with a lower mean SES than Tui College had changed so rapidly in their SES composition over the last few years because of the removal of zoning that the processes in the school were likely to be very unstable and not necessarily related to their present socio-economic mix. At the other extreme, those with a higher mean SES than Plimmer College did not have enough SES 4.0–5.0 students for matching purposes.

Table 3.2 also provides the ethnic composition and number of students[10] in each of the schools. Tui College is typical of many low-SES New Zealand schools in having relatively high proportions of Maori and Pacific Islands students. Furthermore, whereas parental unemployment was negligible at the other schools, it grew at Tui College from 16 per cent to 30 per cent of the Year 9 intake over 1990–3. Tui College was also much smaller than most of the others by 1993, reflecting a declining white middle class roll over the previous decade as the school had become increasingly working class and non-Pakeha. Wakefield College was the smallest of the middle class schools. This reflected less a decline in its popularity with middle class families than the aging demographics of the suburb in which it was situated. However, size differences between the schools of the magnitude indicated did not appear to have much impact on their organization or ability to access resources.

Table 3.3 presents examination attainment data for the four schools (Minister of Education 1995).[11] What is apparent from the School Certificate (SC)[12] figures is that the middle class schools all experienced considerably more national examination success than Tui College, with up to twice as many students gaining B passes or better. Moreover fewer students at Tui College chose or were allowed actually to sit the exam than at the middle class schools. The proportion of students at the middle class schools gaining Year 13 (usually university entry exam) qualifications was much higher, especially at Plimmer College. Compared with Tui College fewer of the students at the other schools left school with no qualification at all. These figures do not, of course, point to

Table 3.3 The Wellington schools' 1994 examination results and school leaver qualifications (%)

	School Cert. grades B or higher	Candidates of Year 9 entrants	School leavers	
			with Year 13 qualification	with no qualification
Tui	24	77	25	18
Wakefield	40	100	39	12
Victoria	48	95	49	10
Plimmer	45	100	63	11

a school mix effect because much of the difference between the schools may be due to individual class backgrounds or differences in school effectiveness, independent of mix. Nevertheless the varying numbers of students experiencing academic success in the schools should be kept in mind.

Victoria College was the only school to formally group students. It had a longstanding practice of creaming off two 'high-band' classes of 'able' students at junior levels and mixing up the remaining students into 'low-band' classes. The inclusion of Victoria College allowed the study to explore whether within-school differentiation (in this case by partial banding) had any impact on a school mix effect.

Gender and ethnicity

Although the Wellington study's emphasis on social class is clearly defensible given the erasure of social class already noted, the extent to which issues of ethnicity and gender should also be addressed was an important consideration. Flanagan rightly points out:

> In research that is relevant to achievement, a main effects paradigm has predominated . . . [even] work that is motivated out of an interest in increasing equity has failed to treat race, social class, and gender as intersecting issues. Consequently, the literature tends to oversimplify issues and presents partial, inadequate solutions for addressing equity.
> (Flanagan 1993: 359)

However, any study which tries to give full expression to the intersecting issues of gender and ethnicity as well as social class will be extraordinarily complex. The problem was addressed in this study by locating it in suburban schools which were coeducational and, to varying extents, ethnically diverse. The matched students were then selected within those schools on the basis of the SES and prior achievement characteristics noted earlier, regardless of ethnic and gender characteristics. In this way gender and ethnic factors were able to be acknowledged where their influence was apparent while retaining a focus on the influence of social class. Chapters 5 and 6 include discussion of how gender and ethnicity led to different experiences for some of the matched students.

A nested approach

The idea of schools comprising hierarchically nested layers of effects on student learning was popularized by Barr and Dreeban in their study of 'ability' grouping in primary school classrooms, *How Schools Work* (1983). The challenge of statistically modelling nested layers of effects was then promptly picked up by quantitative researchers so that Hierarchical Linear Modelling (HLM) has become the dominant approach to modelling school effects today

(Raudenbush and Willms 1991). Yet it is difficult to find qualitative studies which have attempted to follow the central idea of a school comprising nested layers to structure the examination of school data. There are likely to be at least three reasons for this. First, ethnographies that have tried to examine potentially school-wide factors are rare in any case. Second, this is probably yet another case of the 'soft folks' never reading the 'number crunchers' (Apple and Weiss 1983). Third, qualitative relationships between the different layers of school activity are not as 'apparent' in qualitative studies as they are often thought to be in quantitative studies because, as noted earlier, meanings and power relationships are not observable. The value of such an orderly view of schools may therefore have been discounted by qualitative researchers as too inflexible for the messy work of collecting qualitative data and making sense of it.

Nevertheless if we are to respond to Dreeban and Barr's (1988) argument that compositional effects are likely to reflect processes throughout schools (but not limit this insight to the instructional sphere as they have), then a nested approach does seem to be a useful way to structure data collection and analysis for this study. The value of a nested approach lies in its ability to bring together data at different levels of the school to indicate patterns across it. In this qualitative sense it would not matter if the data could not show clear relationships between the levels of the school or the relative strengths of factors at different levels. Rather the key issue would be that evidence would exist at different levels and that it would mostly point in similar rather than conflicting directions. For instance, if it were found that all of a matched student's reference groups at different levels (the student body as a whole, yeargroup, classgroup, friends, schoolmates, seatmates and so on) were higher SES (or *all* lower SES) than the ordinary pupil, this would constitute more powerful evidence with respect to a school mix effect than if some reference groups were higher while others were the same or lower. In a similar way, if a school was found to have a common approach to curriculum across class-rooms, departments and the school as a whole, this would speak more powerfully to the causes of the effect than discovering substantially different approaches at levels within the school.

The Wellington research therefore attempted to examine school processes in a nested way. This was most apparent in Thrupp (1996) where nested case studies allow the reader to see patterns across different levels of each school. Space does not permit the same approach here but it is hoped still to provide some sense of the study's nested approach.

A comparative approach

Along with comparing levels and different forms of data, the research design was also overtly comparative in three other ways. First, it compared the experiences of several matched students in two different teaching groups within each of the schools to identify common reference group and instructional processes. Second, although I concentrated on English and Social Studies classes, processes were also compared, albeit at lesser depth, across all of the matched students' subject classes. The issue here is that in many studies a path is mapped out for the reader but one is left wondering what was happening off the beaten track. In the Wellington study an attempt was therefore made to view the matched students 'in the round' as recommended by Delamont (1981) and Delamont and Galton (1986). The final level of comparison was across the schools to determine similarities and differences that might relate to school mix.

Data collection

Many kinds of data were collected to gain a broad view of the processes to which the matched students were exposed. The main forms of data collection are summarized below.

Student interviews

Recorded group interviews with the matched students and their friends were used to gain insights into student experiences. Group interviews were used to give students support and encourage discussion. A group approach also usefully retained the anonymity of the matched students and gave important insights into their reference groups. The questions asked were open-ended with a series of prompts if conversation lagged. However, I generally found that after some initial shyness, the students were keen to tell me what they thought about school and life in general. Thus the interview schedule ended up forming only a very loose framework.

Student questionnaires

A simple questionnaire was administered early in the year to all students in the matched students' form classes. This provided useful information about the matched students' friends and contacts around the school and was also used to help to select students for the group interviews. The questions were then repeated late in the year as part of an extended questionnaire which also asked students to comment on their teaching classes, out-of-school activities and future aspirations.

Classroom and school observations

Classroom observations involved constructing a record of what was occurring through field notes. I took notes on the activities of the matched students, others they interacted with, the class as a whole, and its teacher. I recorded tasks given to students, collected copies of worksheets, assignments and tests and noted any texts or other resources used. I also taped some class questioning or discussion sequences to compare the nature of teacher–student interaction across the schools. In total 261 (generally one hour) lessons were observed. In general I found that observation of one lesson in any subject class could be misleading but after observing several lessons, a 'picture' of what usually went on began to develop. This was then able to be tested through further discussion with students and teachers. I also spent many hours around the grounds and classrooms with the matched students and their classmates, in the staffroom talking informally to teachers or in departmental or school meetings. I also attended parents' evenings, prizegivings and other school events.

Staff interviews

Like Brown *et al.* (1996a) I felt that discussion with teachers would be essential for understanding teacher behaviour with the observed classes. To this end I interviewed the matched students' English and Social Studies teachers, using open-ended questions about the teachers, their teaching approaches, and their views on the school and its students in general, and towards the observed classes in particular. Late in the year I also asked teachers to rate the chances of individuals passing examinations in their subject and to comment on students' likely futures. Interviews were also held in all schools with heads of departments (HODs), deans, guidance counsellors and senior staff.

Staff questionnaires

A questionnaire was also distributed to all teachers in all the schools. This asked questions about their personal and teaching backgrounds, their involvement in the school, what they thought was good and bad about their school and about their general approach to teaching. The initial, relatively closed questions gathered useful information about teacher characteristics across the schools, while responses to the latter, open-ended questions were used to add depth to my observation data.

Student work samples and teacher evaluations

I collected samples of written work from the matched students' English and Social Studies classes. The aim was to get a full record for comparative analysis of the written work set. Towards the end of the year I held a meeting in each school with Social Studies and English teachers (those whose classes I had observed as well as others) and asked them to comment 'blind' on the work samples I had collected from schools other than their own. I particularly asked them to look at the quantity and quality of work demanded and the suitability of the curriculum if it were for their own students. This provided some useful comparative data on teacher perspectives of curriculum across the schools. Independent comments were also gathered from five teachers from another region. Other single measures of academic difficulty might have been used instead (such as measuring the complexity of language) but these would not have provided such a *general* overview of what was being done.

School documents

Considerable information was also gathered from school documentation, including minutes of departmental, deans', staff and Board of Trustees meetings. School development, policy and financial documents were also useful. Information was also collected from school records, timetables, detention books, absence registers, student reports, referral slips, deans' notes, newsletters, student magazines, staff bulletins and staff handbooks.

Gaining access and carrying out the research

Gaining access to schools and classrooms for the Wellington fieldwork was potentially difficult. To begin with, it was examining classroom practice at a time when matters of teacher competence and accountability had a high public profile. Second, the research was also taking place in a wider context of market competition and curricula reforms with their attendant sensitivities and pressures. To complicate matters further, the number of schools and teachers involved in the study was considerable for a study of its kind and the research design rather inflexible. As I was following particular matched students I simply had to gain access to specific schools, classes and teachers.

The difficulties however were not as great as anticipated. Initial consent turned out to be straightforward because many principals knew me from my work on the Smithfield Project. Nor did I encounter the antipathy I feared from teaching staff. Requests of specific teachers, for instance to observe their classes or to be interviewed, were usually willingly acceded to.

Formal permission to conduct research in schools is of course only the first step in gaining access – access may have to be negotiated not once but many times over (Delamont 1992). During the period of fieldwork I therefore made every attempt to build positive staff relations in the four schools. Although this was limited by the fact that I was working across four schools, the fact that I had been a secondary teacher was very useful for developing credibility. I attended several staff social occasions in each of the schools. Some of my best interviews with teachers were held in pubs!

Gaining access with students was also not as difficult as anticipated. I used the usual secondary school ethnographer's persona and told students I was writing my own book about schools. In general the classes listened quietly while I introduced myself, expressing neither hostility nor acceptance, as they grappled with understanding my role and my likely relationship with them. Only at the contributing school to Tui College did I get challenged directly (by one of the matched students as it turned out):

Teacher: This is Martin Thrupp, he'll tell you what he's doing here today.
Terry: He's looking for marijuana! [Class laughs.]
MPT: Well no, I'm not looking for marijuana . . . actually what I'm doing . . .

However, questions and more subtle challenges invariably followed later as I started to interact with the students:

Student: What do you actually do?

Student: Are you one of those training teachers?

Student: Mr, — threw my shoe up there, can you tell him off?

Nevertheless, on the whole students didn't seem concerned about my presence. Often I was welcomed warmly: 'Come and sit with our group – you haven't been to talk to us yet.'

I was also surprised by the fact that some students, even at the outset, did not seem to modify their behaviour when I was present. For instance, while doing some preliminary observations of the matched students in one of the contributing schools to Tui College, I witnessed an assault on my first day in the classroom. The class observed had a relieving (substitute) teacher whose attempts to teach were being largely ignored as many students talked and wandered around the classroom. I had been talking to two of the matched students and their friends when suddenly one boy sitting at the same group of desks started to swear profusely at his seatmate. In no time the boy being sworn at was in a headlock and being quietly and repeatedly punched in the face and head, very hard. After some time, the watching group, sensing perhaps that the situation was getting out of control, started to make a noise to attract the teacher's attention from the other side of the room. 'Miss, we have a rumble' someone called out. The punching ceased as the teacher looked up, although the verbal abuse continued for some time. Thus although the students involved clearly had a measure of concern for the authority of the teacher, they obviously did not expect me to intervene even though I was unfamiliar and sitting only a few feet away.

This indifference to me seemed to be more the rule than the exception during fieldwork. The classes continued under their own momentum, while I took notes. I chose a friendly but unassuming and non-judgemental role and this seemed to work. Even initially cautious students didn't seem to worry about me once they realized that I would not respond negatively to their swearing or misbehaviour. Occasionally individuals or groups of students would enquire what I was writing down. I would say 'everything and anything' and assure them it would remain confidential. When students asked for help my advice was deliberately vague so as not to be unfriendly but not to encourage the practice either.

Although I had the general permission of the matched students' parents for them to be involved in the study (through its affiliation with the Smithfield Project), the matched students were not themselves told that I was more interested in their experiences than those of anyone else in their classes. In part, this was because I was concerned that they would be intimidated by my presence in the classroom if they knew I was observing them. Moreover, it was almost inevitable that their friends and teachers would find out that they were the focus of my research. If this had happened it could have changed the students' relations with friends and teachers when I was present, perhaps in undesirable ways. For instance, their friends may have teased them or their teachers given them more attention than would normally be the case.

Although treating the matched students as just members of their teaching class may have resulted in a more distant relationship than an individual approach would have done, it was a relationship I felt I needed to maintain. First, as the students were in their early adolescence and mainly female, I did not feel I could count on achieving the confidence enjoyed by school ethnographers with older pupils or pupils of the same gender as themselves. (I was however surprised and pleased about the frankness with which nearly all the matched students and their friends were prepared to talk about themselves and their school experiences.) Second, given that I had four schools to cover and would therefore be out of each school more often than in it, my relationship would inevitably be more distant anyway. Third, and most important, while the matched students were an important focus of my study, the research design went beyond them to the reference group, instructional and organizational/management processes to which they were exposed.

It was this broader focus that usefully allowed me not to single out the matched students in any way. For example, I always gave questionnaires to the whole class and collected in full class sets of their exercise books. I also always interviewed in groups. I aimed to build a general rapport with the classes I observed within which my discussions with particular groups and individuals would not seem out of place. As far as I could tell this strategy was successful with no one suspecting that I had a greater interest in some students than others.

PART II

THE WELLINGTON SCHOOLS

 **4**

Setting the scene

This chapter gives a brief introduction to each of the schools and an overview of their major features. It may also provide a corrective to the following thematic chapters which, through stressing the differences between Tui College and the three middle class schools, at times tend to overgeneralize the features in common among the latter.

Tui College

Located in an area of low-cost housing, Tui College had by far the highest proportion of working class and Maori and Pacific Islands students of the four schools. Things had not always been this way, however. In the 1970s the area was home to upwardly mobile working and middle class Pakeha families, slowly displaced as waves of Maori and later Pacific Islands immigrants arrived in the area. Over the last decade in particular the school had slowly became smaller and increasingly non-Pakeha as many middle class families moved away and those who remained sent their children to other schools. Now the remnants of the former school were only manifest in the amount of surplus space the school had, old photos of predominantly Pakeha students, stacks of dusty textbooks which were no longer appropriate, and an impressive honours board, now also disused.

Tui College's current pupils and most of the teachers did not remember this earlier, different school. The current student intake was primarily character-ized by its ethnic diversity and poverty. The first was more obvious to the casual visitor as large groups of Pacific Islands girls sang songs as they drifted along and the sounds of Maori culture group practice came from the school hall most lunchtimes. Yet there were also subtle signs of poverty. Many students walked a long distance to school regardless of the weather, and uniforms, while clean, were often well worn. The school facilities looked pretty much like those of any other state secondary school in New Zealand except for more than usual litter and peeling paint. The vinyl bench seat opposite the deputy principal's office had been worn shiny and was covered in graffiti.

The principal of Tui College was frank about the intake the school had as a result of white and middle class flight:

> From a student point of view, to be blunt, there are few kids here who have a clue how to work. The output and the tools that enable that output, and the profile of the students coming in, is very much at the bottom end.

The school's focus was consequently on dealing with students 'at the bottom end'. It had a wide range of interventions designed for students with low levels of prior achievement. Almost half the senior curriculum was taken up with vocational 'Transition' courses. The school also placed heavy emphasis on pastoral and guidance activities. Indeed the school's 'social welfare' role was almost as important as its instructional role.

In terms of reference group processes, a central feature of Tui College was the modest range of experiences and expectations/aspirations that the matched students' peers brought to school. A second important factor was that while the Tui matched students usually associated with the relatively 'good' and 'able' peers available to them, their informal reference groups nevertheless reflected the working class nature of the school as a whole. Also of relevance was the strong presence of 'homie' and 'metaller' subcultures within the school which some of the matched students became involved in. Homies are a New Zealand variant on Afro-American urban youth cultures (complete with names such as 'Crypts' and 'Bloods', tagging and rap music) while metallers follow thrashy 'metal' music.[1] One of Tina's friends at Tui College described these groups as follows:

Friend 5: Metallers wear black with metal tops like 'Metallica' [i.e. black T-shirt or sweatshirts emblazoned with the logos of music bands and tight black jeans]. Homies wear 'Origins' tops and baggies [Origins are a cheap sweatshirt brand, 'baggies' refers to extremely oversize jeans] . . . Homies are mainly into rap and that, they are mostly Samoans and Maoris. Metallers are mostly white.

There were also numerous instructional features at Tui College which might help to explain a school mix effect. Low or very low student engagement and academic difficulty was usual in classes across the school. A demanding academic curriculum was missing here apparently because of low levels of student 'ability' and compliance. In many cases teachers were unable to control student behaviour, and those who could were generally only able to achieve this by aiming their teaching strategies at the needs of the 'low-ability' students who dominated. A heavy emphasis on the needs of the 'less able' permeated departments and the curriculum programmes of the school as a whole.

It was also apparent that the nature of the student intake posed enormous problems for school organization and management. Daily routines were very difficult to sustain – pastoral issues dominated. Many teachers were stressed and disillusioned. Staffing the school, keeping up staff and student morale, marketing and fundraising were all persistent problems.

Wakefield College

Wakefield College was located in a predominantly white, middle class, commuter suburb. Faced with a serious decline in student numbers in the early 1980s because of an aging local population and competition from even higher SES schools, Wakefield College had become a market-oriented school. Following the arrival of a very enterprising principal, the school had progressively attracted back not only almost all the available students from within its own suburb but also several busloads of students from nearby suburbs. It was still a small school but one which now seemed to enjoy a very good reputation based on academic and extracurricular successes and a 'no-nonsense' approach to disciplinary matters:

Wakefield teacher: Very dedicated staff, a good school. If I'd known about it previously, I would have sent my own kids here, put it that way.

Unlike Tui College many teachers lived locally and sent their own children to Wakefield College. Despite drawing students from other areas, it was in most respects a neighbourhood school. Most of the students could easily walk to school and had known each other from preschool days. Their parents knew many of the teachers and were often involved in night school classes, entertainment events and fundraising.

Wakefield College ran quite differently from Tui College. There were many systems and structures for organizing students and these were often backed up by punishments for those who did not conform. Yet most students were compliant and diligent and the school ran smoothly. It had an academic course structure to cater for students who were mostly university bound, with an emphasis on extension activities for 'able' students. It also provided numerous extracurricular offerings. Due to its fundraising efforts, the school had excellent physical facilities and resources. It was a school which reflected staff and community pride with staff almost unanimous in their view that students at their college received a very good education.

Reference group, instructional and organizational/management processes differed markedly from those at Tui College. The matched students typically associated with higher SES students. Their peers had many more recreational and travel experiences to bring to the classroom and generally had higher credential and occupational expectations/aspirations than the Tui College reference groups. Subcultures such as 'homies' and 'metallers' were largely absent.

Classroom teaching and learning at Wakefield College were mostly characterized by high or very high student engagement and academic difficulty. Teachers here were advantaged in numerous ways by relatively high levels of student compliance/'ability'. As at Tui College there were a range of instructional approaches but teachers at Wakefield College typically aimed their instruction at the exam success of 'average' and 'able' students rather than 'slow learners'. The same was true of departments and the school as a whole.

Organizing and managing Wakefield College was also more straightforward. With considerable support from middle class students and parents, school routines were efficient and pastoral care issues were not as pressing. There were some staffroom tensions but morale was generally better than at Tui College. Management tasks such as staffing and promoting the school were undoubtably easier. The school's Trustees knew and did what was expected of them. Financial resources were adequate.

Victoria College

Victoria College was also located in a predominantly middle class commuter suburb of comfortable family houses. Like many New Zealand schools, this school had been built to cope with the post-1945 baby boom. The principal suggested that it was a very ordinary school:

> The thing that impresses me most about it is how ordinary it is in the sense that it is a no-frills school . . . We are a basic [school building design] which has had very little by way of extras given to it in the past . . . So we are very much a regular, ordinary state school set in an area for which we can be thankful.

Certainly, the appearance of the school was not unusual. However the strength of the relationship between the middle class community and the school was. For instance, the school worked with local community groups to co-produce a number of annual community events. As at Wakefield many staff lived locally and some had been on the staff long enough to have taught the parents of current pupils. The school unselfconsciously reflected the values of a fairly conservative community:

Victoria teacher: It's a school where the parents reinforce the traditional standards that the school maintains. For example we have this historic prayer, it's been there for years, it's continued to be said in assembly, reinforced by [the principal]. Even if our kids are not Christian, and I think a lot are, it seems to be that wholesome Christian values are the ethos here – 'do good by others, do your best'. Also reinforced by [the principal] . . . 'put yourself forward, serve your community, never be happy with the way things are, always walk around with that feeling that things can be better'.

Victoria College had always had a 'good' reputation. It had an academic course structure and a wide range of extracurricular activities. Many of its students went on to university study.

In most respects, the experiences of the matched students at Victoria College were similar to those at Wakefield College. They also had informal reference groups whose SES was higher than their own and who had relatively high expectations and aspirations compared to Tui College. There was again little evidence at Victoria College of homie or metaller subcultures.

Classes at Victoria College were usually also learning environments of high or very high engagement and difficulty like those seen at Wakefield College. Once again, there was a considerable range of teaching and learning processes occurring in the classrooms observed and, as at Wakefield College, teachers, departments and the school curriculum as a whole centred on the needs of the 'average' and 'able' student.

Daily routines ran smoothly at Victoria and the school was able to maintain a tight guidance and disciplinary system. Staff were generally happy and motivated and enjoyed their work. Cushioned by the nature of the intake, managing the school was also relatively straightforward.

There were, however, some differences between Victoria and Wakefield colleges. Victoria College had an older and more stable staff, more comfortable staff relations and an emphasis on doing things the time-honoured way. There was also less of a focus here on marketing the school and raising funds. This probably reflected both the more secure position of the College with respect to enrolment numbers and the disposition of the principal. However, the differences between Wakefield and Victoria were nowhere of the same magnitude as the differences between these two schools and Tui College.

Partial banding at Victoria College did not appear to make much difference to the reference group or instructional processes that the matched students experienced there.

Plimmer College

In terms of its intake, physical plant and resources, Plimmer College at first glance seemed similar to Wakefield and Victoria colleges – another mainly Pakeha, middle class suburban high school. However, in addition to serving a community similar to those of Wakefield and Victoria, Plimmer College also drew large numbers of 'able', articulate students from relatively wealthy families in other parts of the city:

Plimmer assistant principal: . . . and then you had the young man [student] who came along [to my office] and said, could he use my phone and when I inquired why, he said, 'I have to ring my stockbroker'. And it was true! And then the stock market crashed and he had to have two days off school because he was traumatized by the loss of money!

Part of Plimmer College's attraction was probably that this school had an established reputation for being more 'creative' and 'liberal' in its orientation than other local schools:

Plimmer teacher: The kids as I see them are quite demanding in terms of . . . that things should be interesting. They have partly been taught by the school itself that school is supposed to be something better than sitting in straight rows. So they have been encouraged into a kind of questioning type of style. I think partly too . . . they come into this school [as] a positive choice, there are other choices out there – the straight rows, the discipline style . . . so for some people perhaps it is just your local school but I think many have choice and they choose to come here. So they have the expectation that Plimmer will be more liberal – whatever *that* bloody well means.

There was evidence that many processes at the school level at Plimmer were not well planned or executed. One reason for this may have been the longstanding absence through illness of the deputy principal (DP). However there was an important sense in which this school did not need the tight structures of Wakefield and Victoria colleges (let alone the wholesale campaigns of Tui College) to be successful – its day-to-day routines were carried along by the nature of its student body and the attitudes and values they generally brought to school:

Plimmer teacher: Plimmer College has traditionally attracted a high-quality intake, full of the children of rich, upwardly mobile people. We teach those kids well, and it is easy, and the school was consistently one of the top coed schools in New Zealand. When I arrived the structure of the school was skeletal to say the least because those kids are motivated, learning is what their families value, they know its importance.

Plimmer teacher: When I first came here [from a working class school], I thought, 'my God, this is so loose', I couldn't believe it. There didn't seem to be any structures for anything. I'm still amazed that Plimmer operates in this way, it appears that nothing is prepared before but it is always 'all right on the night'.

However this looseness did not necessarily benefit all students. Just as the matched students tended to be overlooked at Tui College because of the number of students with serious learning difficulties, Plimmer College was very much geared towards the success of the middle class and 'able' so that the matched students tended to be left to flounder.

At Plimmer College the matched students mixed with solidly middle class peers who had high occupational aspirations and expectations. There was some evidence that subcultures like 'homies' and 'metallers' existed but they attracted few adherents.

Classes were usually high- or very high-engagement and difficulty learning environments with many of the same instructional advantages noted at Wakefield and Victoria colleges. Once again, a wide range of teaching and learning processes occurred. There was an even greater focus on the needs of the 'able' than at Wakefield and Victoria colleges, with an emphasis on creativity, style and sophistication more apparent in both the classroom and staffroom.

Daily routines ran very smoothly despite the school's 'laid back' approach. The school did not need a tight guidance and disciplinary system. Issues of concern to staff and management revolved more around their own relationships than problems posed by the student body. Overall Plimmer College was certainly less 'straight up and down' than the other middle class schools, but unlike Tui College this seemed more a case of not having to be tightly structured than not being able to be.

5

It's not what you know . . .

This chapter considers reference group processes across the Wellington schools. We saw in Chapter 3 that while some researchers have hypothesized that a school mix effect might be caused by working class students having higher SES peers in higher SES schools, some studies have also suggested that there is little voluntary contact between working class and higher SES students in schools. The key question then is, which view is correct? Does attendance at a school with a large proportion of middle class students make it more likely that a student's informal reference groups are middle class or not? Put another way, do students' informal reference groups reflect their formal reference groups?

The evidence from the matched students in this study was that they do. This can be seen through an analysis of SES data collected across the schools, shown in Tables 5.1 and 5.2.[1] Table 5.1 gives the mean SES of the matched students' various *formal* reference groups by school and teaching classes. A central point here is that in each school the mean SES of yeargroups and classgroups was, as might be expected, similar to the school as a whole. In general then, it seems that within-school formal reference groups are likely to reflect the mean SES of schools as a whole so that the SES of the school a student attends will largely determine the SES mix of his or her yeargroup and classes. In the Wellington study this was the case even in banded Victoria College, where the low-band form classes containing the matched students were not significantly lower SES than the school as a whole. On average, classes in the middle class schools were more than one SES level higher and in the case of Plimmer College, two SES levels higher than at Tui College. The nearest the middle class schools' form classes, banded or otherwise, came to any class at Tui College was a bilingual (mostly Maori class) at Victoria College which was still 0.6 of an SES level higher than Tui College's highest SES class.

Table 5.1   Mean SES of the matched students' formal reference groups

	Tui			Wakefield			Victoria			Plimmer		
	9A	9B	ALL	9A	9B	ALL	9A	9B	ALL	9A	9B	ALL
School	-	-	4.62	-	-	2.92	-	-	2.97	-	-	2.63
Yeargroup	-	-	4.56	-	-	3.22	-	-	2.95	-	-	2.51
Form/Core classes	4.37	4.96	4.66	3.30	3.36	3.33	3.15	3.14	3.15	2.19	2.20	2.20
Option classes	4.37	5.43	4.39	3.60	3.11	3.43	3.00	3.19	3.08	2.81	2.69	2.73

Table 5.2 gives means of the SES characteristics of the matched students' informal reference groups, by school and teaching classes. There was some variation between measures, different time periods during the year, and different types of reference groups. However, the overall pattern, as indicated by the grand mean, was for the SES of the matched students' informal reference groups to reflect the SES of their formal reference groups even where they were not associating with the full range of students. If we compare the grand mean of the informal reference group contacts with the SES of the students' classgroups,[2] we see that the students at Tui College mixed with students who were, on average, slightly higher SES than the school as a whole while the students at the middle class schools mixed with students who were on average slightly lower SES than the mean for their schools.

Although there seems to be some evidence therefore to support the argument that students stick to their own where possible, the data also suggest that school mix is a more important influence on students' informal reference groups. The matched students at Tui College had friends and contacts who were, like their classgroups, roughly one SES level behind the matched students at Wakefield and Victoria colleges and roughly two levels behind those at Plimmer College. The matched students who attended the middle class schools did associate with more middle class students, a pattern which seemed to hold true to varying degrees for friends, schoolmates and seatmates throughout the year.

One problem however with the data presented in Tables 5.1 and 5.2 is the large number of students at Tui College for whom SES data were not available, either because they had not been provided/collected or because parents were unemployed.[3] Table 5.2 shows that close to a quarter of the informal contacts or mentions were uncodeable. For this reason, I calculated best- and worst-case scenarios, by considering all the missing cases as either SES 1 or SES 6 respectively. Given the best-case scenario, the range of SES means are reduced significantly, yet not enough to break through the ranking of school means. Taking the worse-case scenario, the difference between Tui College and the middle class schools becomes acute. Which of these scenarios are likely to be closer to the truth? Given the nature of the community served by the school, it is extremely unlikely that the missing cases at Tui College were high-SES.

Table 5.2   Mean SES of the matched students' informal reference groups

	Tui			Wakefield			Victoria			Plimmer		
	9A	9B	**All**	9A	9B	**All**	9A	9B	**All**	9A	9B	**All**
Friends												
Term 1 self-identified	4.19	3.00	**3.97**	3.42	3.50	**3.45**	3.13	2.83	**3.08**	1.83	2.21	**2.13**
Term 3 self-identified	4.20	5.00	**4.25**	3.84	2.93	**3.45**	3.50	3.00	**3.07**	2.20	3.41	**2.86**
Term 1 reciprocated	4.00	6.00	**4.50**	3.20	-	**3.20**	3.20	3.50	**3.33**	1.83	1.91	**1.89**
Term 3 reciprocated	3.79	4.33	**3.90**	3.38	2.66	**3.07**	2.66	3.79	**3.27**	2.16	3.25	**2.79**
Schoolmates												
Term 1 self-identified	4.34	3.00	**4.21**	3.38	3.50	**3.41**	3.66	2.57	**3.14**	2.50	2.56	**2.55**
Term 3 self-identified	4.11	4.60	**4.14**	3.33	2.44	**3.05**	3.05	3.13	**3.09**	2.30	2.92	**2.79**
Term 1 reciprocated	4.33	6.00	**4.46**	3.29	4.00	**3.44**	3.80	3.90	**3.85**	1.50	1.70	**1.67**
Term 3 reciprocated	3.91	4.00	**3.92**	3.31	2.50	**3.19**	2.93	3.50	**3.25**	2.38	3.17	**2.85**
Seatmates												
Term 1 self-identified	4.05	2.50	**3.95**	3.07	3.21	**3.12**	3.33	3.96	**3.75**	2.20	2.41	**2.31**
Term 3 self-identified	4.31	5.50	**4.63**	3.39	2.88	**3.22**	2.79	3.47	**3.28**	2.15	3.12	**2.79**
Term 1 reciprocated	3.94	4.50	**3.96**	3.07	3.66	**3.18**	3.29	4.25	**3.80**	2.00	2.36	**2.26**
Term 3 reciprocated	4.38	4.63	**4.41**	3.61	3.00	**3.41**	2.78	3.33	**3.15**	2.11	2.88	**2.62**
T1 observed (Eng/ SocSt)	4.78	5.00	**4.79**	3.42	3.19	**3.36**	3.20	3.98	**3.56**	2.00	2.50	**2.29**
T2 observed (Eng/ SocSt)	4.84	5.09	**4.90**	3.08	3.31	**3.11**	2.85	4.08	**3.52**	1.94	2.81	**2.47**
T2 observed (all subjects)	4.72	4.61	**4.70**	3.33	3.08	**3.24**	3.16	3.57	**3.41**	1.83	2.71	**2.35**

	9A	9B	All	9A	9B	All	9A	9B	All	9A	9B	All
All categories												
Term 1 self-identified	4.18	2.88	**4.06**	3.30	3.36	**3.22**	3.32	3.30	**3.31**	2.14	2.44	**2.38**
Term 3 self-identified	4.19	4.89	**4.24**	3.50	2.76	**3.21**	3.02	3.18	**3.13**	2.20	3.08	**2.80**
Term 1 reciprocated	4.04	5.25	**4.13**	3.15	3.80	**3.26**	3.41	3.97	**3.69**	1.91	2.16	**2.09**
Term 3 reciprocated	4.17	4.39	**4.20**	3.42	2.88	**3.31**	2.80	3.47	**3.20**	2.19	3.00	**2.70**
Grand mean[a]	4.39	4.46	**4.40**	3.37	3.06	**3.27**	3.15	3.51	**3.35**	2.00	2.65	**2.43**
Ind. Highest	4.34	4.46	**4.34**	3.31	3.06	**3.06**	3.15	3.51	**3.15**	2.00	2.21	**2.00**
Ind. Lowest	4.44	4.46	**4.46**	3.43	3.06	**3.43**	3.15	3.51	**3.51**	2.00	3.11	**3.11**
Total no.	539	66	**605**	268	127	**395**	142	180	**322**	147	289	**436**
No. Unem/miss	137	35	**172**	10	-	**10**	35	28	**36**	-	21	**21**
Best case[b]	3.27	3.26	**3.26**	3.21	3.06	**3.06**	2.73	3.17	**2.73**	2.00	2.16	**2.00**
Worst case[c]	5.88	5.00	**5.88**	3.51	3.06	**3.51**	3.71	3.84	**3.84**	2.00	3.39	**3.39**

Notes: a All informal categories, measures for terms one to three.
   b Assuming that all unemployed or missing mentions for any ordinary child were from SES 1 backgrounds.
   c Assuming that all unemployed or missing mentions for any ordinary child were from SES 6 backgrounds.

Rather, many probably were unemployed and/or low-SES. It is likely then that the true picture is closer to, but not as bad as the worst-case scenario, perhaps somewhere between this and the grand mean.

The evidence suggests therefore that the higher the mean SES of the school, the more the matched students *did* mix with middle class students, presumably exposing them more to middle class values, aspirations and knowledge. However, not all of the matched students were equally comfortable in the student cultures of their schools. Those at Tui and Plimmer colleges were generally on the social margins of their classes in terms of both their friendship groups and seatmates. At Tui College the matched students were often seen as conforming 'geeks' who were at the respectable end of the 'rough–respectable' working class continuum within the school. For instance, Tina and her friends generally prided themselves on being at the top of their class while many of the other matched students at Tui College distanced themselves from 'rough' students within the school. At Plimmer College the matched students were 'uncool' compared to the school's generally 'able' middle class student body:

Plimmer teacher: There's the 'cool' boys . . . and the 'uncool' boys . . . then there's the alternative 'cool' group [girls] . . . and then there are the 'uncool' girls like [Penny and her friends].

By comparison, the matched students at Wakefield and Victoria colleges felt more accepted and acceptable among their peers. As Wendy put it, 'everyone here is just normal really'.

Yet it would also be wrong to overemphasize the dislocation of the matched students at Tui and Plimmer Colleges. They *did* find friends among others in their classes and they generally *did* get along with most other students. This was because although students were 'hassled' in the schools for any number of idiosyncratic reasons (a strange voice, a propensity to tears, a funny name), they were not usually 'picked on' for general social class or ethnic characteristics. Only sexual matters seemed to warrant systematic harassment, a point to which we will return shortly.

While the study did not set out to prove that exposure to higher SES peers was advantageous to the matched students in the middle class schools, qualitative evidence did point to a range of factors which may have been important. These are discussed below.

Differences between Tui College and the middle class schools

It was apparent that the characteristics of the students with whom the matched students at Tui College mixed in their formal and informal reference groups differed markedly from those at the middle class schools in ways which could conceivably lead to reduced achievement. To start with, the Tui College matched students' peers had a much narrower range of world experiences. An example of this was that their class and friends were less likely to go away for holidays, particularly overseas. They appeared to spend a lot more time just 'hanging around' the local shopping centre (especially boys) or helping with domestic duties (girls),[4] and were not involved in the same range of out-of-school activities that the peers of the matched students at the middle class schools were. As a result of these differences, the matched students at Tui College were probably not learning in an environment as rich in curriculum-relevant experiences (Heath 1983; Alton-Lee *et al.* 1993) or social capital (Coleman 1990) as were the matched students in the other schools. They may have also been less likely to be exposed to new activities through their friends than the matched students at the middle class schools.

The matched students at Tui College were also mixing with students who had much lower levels of prior attainment. Although the effects of this are discussed in more detail in the next chapter, the key point to note here is that most of the matched students in the middle class schools were able to get more immediate support in and out of class from close friends with high levels of prior achievement.

Vicky: It'd be, like there is the half way [in 'ability' in the class] then there is a couple more people then I'd be there and then there is the top. Friend 1's there [at the top], she gives me the answers and I get used to what I'm supposed to be doing, like she helps me with it.

Plimmer teacher: It's a strange combination but they [Penny and Friend 1, 2 and 4] sit in the same place all the time. I don't know if they are actually friends but they sit in the same place and whether or not Penny and Friend 2 hope that something will rub off [the others], I don't know. Doesn't that sound horrible [laughs]. I don't mean to be horrible but let's be realistic!

The matched students at Tui College could not call on this help to the same extent because there were no students in their classes with higher levels of prior achievement. The seatmates and friends of the Tui College matched students were therefore unlikely to be a source of help, indeed they were more often a burden. This was especially the case when compulsory grouping policies employed by some teachers at Tui College, as a way of supporting special needs and 'less able' students, resulted in the matched students often sitting with those who required considerable help.

Tina: It's kind of annoying sometimes, you have to stop and help them, it's really annoying. — gets moody. You try and do your work and she just keeps talking to you and talking to you and talking to you and sometimes you can't even understand what she's saying.

The study was not able to assess whether, at the outset, students at Tui College had similar academic self-concept to those in the middle class schools. It was apparent that most saw school favourably and were optimistic of their chances of academic success despite their relatively low levels of prior attainment. Yet

Table 5.3 Mean grade and teacher comment in the four schools (%)

	Tui		Wakefield		Victoria		Plimmer	
	9A	9B	9A	9B	9A	9B	9A	9B
Grade	54.8	46.9	77.9	77.6	65.3	61.7	79.2	73.0
Comment	68.3	71.9	88.8	84.8	80.4	68.1	81.6	83.3

they did receive lower mean report grades and got more negative report comments from teachers in their end of year reports than the students at the middle class schools (Table 5.3). In contrast, the students in the matched students' classes in the middle class schools usually received higher mean grades and more positive teacher comments.[5] In this way the view that the students at the middle class schools could succeed may have been reinforced.

Another factor to be considered is that the class peers of the Tui College matched students were almost twice as likely to be absent as those in the middle class schools (Table 7.1, p. 107). It was apparently considered more acceptable among students at Tui College not to come to school. For instance, when the teachers called the roll at Tui College, students would often joke of those who were absent 'she's wagging Miss'. However, at the other schools, not coming to school was less acceptable to students. Although there was no evidence that the matched students were unduly influenced to stay away from school at Tui College, low general attendance sometimes appeared to hinder the progress of classes there as teachers announced they would hold off teaching new material until more students were present, or spent time reviewing material that students had missed through absence.

Student views of likely future qualifications and occupational destinations also differed in arguably important ways. To begin with, although most students at Tui College intended to stay at school to the highest level (Year 13), this was more often a case of marking time until a job could be found than of going on to further education. Students at Tui College thought about qualifications in terms of passing Year 11 School Certificate rather than other senior secondary school or tertiary qualifications. At the middle class schools on the other hand, large numbers already saw the Year 13 Bursary (the highest New Zealand school qualification) as their goal, often to gain entry to tertiary courses.

The reference groups at Tui College also had lower SES occupational aspirations than classes at the middle class schools. Although there was some interest in occupations across the SES spectrum in all the schools, Tui College students typically aspired to trade or service occupations whereas most students at the middle class schools, especially Plimmer College, hoped for a future in managerial and professional fields. Another difference was the extent to which students expected to be able to attain their desired occupation. In a similar way to low-SES students in Brantlinger's (1993) study, only about half of Tui College's students expected to reach their (mostly modest) occupational goals, while students at the middle class schools (especially Plimmer College) were generally more confident they could reach their chosen higher SES occupations.

The matched students and their friends at Tui College also often expected to get relatively unskilled work to start with and then 'work up'. Tony aimed for 'just a small job till you stabilize your family and that, then go on'. They appeared to believe (or wanted to believe) that this kind of incremental occupational mobility would be possible. This view may of course also have been a realistic response to being aware of the inability of many of the families at this school to fund tertiary study. Terry had plans to be a lawyer but said, 'I might not be able to stay at home, I might have to go to my brother's, I might not be able to go to university.'

As they grew older, it is likely the matched students at Tui College would find little support among their peers for the view that further study and entry into higher SES occupations was feasible or even desirable. The matched students in the middle class schools, perhaps because their peers at these schools had higher SES occupational hopes and expectations, expected to do much better:

Vicky: Me and Friend 1 want to be marine biologists . . . I've been reading this book and this girl . . .
Friend 1: It's my book Vicky.
Vicky: . . . this girl saves a baby seal and then she wants to be a marine biologist and I thought, 'Oh yeah, that's quite good' and then I'm walking home with Friend 1 and she says, 'I want to be a marine biologist' and I thought you see, I [had] wanted to be an interior decorator and I [thought] a marine biologist, that would be pretty choice.

The matched students attending Tui College were also much more exposed to 'homie' and 'metaller' subcultures. By the end of their first year at Tui College, the matched students had developed a considerable awareness of these groups. Like those interviewed in Brantlinger's (1993) study, the matched students could explain their characteristics and map their locations around the school:

Tony's Friend 4: The Metallers have took our place now behind D Block . . . they used to be up on the bank, then they come down by that river thing, come on the corner of D Block and now they are behind D Block . . . the Samoans are down by that tree, the ones down by B Block are all Maoris.

Some were attracted to these groups:

MPT (term three): So what else has happened since I last talked to you?
Tina: And I hang around down by the bank, it's really cool, that's where heaps happens, yes, well, everybody smokes and that . . .
Friend 2: We used to hate going down to the bank but after a while you get hooked on it . . .

Tina: You know everyone.

Friend 2: And it's really fun.

Tina: And there was this guy who told me I look like a good rooter. And I went, 'Yes, well' . . . [others laugh] . . . I felt really cool eh.

MPT: So what are they like down there?

Friend 2: They are cool.

Friend 3: They are rude.

Friend 2: They are metallers, they all wear tight jeans. They're mostly fifths. There is kind of a war going on at the moment between the homies and the metallers. The metallers kind of hate the homies . . .

Tina's involvement in the 'bank' 'metaller' group appeared to have little effect on her schoolwork but Trudy left school six weeks before the end of the school year when she came into conflict with her own (different) metaller group:

Trudy's Friend 1: They don't like homies who wear 'Origins', right, and she [Trudy] goes '[Friend 2], you can't come down to the beach if you are going to wear 'Origins' otherwise — [a metaller] will give you the bash.'

Friend 2: And I go [makes a face], 'Oh OK'. My [homie] friends heard about it and they were going to beat up — and he got a hiding. And so the metallers then blamed Trudy and now she is going to get a hiding.

These groups were also present at the middle class schools but small, apparently because there were too many pro-school students to provide much support. Certainly none of the matched students in the middle class schools had anything to do with metallers or homies and rarely mentioned their existence. At Victoria College Vicky became involved with the 'steps' group (this consisted of mostly older students who sat together on the same concrete steps in the school grounds each lunchtime) but the values of this group were much more pro-school than Tui College's metallers or homies. At Wakefield College, some sixth formers were vaguely thought by the matched students to be metallers while at Plimmer College, homies and 'wannabe' homies formed only very small, if distinctive, subcultures. At the middle class schools, conforming 'geeks' were by far the majority!

Perhaps because of the influence of the metaller and homie groups, there appeared to be more physical violence and intimidation among Tui College students which may have had a negative effect on the matched students' achievement there. Many were already concerned about violence in the school before they arrived:

Trudy's Friend 1: All my other friends who go to other schools, they go, 'Oh, Tui College, all the people smoke, you're going to get beaten up.'

There was certainly some intimidation. Fights, which were common, were mostly but not always able to be followed up by teachers or senior staff. The threat of physical violence at Tui College was summed up by the phrase 'getting the bash'. This expression was not heard at any of the middle class schools, where being physically threatened was generally not a part of school life for the matched students.

At a less physically serious level, but one which may have been just as important in terms of achievement outcomes, the reference groups at Tui College also saw a more intense level of inter-student conflict in terms of general 'hassling'. For the boys this involved fighting with other boys for dominance in what seemed to be habitual pecking order behaviour. Tony's regular 'bum outs' (put downs) and 'hidings' (beatings) were a point of amusement to his friends:

Friend 1: Mostly we just talk about rubbish.
Friend 2: Sometimes we have fights.
Friend 4: Most of the time they gang up on Tony.
Friend 2: Everyone bums him out.
Friend 1: Tony got a hiding at lunchtime today.
Tony: I didn't!
Friend 1: You did, you got a hiding from — by the library! [They start to talk about Tony's other hidings and how he had chewing gum put in his hair.]
MPT: You guys give each other a pretty hard time these days don't you? [They laugh and nod, including Tony.]

When the female matched students at Tui College hassled one another it was more to do with rivalries over boyfriends and their own friendships and allegiances. Trudy and her friends provide a good example:

Trudy: We just hang around and go to the library and follow boys [laughter], sit in the garden and talk about our problems and boys and have fights . . .
Friend 1: Arguments! . . . The boy Friend 3 is going out with now, Trudy used to like. They fight over him.
Friend 2: And then Trudy goes, 'Have you noticed every time I like someone, Friend 3 likes him too.'
Trudy: Well it's true! I liked — first then she did.
Friend 3: But before you even said it, I thought, 'He's cute!' And you go, 'Look at him, he's so cute' and then I go, I go, 'No, he's ugly', 'cos I know what she's like.
Friend 2: And then next time Friend 3 admits that she likes him.
MPT: And then it's all on, I suppose.
Friend 4: 'I liked him first!', 'No I did!', 'No I did!'

It sometimes seemed that for Trudy and her friends this kind of activity was the *raison d'être* for being at school, far more than any formal learning goals:

Friend 1: When I'm sick I just want to come to school anyway, sometimes my mother has to force me to stay home.
Friend 2: Home's boring.
Friend 3: You want to know if your friends are going to talk about you or something behind your back.

Friend 1: That usually happens in our group.
Friend 2: If we take a day off and like, something major happens and you're
   not involved in it, like someone's not friends with someone, we don't
   know what's happened, they won't tell us.

However, whereas some studies have suggested that student relations of a
romantic or sexual kind might be a stronger part of school culture in working
class than middle class schools,[6] there was no evidence this was the case in the
four schools studied. Such relations were a part of school life for many of the
matched students and their friends regardless of school mix.[7]

Differences between the middle class schools

Compared with their differences to the reference groups at Tui College, the
differences between the matched students' reference groups at Wakefield,
Victoria and Plimmer colleges were small and only the effects of partial
banding at Victoria College will be looked at here.

The partial banding or streaming at Victoria College appeared to have less
effect on the matched students' reference group processes than might be
expected on the basis of UK 'differentiation–polarization' studies (Hargreaves
1967; Lacey 1970). We have already seen that the partial banding made
(relatively) little difference to the SES mix of classes in the school compared to
classes at the other middle class schools. There was also little evidence that the
matched students or their friends were defining themselves in relationship to
students in high-band classes ('bandies'). I never got the sense of an anti-
school subculture developing as a result of the partial banding although this
may (Kealey 1984) or may not (Jones 1991) have occurred had the school
been fully banded. Rather, for the most part the 'bandies' were 'out of sight
and out of mind', and only discussed when asked about. Certainly Vicky's and
Vince's friends were mostly drawn from their own class, but this was typical of
most of the matched students in all the schools. They may not have had very
high-SES, high-'ability' students in their classes as did the matched students at
Wakefield and Plimmer, but at the same time neither they nor their friends
expressed any real hostility towards those in the high-band classes. Rather
they often seemed confused as to whether 'bandies' were OK or otherwise.

Differences related to gender[8]

Even for students with similar social class backgrounds, reference group
influences sometimes differed considerably because of gender factors. The
approaches of the female matched students to their schooling were very
complex. Sometimes it seemed that they were both academically oriented and
pro-school, while at other times they seemed to enjoy learning but not being
at school, and at yet other times they seemed to like school but mostly for its

social opportunities.[9] Nevertheless all the female matched students complied with the demands of the school. If they resisted, it was resistance of the more passive kind (Stanley 1986).

However as a number of other studies have found, the male matched students were more likely to form highly cohesive 'anti-school' groups along the lines of Willis's 'lads' (1977). 'Having a laugh' and getting into trouble was a relatively large part of these boys' day, adding excitement. This was especially the case for Vince at Victoria College. In English he and his friends 'wound up' their teacher, calling out abuse to her, and eventually even tied her to her chair! When isolated in a classroom for misbehaving during physical education they sneaked out of a window to urinate behind a tree. In their technical class they used a can of deodorant and a cigarette lighter to create a flamethrower which scorched the wall of the classroom. Yet because Vince and his friends were much more compliant and hardworking in other classes the 'resistance' of these boys seemed transitory. Arguably much of their 'misbehaviour' would never have occurred had they experienced other teaching approaches. In a similar way, their degree of compliance changed during the year as they came to the attention of the school's pastoral network. Once it was realized the boys were creating problems for teachers, the deans and deputy principal successfully curtailed many of their activities by putting pressure on them through report systems, threats of suspension and so on.

Another feature of the boys' reference groups in all schools was a 'staunch', macho view of masculinity (Rout 1992). This was partly marked by an exaggerated aversion to homosexuality as a means of defining their masculinity (Buchbinder 1994; Mac An Ghaill 1994). 'Homo' was a generic form of abuse among these boys. They gave any suspected homosexual teachers a difficult time:

Vince: Mr —, where did you go to school?
Teacher: X High School.
Seatmate 8: That's a gay school.
Friend 3: Yeah, gays go there.
Teacher: Comments like that are not necessary.
Friend 3: Sorry, just joking – not.

Vince: Mr —, we really think he's a faggot, he's a Julian [Clary]. He just acts like one, sounds like one too I think.
Friend 3: Everyone thinks he's gay and he bums little boys in his back room.
Seatmate 8: [He] bums you in the back room, he's a fucking cunt.

The male matched students also generally had very sexist attitudes to girls and women. In particular, Vince and friends teased each other mercilessly about prospective sexual partners. For instance, during one library session, Vince ripped a picture out of a book of a cowboy standing beside a horse out of a book and drew a huge penis on the cowboy who was then depicted penetrating a vagina drawn on the horse. He annotated the cowboy and the horse with the names of his Seatmate 8 and that boy's current girlfriend. Vince was very pleased with his handiwork in this instance:

Vince: He's a dreamer, he thinks he is real cool. He goes out with a girl called —, God, she is a dog. But like we shit-stir, we get him into heaps of trouble.

Friend 3: Like that time they nearly broke up because of Vince . . .

Vince: I tell — that Seatmate 8 likes lots of other girls. She gets really jealous and that and just cracks a big mental . . . I showed her this picture and said, 'Look what Seatmate 8 drew' and she goes, 'Oh the bastard' and all this. I also told her [he] smokes, to get him into heaps of trouble.

In some instances the female matched students were sexually harassed by boys in their classes. In most classes the number of boys and girls in each class was similar and the female matched students reported and were observed getting along reasonably amicably with the boys in their class. While being called names like 'slut' and 'bitch' must have had some effect (Lee 1983; Lees 1993), the girls were usually able to shrug off such abuse, sometimes arguing that they could give as good as they got. However this was not the case in one class at Plimmer College where Pauline, Polly and other girls in their class were subjected to intense harassment by several boys in their class despite the school's attempts to resolve the situation through counselling. Pauline and her Friend 1 seemed to get an especially hard time and were sometimes angry about it:

Friend 1: All the boys, except for —, they are really stupid, they hassle . . .

Pauline: Some of them get on my nerves . . . — really annoys me and I get angry with him and want to punch him and all that. — talks about really gross stuff. — is really disgusting, he's really rude.

Friend 2: — says to Friend 1, 'She [Pauline] has got big tits, I want to see her pink nipples.'

Pauline: They make up all these boys and ask you if you like them, they call you a slut and that . . .

Some of the boys in the class had developed a conscious strategy to divide and intimidate the girls:

Boy: They [Pauline and Friend 1] think they are great, but now me and — [boy] hassle them really bad, quite a few boys do now . . . like what I do, I've done this three or four times, if Friend 1 is sitting with — or — [two boys], I'll go and sit over there if I see Pauline coming, so like Friend 1 is in with all these boys so I'll get [force] Pauline to go and sit somewhere else and then Friend 1 will have to move.

It would be easy to see a gender imbalance in the class as the major factor creating the degree of harassment these girls suffered. However in Tony's class at Tui College, where boys also outnumbered girls, the latter were not abused to the same extent. Rather the gender relations at Plimmer College seemed to revolve around the combination of individual personalities within the class as well as the gender imbalance.

Summary

The evidence from the four schools does seem to support the existence of reference group mechanisms for a school mix effect. Table 5.2 indicates that the matched students were mixing with more middle class kids at the middle class schools and the qualitative evidence suggests numerous advantages that could accrue to them as a result. This analysis does not refute the findings of earlier studies that suggest students stick to peers of their own social class in schools where possible. Rather it suggests that informal student reference groups necessarily represent a selection from the available formal reference groups. If these vary, so will the informal reference groups. Those in the middle class schools would have been hard pressed to find working class peers had they wanted to. At Tui College there was little other choice. Student cultures also appear to reflect the characteristics of the dominant student group in the school. The concept of critical mass is clearly useful here. It seems likely that a large number of working class, disaffected students would be necessary to support the kinds of homie and metaller cultures evidenced at Tui College.

Overall, the evidence from the four schools suggests that reference group processes could underpin a school mix effect. However, since school policies and practices (instructional, organizational and management) may also be influenced by mix, these now warrant examination.

6

The negotiated curriculum

There were two parts to the question of whether or not school mix affected the nature and quality of instructional processes. First was the issue of whether the nature and quality of instruction did vary between the schools, and second, if this were the case, whether this was caused by school mix. To engage with the first issue I needed to make a judgement about the quality of instruction in classrooms across the schools. However such judgements are controversial. To start with, there are many classroom factors which may cause differences in student achievement. Instructional literature suggests a host of matters such as student 'time on-task', the order of the concepts to which students are being exposed, questioning types, the amount of home-work being set and so on. Pedagogy, curriculum and assessment all clearly warrant consideration and both their quantitative and qualitative dimensions are of interest. It is not enough, for instance, to analyse the amount of time devoted to the academic curriculum in any lesson (as against, say, pastoral or disciplinary issues) without saying something about the academic demands of tasks.

A related difficulty is that not all the factors which should be taken into account are easily recorded. For instance, there were considerable differences between classrooms in the study where teacher and students seemed to be either at blows or just marking time, and those where there were positive classroom relations and an intensity that seemed to signal genuine commit-ment. Yet these kinds of differences are difficult to describe, let alone measure. The problem also needed to be addressed in a way that could meet the very broad nature of my enquiry. For not only was classroom instruction only one aspect of the Wellington study, but in order to investigate students' instruc-tion 'in the round', multiple classrooms were observed across each of the four schools.

My study therefore took two quite different approaches to the problem of assessing instructional quality. One, noted earlier, was to obtain teacher evaluations of student work, the findings from which will be discussed shortly. The second approach was to carry out my own assessment of instructional quality based on classroom observation. This approach considered multiple factors in order to make judgements about two broad dimensions of classroom life – *student engagement* and *academic difficulty.*

Student engagement refers to the extent to which students appear to be committed to classwork. The following factors were taken into account:

- the tone/ethos/climate of expectation/intensity in the classroom;
- the amount and type of on-task/off-task behaviour (including homework as appropriate);
- the amount and type of misbehaviour;
- the amount and type of independent student questioning.

Clearly, some classroom activities might generate greater student enthusiasm and engagement than others. Thus the second aspect of lessons considered was the academic difficulty of the instruction or the extent to which lessons appeared to be more or less academically demanding.[1] Factors considered were:

- the amount of time spent by the class on activities related to the formal curriculum (versus other activities such as waiting, discipline, pastoral or administrative matters);
- the pace and complexity of tasks related to the formal curriculum including listening to teacher talk, answering questions and discussion tasks, the use of texts and other resources, written tasks (including homework as appropriate) and assessment tasks.

One of the strengths of this approach is that it paints with a broad brush in the way required for this study. In addition, no causal direction is implied by the engagement/difficulty assessments – they can be seen to stem from either the characteristics of the teacher or the students. The approach also acknowledges that a highly engaged classroom is not necessarily one where the tasks are very demanding and vice versa. The assessments involve considering multiple factors and gauging their relative importance in each particular classroom context. Since this is an approach which essentially takes each classroom on its merits, the assessments will be too subjective for some. They nevertheless represent the observations of a single researcher. In Thrupp (1996) they are also accompanied by hundreds of pages of case study material, allowing readers to view for themselves something of the evidence on which the assessments have been made.

Figure 6.1 represents a global assessment of the matched students' classes in each school along the lines described above. The letters T, V, W and P each indicate one of 57 different subject classes attended by the matched students at Tui, Victoria, Wakefield and Plimmer colleges respectively.

Two trends emerge from the data. The first is a substantial variation in

		Academic difficulty			
		very low	low	high	very high
Student engagement	very low	TTT	WVP		
	low		TTTT WPP	WWV PPPPP	P
	high	TTT VV	VVVP	WWWVVV P	WPP
	very high	T	TWWWPP	WWP	WW VVVV

Figure 6.1   Engagement/difficulty assessments across the schools

academic difficulty and student engagement *within* each of the schools. Even for the same group of students there was considerable difference between subject classes in terms of the instructional conditions the matched students experienced. For instance, Wendy's Social Studies class was characterized by students working hard on demanding tasks with tight deadlines but in her English class, students 'mucked around', were provided with relatively simple tasks and had elastic deadlines. As noted in the last chapter, Vince and his friends were spectacularly off-task in some classes while in others they worked diligently. Similar variations between subject classes were observed across all the schools:

Tui teacher aide: Would you believe this is the same class as in Integrated Studies?

The second trend to note, however, is that, despite this variation, Tui College classes were more likely to be characterized by lower academic difficulty and lower student engagement than the middle class schools. The middle class schools all had some very high-difficulty and/or very highly engaged classes whereas subject classes at Tui College were rarely characterized by either and never by both. This raises the question whether the difference was caused by instructional processes *independent* of school mix, or whether it *reflected* school mix. The evidence from this study suggests the latter – that curriculum management and course offerings, classroom discipline, teaching approaches, curriculum content, assessment, teaching resources and teacher character-istics may all be diverse within schools but that this diversity is nevertheless bounded by school mix.

Curriculum management and course offerings

At Tui College so many students had severe learning difficulties that curricu-lum issues most often came to the fore in the context of addressing disaffection and learning failure across the school, rather than in particular subject areas.[2]

As a result, traditional subject departments were weak and the idea that Tui College teachers had to be generalists first was widely accepted:

Tui principal: We have . . . said quite strongly, and for positive reasons, that teachers are generalists first and [subject] specialists second. When you are dealing with the kids in this community, the bottom line is, what do we have to do to increase the life chances of these kids? That's all to do with qualifications and achievement. But there are a whole lot of preconditions and without understanding the context you are working in you won't even get to the starting point.

The view of teachers as generalists was reflected in strong support for those who were seen to have cross-curricular solutions to dealing with students – those running the host of special programmes, committees and action groups the school had developed to address learning issues and provide alternatives to the academic curriculum. These included large special care and special needs departments, a literacy committee, a special curriculum programme intended to provide time for diagnosing and addressing learning and pastoral problems, Maori and Pacific Islands programmes and a large vocational programme. Tui College was justifiably proud of the strength of these programmes. It claimed that its 'least able students were very well served' and staff were positive about how the school was addressing bicultural and multicultural issues. However, it was clear that these programmes took up much energy and that, in general, staff were too caught up in dealing with the mass of low prior achievement students to give the advancement of its smaller groups of 'average' and 'able' students much thought.

Staff ambivalence (if not hostility) to addressing the needs of these students when the great majority of students clearly had far more pressing needs became apparent when a programme for 'able students' was proposed at Tui College. There was general support from teachers for the programme as a means to 'help bring up the standard for everyone' but this was tempered by concern about taking resources from programmes for the more numerous 'less able'. For instance:

Shouldn't compromise programme for less able students. It's an add on, not an alternative.

Needs to be marketed to the community. If the emphasis is placed here, some of the community may be put off sending their students here – elitism.

Extra tuition at the expense of other curricula?

'Disabled' programme should not be compromised in order to put this in place.

In the event the school did start to set up an 'able students' programme but the team charged with it expressed reservations that the idea would not take off because staff were already too busy and, in general, not very interested:

Tui teacher: I suppose your middle and your bright kids are expected to get on with it . . . it's an issue of staff time, they haven't got the time or energy to give up x number of hours to help a relatively small number of kids, they have basically got their hands full.

The tension between providing an academic curriculum and catering for students with low levels of prior achievement could also be seen in the senior curriculum at Tui College. Many students wanted to take vocational subjects rather than fail academic courses. Transition (vocationally oriented) courses therefore made up almost half the senior curriculum. Student preference for transition subjects was forcing the school to reduce its senior level academic offerings as courses became non-viable. The school was attempting to respond to this problem by rationalizing its senior academic offerings and strengthening prerequisites to get students to repeat failed subjects. However, many teachers were opposed to tightening up the academic curriculum with their main concern that 'non-academic' students would be left without enough options:

Tui teacher: They haven't considered properly the implications of tightening up the criteria for entry into senior subjects – there will be the 20 students who can do it, and the rest. We are not yet catering adequately for most students in non-academic subjects.

In contrast to Tui College, at the middle class schools academic success was considered paramount. Most seniors were university-bound and took a full academic programme. Student and parent demand largely dictated this focus:

Victoria principal: Well in large measure it comes back simply to the choices that students want . . . I mean for a school this size to have [so many] seventh form [Year 13] Maths with Statistics and Maths with Calculus classes gives you an indication of where people put their priorities.

Most parents at these schools took a keen interest in the academic progress of their children. They asked for special reports on their child's progress and complained forcefully about lack of homework, other students disrupting their child's lessons or perceived teacher incompetence. An indicator of parental interest was the strength of report night attendance:

Victoria dean: Most come, especially if the form teacher sells it well. There are usually only a couple of kids in each class whose parents don't turn up.

These were not schools where teachers saw themselves as generalists. Subject departments were a key organizational structure of all the middle class schools. There was competition between departments for high examination results:

Wakefield HOD: If a department does well in exams it is seen as a good department.

The middle class schools all had extension programmes which were well supported by staff. Dissent on the grounds of equity for students as was seen at Tui College was rare. On the other hand only a small range of vocational courses were offered:

Victoria transition teacher: The community drives the school towards academics, the staff have bought into that, it's like barrowing cement up hill to [get transition classes established]. The 'tail' is not attended to.

Overall there can be little doubt that the main curriculum emphasis of the middle class schools was towards those students who could succeed in external exams and uphold the academic reputations of their schools:

Wakefield HOD: I mean at [a low-SES school] the fact that 25 per cent of kids in your class couldn't read meant that if you ignored them it was at your peril – literally! Whereas [here] it is easier not to be forced to cater for that small group at the bottom. The expectations of parents here . . . the brighter ones have more say, the brighter kids are the saving grace of the school so you cater for them. They probably have an undue influence though.

A much wider range of extra-curricular activities was also offered at the middle class schools. This did not appear to be so much because of greater staff support at those schools but because a wider range of activities found support among their student bodies, making them viable school offerings. At Tui College, money (in some instances) and enthusiasm (in others) would have been difficult to raise for activities such as horseriding, skiing, debating, theatre sports, chess, bridge, astronomy and overseas tours, all of which were popular in the middle class schools.

Classroom discipline

Maintaining control of the classroom environment to motivate or enforce student engagement with the curriculum appeared to be the most fundamental classroom task for most teachers across all the schools. While some might question such emphasis on control rather than learning, the matched students and their friends across all schools had little doubt that the ability 'to control us' was most often the difference between a good and bad teacher. The ability of the teacher to exert his or her influence on the class was seen as an essential prerequisite to creating an environment where students felt safe and comfortable and where they would learn:

Terry: Mr —, he should show the people that he can give detentions, he can be mean.

In a sense, however, the necessary emphasis on classroom control with this age group is hardly surprising. By early adolescence, most students no longer see their teachers as proxy parents – the teacher's authority must rest on other, less certain grounds. There is considerable evidence of even quite compliant students in this age group initially 'sussing out' their teachers in terms of testing the limits of classroom behaviour (Woods 1990). In a situation where the teacher is outnumbered and individual needs can rarely be adequately met on a one-to-one basis, teachers are forced to find motivational or disciplinary strategies to keep students 'on-task' even where they are not particularly interested. In short, whatever learning activities are planned, teachers also have to 'handle' their classes.

In this respect classes at the middle class schools presented their teachers with significant advantages. The teachers there were able to create settled, purposeful classroom environments with relatively little effort. At Tui College, however, most classroom environments were much less conducive to work despite the efforts of teachers. The 'sussing out' period continued throughout the year:

Tui DP: After five years in this school, I'm having to drive classes I teach in a way that in other schools I'd only have to drive them the first month of the year. I'm talking about homework, focussing in class, staying on-task . . .

One reason students were easier to teach at the middle class schools was that the majority appeared intrinsically interested in the lessons. For instance, like the children in Davies's (1983) study, they facilitated the teacher's presentation by telling one another to be quiet if they noticed the teacher waiting for silence or if they couldn't hear. Teachers sometimes overtly tapped into their enthusiasm:

Wakefield teacher: Shall I explain? You are probably itching to start.

Victoria teacher: I think we should practise these – do you want to do that? [Most students nod.]

On the other hand, at Tui College, students were less likely to facilitate lessons. Their fewer curriculum-relevant experiences probably allowed them to identify with less of the material teachers wanted to discuss in the classroom. If teachers simply waited for silence, they could have waited all day in some of the classes observed! Occasionally a student would tell a particularly noisy student to be quiet, but this was not common. Most Tui College teachers put up with talking over the top of a barrage of off-task noise.

Teachers in the middle class schools could also draw more on the instrumental value of what was being done by tapping into the desire of middle class students to succeed academically. For instance, Wendy's English teacher used a brief test to quieten the class while Vince's English teacher found that just putting work up on the board soon engaged the class and made them quiet. Teachers at the middle class schools frequently appealed to the instrumental value of the work at hand, telling the students, 'This is important' (without specifying why) or that the information was necessary for study at more senior levels. The advice seemed to be taken seriously and could reduce a restless class to silence. In these ways teachers at the middle class schools were able to link their control of knowledge to the control of students (Delamont 1983). However, at Tui College this kind of strategy was less likely to work, perhaps because many students saw little of relevance in the academic curriculum to their futures.

Nevertheless there were times when motivational approaches were not enough to settle classes in any of the schools. Especially during the afternoon on hot or rainy days or when students were upset, tired or excited, teachers were often forced to apply sanctions. But once again, teachers at the middle class schools had advantages over those at Tui College. For instance, if a teacher at one of the middle class schools threatened a detention, this was usually enough to settle the class and it was often not necessary to follow the action through. At Tui College, being threatened with a detention or similar sanction had relatively little effect on most classes. If carried through, many students would simply not turn up.

Part of the reason disciplinary efforts were more successful at the middle class schools was that teachers seemed to carry more moral authority with the students there. Vicky's class 'played up' while their Maths teacher was out of the room, but posted a guard at the door and quickly returned to their seats when given a warning of the teacher's impending return. Wilma's friend at Wakefield College spent one lesson hiding in a cubicle in the toilets because she was late for class. To avoid getting into trouble, students at Wakefield College would do the non-assessed homework of teachers they feared ahead of assessed homework in other subjects. Teachers at the middle class schools could, if necessary, shock their class into complete silence by yelling at them. Students' fear of the authority of the teacher in the middle class schools was sanctioned by the expectations of middle class parents who generally supported the school in its disciplinary efforts.

But more than this, there was also evidence that teacher strictness was understood by the students in the middle class schools. Penny's friend suggested that her teacher would be a 'nice' person if she didn't have to be a teacher, and Wendy argued that her 'nice' teacher only got 'aggro' when 'provoked'. These kinds of comments suggest that the students at the middle class schools were able to make a distinction between the teacher as a person and his or her role in the classroom. Their ability to do this was no doubt helped by the fact that they often knew teachers out of school and mixed with their children. They understood the disciplinary game and usually accepted it as fair and necessary, even if at times they didn't like its consequences.

On the other hand, teachers at Tui College found it more effective to be firm but 'low-key' because students there often just didn't seem to understand the point behind teachers' disciplinary actions. To yell at Tui College classes was often to invite bemusement at best or an angry and aggressive response at worst. Disciplinary action was often seen as malice on the part of the teacher. Teachers, after all, were mostly people who lived other lives in other suburbs and who sent their children to other schools. Perhaps for much the same reason, the school was frequently not backed up by parents over disciplinary issues. It seemed that few students or parents understood the rules of the disciplinary game here in the way that they were understood in the middle class schools.

The disconnectedness between middle class teachers and working class students at Tui College was underlined by the way students there called their female teachers just 'Miss' (regardless of marital status) and their male teachers just 'Mr'. While some teachers seemed to be attempting to close the gap between their experiences and those of the students through a highly informal approach to student–teacher relations, they could rarely carry it off successfully. Conversely, at the middle class schools teachers could afford to be quite formal, because their underlying relationship to students was more organic.

Like student subcultures, teacher–pupil relations across the schools need to be seen as a matter of critical mass. Even in the middle class schools there were some students who didn't understand or accept the disciplinary 'game', just as Tui College had some who did. However, where numbers of non-compliant students are small, it is easy for teachers and senior management to concentrate their energies on those students, while it is more difficult, perhaps impossible, in a situation of more widespread non-compliance. When only one or two students are misbehaving in class they can easily be picked off:

Plimmer teacher: The behaviour problems in this class – there are only one or
   two of them, they are on their own.

As a result teachers at the middle class schools frequently used disciplinary strategies which involved isolating misbehaving students and making them look foolish among their peers such as using sarcasm or making students stand up in class. However these approaches were rarely used at Tui College. There student allegiances were sufficiently powerful to unite groups of students against the teacher.

Overall, teaching in the middle class schools was much easier in terms of motivating or disciplining students and avoiding disruption.[3] Unless teachers were particularly unfair or confrontational, students were compliant and motivated enough to allow classes to run reasonably well even where the teacher exerted relatively little influence. For instance, a number of classes ran remarkably smoothly despite very low-key teaching styles. As one teacher commented, 'You don't really get the discipline problems here.' There were always a large number of students in these schools who were able and willing to work. However, to have taught in such an unstructured way at Tui College would have been to invite chaos because few students were sufficiently 'able' and willing to carry on with their work independently. Some teachers at Tui College were able to keep a very structured classroom environment but only through extraordinary effort and at the expense of the formal curriculum.

Teaching approaches

The compliant and 'able' nature of most students at the middle class schools also presented other advantages to teachers, such as the amount and type of discussion and questioning. The importance of this was signalled by the principal of Victoria College:

> After all, what is it in a classroom that sparks the lesson along? What sparks it along is the prior knowledge those kids bring to the classroom. And it is that which you tap into as a teacher. That's what kick starts it. That's the question and answer, the discussion . . . where you have kids with prior knowledge of the world, you have enormous advantages. Where you don't have that, you have enormous disadvantages . . .

In the middle class schools the formal curriculum was indeed dealt with much more interactively than at Tui College. Teachers at the middle class schools tended to ask numerous questions and to receive a lot of substantive and knowledgeable answers. The many student contributions received by teachers at the middle class schools were advantageous in a variety of ways. They could be used to build a discussion to a summary position and the responses of more 'able' students could also be used to correct less 'able' peers. Teachers could be demanding of classes and hold out for quality answers. Spontaneous student questions could be used by teachers as spurs to further discussion, or could serve as reminders of points to cover. Knowledgeable student contributions meant that teachers didn't have to be 'fountains of all knowledge' – classroom relations could be more reciprocal.

At Tui College, by comparison, teacher questions and comments often met with little response. Teacher jokes usually fell flat because they didn't connect with the students' sharp, but quite different, sense of humour. Even where teachers had encouraged a supportive atmosphere where students would speak out, answers were much less likely to be 'correct enough' to use to continue the discussion/questioning sequence. Teachers at this school had to be grateful for any answers and could not afford to 'hold out' too long because students quickly tired of the questioning game. Perhaps because it was difficult to get 'useful' responses, teachers also asked fewer questions at Tui College than at the middle class schools.

As a result of the generally higher level of student understanding and compliance, teachers in the middle class schools were also able to talk and question classes for much longer periods of time, in some cases most of a lesson. At Wakefield College, for instance, I observed Wilma's Social Studies teacher 'lecture' for 25 minutes on the importance of the coconut in Pacific Island societies. Wendy's Japanese teacher ran a whole-class discussion for 45 minutes supported mostly by independent student questions. In contrast, talking to or questioning a class at length at Tui College was to invite disaster as students became noisy and restless. 'Successful' teachers in this environ-ment kept their whole-class talk 'short and sweet' before giving students a written task. Tasks were also introduced by Tui College teachers much more carefully and specifically with little left to chance:

Tui teacher: Now I need you all to listen carefully. That means you can't be concentrating on whether the New Zealand cricket team will win or what you are going to have for lunch. You need to be either reading or listening or both. OK, is everyone listening now? Has everyone got their books? OK let's go . . .

In some instances a whole raft of approaches was used to get the message across. Instructions were given orally, then re-emphasized and then checked with a 'guinea pig' in the class, then written on the blackboard. Such instructions were further reinforced by teacher checks on whether they were being followed. The particular problems presented by some low-'ability' students help to explain why teachers saw a need to give such simple, clear instructions:

Tui teacher: You say to him, you say [to a small group], 'Now look, right, now put your pens down, look at me. It's important to listen because if you don't listen you won't know what's happening. Right, now are you listening . . . right.' And then you draw on the board, you are working with a small group. 'So what are you going to do when you leave here? Right now, first thing you are going to do is get out your skills book and head up the date. —, what are you doing? . . .' [Imitates the student concerned.] 'What book do you use?' [Laughs.]

By comparison, at the middle class schools directions were often given quickly and briefly. Teachers appeared to rely on students' prior experience and their 'ability' to know exactly what to do.

A related difference between Tui College and the middle class schools was the size of written tasks assigned to students. At Tui College, many students could not make much progress independently of teacher assistance so teachers learned to 'feed' the curriculum to students by breaking it down into small tasks which could be easily completed. For instance, Tony's Integrated Studies class demanded structured work that required frequent teacher intervention. When his teacher helped individuals, others who were also struggling with the task soon demanded her attention or started to misbehave. The class as a whole quickly became too noisy for the teacher to continue with individuals, and she had to revert to a whole-class approach to explain the task. Teachers, knowing that giving individual attention to one student for very long was fraught with peril, tended to keep moving around the class, giving students snippets of immediate information needed and keeping a watchful eye out for misbehaviour.

By comparison, the use of extensive assignment work, often of several weeks' duration, was more common at the middle class schools because students there were mostly 'able' and compliant enough to work independently for long periods of time. Vicky's English teacher, for instance, could set the class lengthy, on-going assignment work that did not require frequent teacher intervention because most of the students could read well enough to cope with the work. The result was that this teacher was able to be more relaxed and less watchful, and to provide more individual help to students in need. She often spent ten minutes or more with individuals while the rest of the class worked silently. Most other teachers in the middle class schools could also get their classes working either silently or with a reasonable level of 'working noise' that would provide the teacher with the necessary space to help individuals.

A further difference in the nature of classroom tasks involved the seating of students. In most of the middle class school classes, students worked individually because teachers felt that students worked better on their own with fewer distractions.[4] They often argued that groupwork didn't suit some students:

Wakefield teacher: Some kids don't like groupwork, the fact that they are physically sitting in a different place, having to help other people, they resent it. Sure it's a laudable aim but it's not them.

Where groupwork was used in the middle class schools it was either used only for particular activities which were monitored very carefully by teachers or it did indeed result in a lot of off-task behaviour. At Tui College, by comparison, groupwork was mostly used to support students who could not cope on their own. While there was evidence that this strategy was at least partially successful, students here were just as likely to drift off-task in their groups as at the middle class schools. Tui College students only appeared to be able to cope with groupwork where tasks were plentiful and easy. Overall it seemed to be an advantage in the middle class schools that students could work more independently because in this situation the greatest time was spent 'on-task' on the formal curriculum.

Nevertheless classes in the middle class schools were also more likely to stay 'on-task' *whatever* the nature of tasks. Although the work needed to have some substance, it was not necessary for it to be as stimulating as Jones's (1991) report of 5 Simmonds suggests. Students in the middle class schools were usually quite happy to copy notes for example. On the other hand, at Tui College (and again, unlike Jones's 5 Mason), providing highly structured work such as copying certainly helped to get students 'on-task' but was still often not enough to engage the class. One teacher who transferred from Tui to Victoria College during the year commented:

Some of the kids here really whinge at you if you don't give them the notes, it's like, 'You are the teacher, why aren't you giving us the notes?' At Tui College, they would never ask for work. At Tui College the lazy ones just muck around.

Curriculum content

Along with the preceding differences in the way in which the curriculum was

Table 6.1 Average teacher ratings of student work samples (transformed to a scale of 1–100)

	Tui	Wakefield	Victoria	Plimmer
Relative level of work	46	55	58	62
Suitability for own school	63	71	65	70

delivered, there were important differences in the *content* of the curriculum across the schools. To gain independent views of the different curriculum, groups of teachers at each of the four schools were invited to participate in blind evaluations of English and Social Studies student work samples from schools other than their own. Their views support the idea that curriculum content at the middle class schools was more demanding than at Tui College.

The teachers were asked two questions, first whether the general level of work being set by teachers at the other schools was 'much lower', 'lower', 'similar', 'higher' or 'much higher' than they would typically ask of a Year 9 class in their own school. Second, they were asked whether the work being set would be 'very unsuitable', 'unsuitable', 'suitable' or 'very suitable' for classes in their own school. Table 6.1 gives their aggregated ratings on a scale of 1–100.[5] Here the higher the score, the more difficult the level of work/greater suitability of the work respectively.

This suggests that the Tui College students were seen by teachers to be doing less demanding work than those at the middle class schools, which were seen to be more similar in their levels of work. There was however less variance in the perceived suitability of the work for students in the respondents' own school. This was probably because teachers from *both* the middle and working class schools saw each other's curriculum being of limited value for their own students.

A further evaluation of the same work samples was done by five subject specialists from another region (the Waikato) who were asked to rate the relative difficulty of the work samples as 'very low', 'low', 'high' or 'very high'. Table 6.2 shows their ratings by school, again converted to a scale of 1–100.

Again a pattern by SES mix is discernible although the Wakefield College ranking is surprisingly low in this case. Closer investigation suggests the Waikato teachers felt that while the Wakefield College work demonstrated 'a huge work output', much was textbook-based which they argued was less creative than the work taught at Victoria and Plimmer colleges.

Teachers' comments on the work samples were also illuminating. In general, while the teachers at the middle class schools commented that the work done at Tui College involved a range of high-interest activities and attractive and varied presentation of work, they also argued that lesson content was 'thin' or 'shallow' and they expressed doubts as to whether syllabus requirements were met by the work covered. They also commented

Table 6.2   Average Waikato teacher ratings of student work samples (transformed to a scale of 1–100)

	Tui	Wakefield	Victoria	Plimmer
Relative difficulty	53	58	73	79

that the samples showed a lack of critical analysis, a narrow range of (subject specific) skills, and little marking of student work.

Teachers at Tui College tended to emphasize different strengths and weaknesses when commenting on work from the middle class schools. They praised the depth and comprehensiveness of the work, the scope for expression of student ideas and values, and the amount of marking done in some classes. However, they frequently commented that the work indicated 'conservative', 'traditional', 'prescriptive' and 'boring' classes that were too 'content driven', 'textbook orientated', or 'bookish'. Tasks were often seen to require too much recall of content, lacked 'graphic transformations' and were unnecessarily wordy.

These differences suggest that teachers in the middle class schools and Tui College had different sets of curriculum priorities and goals. They clearly had differing emphases on 'content' and 'skills' which they tended to pit against each other. While the teachers at the middle class schools usually felt that teaching curriculum content was important, teachers at Tui College typically argued that if students had the literate/information skills to access content, they could pick this up at any time. So while on the one hand, the assumption at the middle class schools was that students were reasonably literate and needed knowledge and ideas for exams, on the other hand, at Tui College the possession of such skills was not assumed but instead it was believed curriculum content would fall into place if students could get these skills. The middle class teachers stressed the need for a relatively tightly framed academic knowledge base emphasizing recall of knowledge and understanding of ideas – Tui College teachers focussed on relatively loosely framed 'relevant' high-interest skills such as taking information in one form and 'transforming' it. This did not require as much recall or understanding of ideas because resource material was nearly always provided.

This difference in emphasis did appear to be driven to a large extent by the characteristics of the student body. Students at the middle class schools thrived on new knowledge and concepts and, in some cases, would complain if work was not demanding enough. In the evaluations their teachers claimed that the students would have found much of the Tui College work too easy:

Straightforward – little creative engagement.

There's simply not enough depth.

Easy to cope with.

Work is simplistic. Too much emphasis on diagrams.

Suitable but would probably bore them. Little chance for individuality and creative development.

Standard three or four [Year 5–6] level.

On the other hand Tui College teachers argued that there was no point in drumming a lot of content into students if they didn't have the literacy skills to understand it. This point was also stressed in the Tui College evaluations of the middle class school samples:

Pointless writing out things the kids don't understand.

More independent, on-task, self-motivated behaviour [would be] required.

Students here would find much of it irrelevant/boring.

The teachers argued that, if pushed to complete this kind of work, Tui College classes would resist:

The bookish nature of it would make most kids here spin out.

These responses indicate that it is student characteristics which largely explain why the Tui College teachers did not attempt to teach the same type of, or as much, curriculum as the middle class schools. While Tui College teachers were impressed by the amount of work covered at the other schools, teachers in the latter often criticized the limited curriculum coverage at Tui College.

The differences in the taught curricula between the schools were also reflected in departmental policies and practices. Management documents of the middle class schools' English departments (with the exception of Plimmer College, to be discussed shortly) tended to be much more demanding and specific than at Tui College. The same pattern was observed across the Social Studies departments. In complete contrast, Tui College's HOD Social Studies was concerned with cutting back course content to give more time to basic literacy skills:

. . . the reality is that there is no point in just pushing content at them. If the kids have got nothing to hang it off it's just irrelevant, you might as well be teaching them Arabic. So I'd rather reduce the content, slow it down, do it properly . . . I still think the syllabus needs to be pared back, there is still too much to cover.

The middle class schools also tended to use class sets of textbooks more, on the general assumption that most students could cope with even quite difficult texts if they were interested in the material being covered. However, Tui College found textbooks of limited use and tended to rely more on resources that teachers were forced to make or modify themselves such as handouts and work cards. The departments at Tui College did buy some textbooks, but struggled to find suitable ones.

Overall the differences between the taught curriculum at the middle class schools and Tui College were considerable. The day-to-day advantages of academic teaching in a middle class school were summed up by a teacher at Wakefield College who had recently moved from a working class school:

> You can go further with a brighter group on less juice. You can get a topic and go deeper into it and unpeel the layers. You can't get into that level of analysis with the less able, they like their activities, bang, bang, bang, move on. If you are looking into a story with brighter kids you can look at the theme, its wider application to society, [with] the less able students you can't go down to that level . . . they don't give me the signals or feedback that they understand that level, or [they] want to go down a notch . . .

Assessment

There was also some difference in the number and nature of assessed items carried out across the schools. This study used the mark books of English and Social Studies teachers to examine the relative amounts of formal assessment done across the schools at the classroom level. These data are presented in Table 6.3 but need to be interpreted with care because not all assessed items were of the same order. For instance, Vicky's English class had only ten formal assessment marks recorded but these were summary grades of substantial assignments involving numerous smaller tasks. On the other hand, many of the grades recorded in other classes were for minor tasks, for instance, five or six small assessments for one assignment.

Taking these factors into account (note that Tui's Integrated Studies should be compared with the totals of both English and Social Studies at the other schools[6]), Table 6.4 points to the same conclusion as the qualitative evidence – that more assessment was done at the middle class schools. At Tui College, the amount of assessment in 9A was minimal and while considerably more was done in 9B, items assessed in this class were less substantial. In any case the number of items assessed in this class (26) was also still relatively small compared to most classes in the other schools when both English and Social Studies assessment items were taken into account.

While it may be argued that Tui College was doing just as much assessment, but more informally, there was little evidence of this. Not much student work at Tui College was marked, perhaps because there was neither parental nor student pressure to do so. By comparison most (not all) of the teachers in the middle class schools did a lot of marking and clearly saw this as part of their job.

A greater emphasis on assessment at the middle class schools can also be seen at the department level. While assessment at Plimmer College (discussed

Table 6.3   Number of items assessed in English and Social Studies (1994)

	Tui	Wakefield		Victoria		Plimmer	
	Integrated Studies	English	Social Studies	English	Social Studies	English	Social Studies
9A	7	27	20	10	12	20	22
9B	26	27	12	13	37	20	16

further shortly) was as unstructured as at Tui College, departments at Wakefield and Victoria colleges tended to have specified common tests or common assessment items which teachers were required to administer. These seemed to be used in part to specify and control what teachers were teaching within these departments. In the Social Studies department at Victoria College for instance, every topic had an accompanying common test and there was also a departmental exam at the end of the year. This emphasis also seemed to reflect the HOD's belief that Victoria College students took assessed subjects more seriously.

Although Tui and Plimmer colleges did not have junior examinations, these were a feature at Wakefield and Victoria colleges. Tui College reported to parents on a range of basic classroom behaviours (such as bringing books to school or being ready to start lessons) which were not reported at the middle class schools. Tui College reports allowed no room for individual teacher comments. When summary comments were provided by deans, they tended to be fairly neutral and to emphasize the chance to improve in future:

> — has reached a pass in only two subjects . . . his other grades are fair. He will have to build a wide variety of skills next year. Absences will have contributed to a lack of task and homework completion but he does show interest in all subjects. A big effort is needed [next year].

The Tui College reports generally avoided the franker judgements of individual subject teachers in reports at the middle class schools:

> — does not stay on-task and so he rarely completes his work. Homework is also often missed and so he gets further behind. When these matters are brought to his attention he becomes defensive and will not accept the responsibility for his own learning.

Classroom resources

Some differences between classrooms at Tui College and the middle class schools clearly had to do with basic disparities in classroom resources. For instance, students at the middle class schools typically had their own personal classroom resources such as paper, pens and rulers. In contrast, the start of lessons at Tui College was often characterized by students 'hunting' for these items from their classmates. Tony was advised by his Science teacher to 'buy a little one [ruler] and keep it down your sock' after he claimed his ruler had been stolen. Teachers at Tui College had resorted to holding class sets of some personal resources for student use. By comparison, the students in the middle class schools usually had their own resources and there were nearly always enough spares among them to cover those who didn't.

The teachers at the middle class schools could also rely on students to have or to bring to school additional resources needed for lessons. For instance, in Wendy's Science class students made 'hokey pokey' (honeycomb in Crunchie bars) to illustrate a chemical reaction and were asked to bring pots, golden syrup, sugar and so on. Almost all the students brought these items along, carrying them with them throughout the day. Teachers at the middle class schools were also generally able to assume their students had access at home to a telephone and newspaper and often a computer, but this was not the case at Tui College. Some subject classes in the middle class schools also used prepared workbooks which students were expected to buy. On the other hand, Tui College itself had to provide 'homework diaries' for students because this was the only way to ensure all had what was considered a basic resource.

But apart from these personal resources, there was little evidence of substantial inequities in the supply of basic texts and written instructional resources among the schools. Indeed teachers at Tui College seemed to have a more generous photocopying budget than at any of the middle class schools. (This was entirely appropriate – although the school had plenty of textbooks, few could be used directly.) Tui College did, however, suffer a greater loss of textbooks and other materials through student disorganization and theft. Consequently students had less access to textbooks because they were rarely allowed to take them home.

The middle class schools were predictably much better equipped with video cameras, computers and musical instruments. Especially in computing where government funding was not available, community-based funds made a considerable difference.

Teacher characteristics

It is frequently claimed that higher streams/tracks get 'better' teachers but can the same be said of middle class schools relative to working class schools? Table 6.4 is drawn from the teacher questionnaire and shows that teachers at the middle class schools had slightly higher SES backgrounds and were often better qualified, particularly at Plimmer College. There was little difference in the mean number of teaching years, but teachers at the middle class schools were less likely to have taught at primary level and more likely to have taught at higher SES schools than was the case at Tui College.

Evidence from interviews also pointed to teacher morale being lower at Tui

Table 6.4 Characteristics of teaching staff by school[7]

	Tui	*Wakefield*	*Victoria*	*Plimmer*
Age				
% 20–39	50	56	45	50
% 40–69	50	44	55	50
Mean SES of parents	3.35	2.83	2.82	2.81
Qualifications				
% no degree	24	23	11	9
% highest above Bachelors	12	12	31	47
Teaching experience				
No. years teaching				
Mean	12.5	13.5	14.3	13.4
Range	3–29	1–33	1–34	0–32
No. years at present school				
Mean	5.29	4.57	8.45	4.88
Range	1–26	1–10	1–28	0–20
Primary teaching experience				
% some primary	13	8	13	12
% mostly primary	25	0	3	6
Nature of intake of previous schools				
Mean decile rating[a]	3.91	5.00	5.83	6.00
% uncodeable[b]	19	43	31	17

Notes: a From Minister of Education (1995) 1 = lowest SES, 10 = highest SES.
b Uncodeable responses were all of those which were not NZ state or integrated schools such as NZ tertiary institutions, NZ private schools and schools and other educational institutions in other countries.

College, with numerous staff looking for other jobs or applying for study leave:

Tui teacher: I was at teachers' college the other day with [another teacher] and we were talking about school and we realized we were talking about basically a slum school. It sounds awful, but that is what I think we have become. I want to get out, get some study leave or something.

Tui teacher: Morale is dropping, it's absolutely rock bottom. So many people are applying for leave or study courses or wanting to move on. Staff feel drained, and had it, and worn out, and where do we go from here. It's a battle.

The morale of teachers was affected by the nature of their workloads. Although it is doubtful that Tui teachers were working harder than teachers at the middle class schools, they saw less reward for their efforts because they were almost always overwhelmed by student needs. This meant that even the programmes in which the school had strengths were not being as well delivered as those in the middle class schools. For instance, despite the evident emphasis on the needs of the less 'able' at Tui College, special needs staff in the middle class schools were under less pressure and were able to do more for their students in difficulty than Tui College staff could for theirs. Indeed many 'special needs' students at the middle class schools would not have been considered as such at Tui College.

Teachers at Tui College also felt less effective because they were not rewarded for their efforts by their students' exam sucesses. While they did take comfort in the concept of value-added achievement and successes in sport and cultural performance activities, these, after all, are not the measures by which society at large judges school success or failure. Teacher comments suggested that the constant failure of students in exams was depressing. For instance, in one staff meeting a Tui College teacher noted that results in the recent mid-year exams in her subject had been 'appalling' and suggested that the exam timetable needed to be brought out earlier. The principal responded that it had been out for three weeks prior to exams and 'lots of kids still didn't have a clue the day before when their exams would be'. Someone else noted that: 'There is minimal philosophy among the students that they have to do anything to prepare. I feel very frustrated at the lack of student ownership of their progress and work.' There was general agreement with this point and discussion then continued for some time as to what might be done about the problem, but no solutions were forthcoming. Eventually another teacher said: 'The horse has bolted. I asked students to sign up for [after school] School Cert revision, drink and biscuits provided. Only six signed up and today four just remembered they had other commitments. What else do you have to do? Hash cookies?'

Teachers at Tui College were also generally less positive about the quality of their school than teachers at the middle class schools. Whereas the latter often had concerns about aspects of school organization and their own conditions of work, they were invariably confident that their students received a good deal. Staff at Tui College had less confidence about this and in some cases were very critical of what their school offered.

Effects of partial banding at Victoria College

It appeared that banding did have some effect on instructional processes, as other studies have shown, but within Victoria College this was relatively small compared to the effect of school mix. Interviews with teachers at Victoria College who taught both low- and high-band classes suggest that they taught them a somewhat different curriculum. While they covered a similar syllabus, high-band classes did more in-depth work and were taught using a wider number of teaching activities:

> Some assignments are the same, I expect the top of [the low-band class] to fit in with [the high-band class]. There are differences in their work ethic[s], [the low-band class], the bottom ones are lazy, there are vast

differences in the amount of work handed in . . . I modify some work for [the low-band class], reduce the word limits of assignments, [the low-band class] have to do 500–1000 words, while [the high-band class] get asked for 1000 words.

By Victoria College teachers' own admission then, it seems they did not teach high- and low-band classes the same, nor did they expect the same quality of work from them. This finding is consistent with much of the literature on the tracking mentioned earlier. On the other hand, and more importantly here, the engagement and difficulty of the low-band Victoria College classes was similar to those at Wakefield and Plimmer colleges and considerably different from the Tui College classes. The likely reason for this was that Victoria College low-band classes were nevertheless still dominated by middle class students because of the largely middle class nature of the school.

This finding does not refute previous findings about the effects of within-school differentiation. Rather it suggests that it is the characteristics of a particular school/yeargroup/class that has the most important implications for its instructional processes. Whether there is within-school grouping is probably not so important as such except insofar as it alters the compositional characteristics of classes and thus the qualities of the learners in a particular class, and the messages this group consequently gives its teachers.

Having said this, for various reasons, being in a low-band class in a higher SES tracked school would probably be more advantageous than attending a class of the *same* SES mix in an untracked but lower SES school. (This is assuming low- and high-track classes are shared around teachers as was the case at Victoria College.) This is because, despite the differences noted above, there was some evidence that teachers were carrying over resources and approaches from high-band to low-band classes. Teachers were also able to try out curriculum innovations in the more forgiving high-band classes and teaching these classes was probably also less tiring and more rewarding. Low-band students appeared to benefit from this in terms of greater teacher energy and morale in their classrooms also.

Effects of a higher SES mix at Plimmer College

Although much of what was occurring at Plimmer College in terms of teaching and learning was similar to the other middle class schools, there were features associated with an even higher SES intake which deserve discussion. One of the main differences was the outstanding level of language competence, most apparent during classroom discussions:

Plimmer teacher: [They are] very challenging because they are so articulate about issues. So if you are trying to do a whole-class feedback or discussion it is hard work because you have the very vocal 'what if' type people. If they are having an 'interjecty' day it's really hard . . .

As a result of the high 'ability' of the students, the main job of teachers at this school was to facilitate lessons rather than push students:

Plimmer assistant principal (AP): On arrival here I was going to strut my stuff in a teacher-directed sort of a way which is how I had operated at [a low-SES school]. But I listened to the class and I could detect lots of conversations, not about TV or the party they had been to but actually about Greek mythology. I thought, if you can't beat them join them, and what I realized very smartly was that they didn't want to listen to me, they actually just wanted to be facilitated and if only I'd shut up and let them get on with it, that would be fine.

The kind of teaching approach that was valued among many staff and students here was one which emphasized creativity and style rather than acquisition of basic content and skills. The latter was largely taken for granted. This emphasis was most apparent in the school's English department where staff argued the need for creativity and developed very flexible curriculum guidelines, bought books and made up assignments with this in mind.

Yet a key question is whether students such as the matched students would have been given much help by Plimmer College's facilitating teachers. In general, the answer would have to be no because the needs of the matched students were often overlooked. This was a school where classroom teachers did not seem very concerned about the progress of the 'less able'. For instance, a number of teachers expressed the view that while they had a responsibility to extend 'able' students, those with learning difficulties were the concern of the special needs department. In a related way, teachers did not exert as much pressure on students as at Victoria and Wakefield colleges. The matched students at Plimmer College seemed to be allowed not to complete, or not to hand in work in a way that arguably would not have assisted their eventual academic success as much as the more 'pushing' approaches of Wakefield and Victoria colleges.

Instructional differences within schools

Although beyond the scope of the Wellington study, many differences within schools *can* perhaps be explained by teacher quality. Certainly, students in all the schools were very clear that there were 'good' and 'bad' teachers, identifying their respective features in much the same ways as have pupils in other studies (Woods 1990). 'Good' teachers knew their stuff, were not too boring and could teach in a way that suited the class. They took an interest in their students as people but didn't pry too much into their personal lives. They had a sense of humour and were fair. Above all they could control the class without resort to sarcasm or excessive punishment. 'Bad' teachers were seriously deficient in one or more of these areas. However, apart from these very broad generalizations, many features of 'good' and 'bad' teachers within the schools studied seemed idiosyncratic. More relevant here, what it meant to be a 'good' or 'bad' teacher appeared to vary by school mix, a point to which I will return in Chapter 8.

Differences related to ethnicity

We noted earlier the fundamental disjunction between middle class teachers and their working class students at Tui College. Terry, the Samoan matched student at Tui College, and his mainly Maori and Samoan friends also viewed the school as hostile on ethnic grounds, often seeing teacher actions as racist. For instance, they thought some of their teachers picked on them:

Terry: They always give us boys a hard time. Like Friend 3 had a black jacket and they hassled him about the colour of his jacket. And this morning, he got told his attitude wasn't acceptable but he wasn't even doing anything. He was just doing his work. If we do one little thing, they just treat it as something major . . .

On the other hand, the same teachers thought Terry had a chip on his shoulder about racism:

Teacher 1: Terry wanted to encourage racism in the class. He wanted to get Samoan to be a separate thing and he was constantly bringing up that teachers were racist. You know I'd go, 'Korero [talk] Maori', he'd go, 'Don't speak that around here', that sort of attitude.
Teacher 2: Yes, he's really got a, he's an arrogant . . .
Teacher 1: He has got loads of ability, he's in the top ten but he has a huge chip on his shoulder and unless he deals with that . . .

Terry was rarely off-task in classes with these 'strict' teachers, but in others he misbehaved. For instance in Maths he was constantly out of his place and being asked to shift back to his group. He was asked in one period to move four times over several minutes before he finally did, then he moved back to the first group later in the lesson, before again being asked twice to move without result. He could barely contain his contempt for the teacher: 'Yeah, yeah, I heard you.' Yet in interviews Terry said he wanted the teacher to take more control:

It would be good if he could control us, it's really us controlling ourselves. We know he can't tell us to be quiet so we just talk heaps.

In Science, Terry was regularly isolated for talking and 'being stupid'. He went reluctantly:

Teacher: Move, Terry.
Terry: I wasn't doing anything.
Teacher: Don't argue with me Terry, just move. [He starts to, very slowly.]
Teacher: Hurry up Terry, move. [He moves, the teacher starts the lesson again.]

Terry: See, I've moved you dumb bitch! [There is no response, the teacher
      pretends not to hear.]
Terry: [to his friends] Shut up, I'm not in the mood.

How should we interpret what was going on in these classes? One possibility
was that the teachers were genuinely racist. Yet there was no evidence from
observation or interviews that this was the case. For instance, the teachers
were certainly doing their best to promote Maori culture and language
although this wasn't appreciated by Terry, a Samoan. A stronger possibility
was that for non-Pakeha working class students such as Terry, the cultural
disjunction between middle class teachers and working class students is
intensified. It seemed that teaching Terry has been something of a tightrope
act for his (Pakeha) teachers. On the one hand, like the other matched
students he wanted his teachers to be in control, yet because he didn't
always seem to understand the rules of the schooling game, and because he
was also sensitive to the possibility of prejudice, he was likely to interpret
teacher actions to keep control as racist.

Summary

Overall, teachers at Tui College appeared to be responding to the needs of
mainly less 'able' and less compliant working class students with often
carefully structured but sometimes not very successful instructional processes
which were necessarily relatively undemanding. The result was that the
matched students at Tui were being 'cooled out' by not being exposed to a
more rigorous academic curriculum. As one Tui College teacher put it:
'teachers here are too busy lifting the 40 per cent students to 50 per cent to
worry about lifting the 60 per cent to 80 per cent'.

At Wakefield and Victoria colleges on the other hand, the matched students
were attending schools which were mainly middle class but where working
class students also constituted a significant group within the school which
could not be ignored. The predominance of 'able' and compliant pupils
allowed these schools to teach a more demanding curriculum, but only
within the supporting framework of tightly organized instructional processes
that ensured all students, not just the most 'able', were being pushed towards
the academic curriculum. As a result, the matched students in these schools
were better supported in their academic progress than at Tui College.

Finally, at Plimmer College, instructional processes seemed to cater almost
exclusively for middle class students. The curriculum was therefore relatively
demanding. Most Plimmer teachers focussed on the demands of more 'able'
students and, because the matched students did not 'fit the mould', they did
not get as much assistance as those at Wakefield and Victoria colleges.

7

The art of the possible

Organizational and management processes also differed markedly between Tui College and the middle class schools. The nature of Tui's intake made most policies extremely hard to implement there:

Tui DP: This school is, the analogy I use is, do you know about Sisyphus's rock that he rolls up the hill? It's in *The Odyssey* somewhere. This school is like that, it makes it hard to teach here. As soon as you take your shoulder off something it goes backwards. You don't ever get to the stage here where you can say that it is in place. It's because the value system you are pushing doesn't sit naturally with the kids – you are trying to impose those values on them . . . Almost anything you put in place, as soon as you stop monitoring it, reviewing it, putting the pressure on, it falls away.

By comparison, organizing and managing the middle class schools was relatively straightforward because they were cushioned by the social characteristics of their students:

Plimmer AP: I think that socially they are probably a bit more advanced, they seem a year or two older than at [previous lower SES school] but that is just the whole socioeconomic deal. If you live in [a nearby high-SES suburb] and are having dinner parties and soirées, I suppose you do have all these social skills that other kids are not exposed to. And I think because of that there is a flexibility about the place here, I mean that in a good way . . .

The differing organizational and management constraints and possibilities can be illustrated through examples of daily routines, guidance and discipline arrangements, and leadership and governance issues.

Daily routines

A continuing problem at Tui College was monitoring and addressing truancy. The school had recently implemented a comprehensive system of checks and employed a part-time truancy officer to ring students' homes. Attendance records suggested the level of absenteeism did drop initially (although the weather over the same period was also exceptionally good). Before long, however, truancy was once again back to its previous levels. Some of those who designed the system blamed other teachers:

Tui teacher: More and more kids have gone back to their old ways. The systems we put in place just don't get followed. Teachers aren't doing what they are supposed to be doing.

Nevertheless observations suggested other reasons for teachers not undertaking their absence responsibilities adequately. To begin with, large numbers of students were frequently absent from daily form time so that their absences could not be checked. (As we shall see shortly, teachers often called for students during form time for meetings of all kinds because the students would not attend at intervals and lunchtimes.) Often half a class or more were either absent from school altogether, drifted in late, or left early to go to some other activity. Staff were also often preoccupied with organizing other administrative, teaching or extracurricular activities during their own form time. In some form meetings there was such a stream of students from other classes to see form teachers that they gave their own form classes little attention.

Attempts to catch up with absences were also difficult – they were time-consuming, unrewarding, and risked confrontation. Teachers often had many students to see about absences in each form time. There seemed to be something of a game played between teachers and students in most of the form classes observed. The game – 'Don't hassle me and I won't hassle you' – had several variations. One was for students to pretend not (or perhaps really not?) to understand the absence system despite having had it explained numerous times. Another variation was for students to appear concerned but baffled by accusations of absence so that the teacher might let them off. A third variation was to offer to bring a note tomorrow so that the confrontation with the teacher could be put off. A further variation was to accept notes for absences even when it was thought that the student had been truant:

Tui teacher: A note is a cure-all in this school . . . 'Where were you?', 'Oh, I had to do something', 'What did you have to do?', 'I'll bring a note' . . . Then we say, 'OK, it's covered.' We don't address the fact that it may well be covered but it's still not good enough.

Similar kinds of patterns can be seen with the problems of collecting in homework and internal assessment work at Tui College. The school had developed a weekly homework timetable for all junior classes which allocated an hour of homework for each subject every week. Yet, despite this attempt by the school to structure homework, it was apparent that it was not being regularly set or checked by many teachers. The majority of teachers observed appeared to be taking the same low-confrontation approach as over checking attendance. Homework was set, but if it was not done by most students, staff didn't make a fuss. In several classes collecting homework was left to the end of the lesson where it was less of an issue if only one or two students handed it in on their way out of the door. Others operated an elastic deadline where it could always be handed in tomorrow.

Although it might be argued that the teachers were simply not trying hard enough, the fact was that *most* students were not meeting homework require-ments:

Tui teacher: A major issue is the whole attitude thing, handing work in, completing homework. If you really wanted to hammer a class here about homework, you would spend your whole time hammering your class about homework. Whereas at [a nearby middle class school] you are picking off one or two or three in a class.

In other areas the Tui senior management team itself was apparently sanctioning a 'flexible' approach. The late work policy for internally assessed work was one of these. The problem here was that many students, seniors in this case, did not hand in their work on time:

Tui teacher: Lots of kids in [a Year 11 class] haven't handed in their internally assessed work – about 20 per cent just haven't done it at all. At [a nearby middle class school] you get one or two, they are normally the kids along for the ride, you tolerate that. Here you have a lot more of those kids as well as those who can't be bothered.

The school had therefore developed a generous late work policy which was attempting to ensure that there were sanctions to encourage students to get the required work in but which also gave students some credit for work done (a residual mark) if they didn't meet the deadline. Some teachers were scathing about this policy which they saw as symptomatic of the school's over-lenient approach to many issues:

Tui teacher: We tend to accept second best, whether it is the white liberal thing I don't know, we tend to sort of think that because some of our kids have a bleak sort of existence outside of school, we make too many compensations.

Another area of student non-compliance sanctioned by the school was the use of class and form time for meetings and practices that in most schools would have been held at interval, lunchtime or after school. At Tui College it was difficult to arrange school meetings of any kind – sporting, cultural, pastoral or disciplinary – between staff and students outside teaching time as students would simply not turn up:

Tui teacher: They have a very relaxed attitude. When I managed sports teams I never got a full turnout. Even when it was important information like telling them what teams they were in there's a very relaxed turn up when you can and if you want to. That really gets to me. You spend an awful lot of time chasing around after students to get messages across.

Tui teacher: Unlike (a middle class school) where the kids actually do turn up, here they just don't – 'You find me.'

As a result, teachers often took students out of classes or form time. In doing so they were forced both to leave their own class if they were teaching and to disrupt the class the student was in. The same difficulty meant last minute panics about preparation for school events which also resulted in disruption of classes. For instance, students were taken out of class to rehearse for two full days prior to a multicultural festival. A drama production also required three full days of rehearsal in school time prior to the event:

Tui DP: Again it's that cultural capital thing. For kids going to a middle class school if you are going to be in a sports team or a choir, that's going to be extracurricular and you'll have to put in the time. Here that is not the case. Therefore whoever is in charge of the event invariably gets near the time and the performance level is not up to scratch. The kids won't put in the time so you have to take them out of class.

The problem of collecting fees to allow students to sit exams is a final example of the extraordinary effort required to carry out many ordinary tasks at Tui College. The exam fees saga began by sending reminder notices home several months in advance to warn parents and students this cost would be coming up. About two weeks before the fees were due, the teacher in charge started his campaign. He began by imploring form teachers in staff meeting to get behind the effort to get the money from students in their form classes:

Tui teacher: The next two weeks will be horrendous . . . point out to (the students) that it's not a school-based fee, it has to be paid if they are going to sit their exam . . .

He had prepared brightly-coloured posters which were pasted up throughout the school. He spoke to a full school assembly:

You have had about three months' notice that we are collecting fees. You have had lots of warning. That money must now be paid. We have given you as much warning as we can. You have had time to organize and plan to get that money in. The time has come now where we need some action.

Despite these efforts only a quarter of fees had been collected by the week before deadline. As added incentive for staff to chase up the fees, the teacher started a 'league table' on the staffroom noticeboard showing the number of students yet to pay in each form class. Some teachers had not collected any fees, most hardly any and only one or two had collected most of the fees. The daily exhortations to staff continued. A special senior assembly was held. Two days before the final deadline the teacher wrote on the staff blackboard, 'When push comes to shove – Exam Fees!' On the day the fees were due 56 per cent of students had yet to pay. The teacher in charge announced to staff wryly:

> Thanks, keep pushing, we might get it all in by a week after it is due. Today is the last day we have given the kids, we have until next [week] then we have to pull the plug.

The final deadline having passed, the campaign went into overdrive. Reminder notices were given to individuals. Form teachers were instructed to ring or visit the students' homes. Another special assembly was called. Two days before the fees were absolutely required, the teacher wrote 'PANIC' above the staffroom fees progress chart. Individuals were counselled and special arrangements were made for 'time payment' for 20 per cent of students. Eventually all fees were accounted for and the cheque sent off on time. '100% FEES TAKE!' exclaimed a message on the staffroom noticeboard.

In contrast, none of these daily routines presented real difficulties in the middle class schools. Truancy was typically of little concern:

Plimmer principal: It's not the big heavy truancy stuff you get in [a local low SES area] where you have kids away for days and days and days and parents keeping them home to babysit younger kids, that's almost unheard of. It's more the seventh form [Year 13] taking a spell off now and then.

There were fewer checks on absences at these schools compared to Tui College. Despite this, the rate of absenteeism in the observed classes at all of the middle class schools was about half that at Tui College (Table 7.1). The small amount of truancy which did come to light was taken seriously and followed up.

Homework was set in most classes at the middle class schools. Whatever their personal views about it, homework was essentially worthwhile for teachers to set because it was expected by many students and could be capably done by most. No instances were observed where, having been given a firm deadline, most of a class at any of these schools had not done, or at least attempted to do, their homework:

Victoria principal: We can set homework and expect that it will be done, at least by a significant number of our kids.

Table 7.1 Mean number of days absent (1994 school year)

Tui		Wakefield		Victoria		Plimmer	
9A	9B	9A	9B	9A	9B	9A	9B
31.9	32.1	16.2	16.3	15.5	19.5	18.0	18.1

For subject teachers at the middle class schools, checking homework was therefore more a matter of picking out the few students who hadn't done the work, rather than a general problem. It was common practice for teachers to check it in class while students were working silently so they could hear the comments of the teacher 'doing the rounds':

Wakefield teacher: Has anyone else not done or attempted their homework so I don't crucify — on his own?

In a similar way all of these schools were able to enforce more demanding policies on assessed work than was the case at Tui College. As one teacher pointed out, this may have been less a matter of conscious self-interest than of general conscientiousness:

Wakefield teacher: At the same time, you ask the kids why they work hard and they wouldn't have a clue. They'll work their butts off but they are not at all, what's the word, clinical. If you gave them a piece of work for homework and went to one class and said, 'This is worth 25 per cent of your internal assessment mark' and went to another and said, 'I want to you to do this for homework' they would go home and spend equal time on it. That's the kind of kids they are.

At Wakefield and Victoria colleges extracurricular activities tended to be held outside form time or class time. It was unusual for students to be allowed out of class either to practise for or to watch student performances. Such interruptions were strongly resisted by the staff:

Victoria principal: They are a matter of concern to a lot of staff, mainly for the teaching staff who find that they can't get on with their work. When you have this expectation of the academic side of the school, things that stuff it up get teachers annoyed . . . we have minimal [sports exchanges]. But teachers want to get on with the job.

However, students at these schools would attend out of class. There was a high level of student attendance at meetings even when held early before school or, for major events, during holidays. Even schoolwide administrative tasks such as collecting sports fees were able to be done out of class time. It was also uncommon for students to avoid disciplinary meetings:

Victoria dean: They turn up, there is no problem. It's a question of how far you get beyond that.

Things were a little different at Plimmer College where traditionally a large number of extracurricular offerings were organized and announced to staff at short notice. However, it was claimed that interruptions didn't affect Plimmer College students much as they could learn as well on their own:

Plimmer principal: Yes, there are a lot (of interruptions) and no, they don't worry me . . . it must be up to the kids to catch up and if the teachers are organizing effective study programmes, it should be OK . . . I think given access to the material, the students will learn it anyway with the occasional question of the teacher . . . In fact, it could be argued that [other activities] enhance their performance by giving them more variety.

Lastly, the collection of exam fees was straightforward at all of the middle class schools:

Victoria AP: We try and fix one day because there is such a lot of money involved. We like to do it on one day and get it processed and out of the school as quickly as possible.

In this school on the allocated day, 84 per cent of students paid their exam fees. The next day, 91 per cent had paid. At Wakefield 66 per cent of fees came in on the two days allocated to collect them and 93 per cent of fees were collected by the school's last date for payment. Some 80 per cent of Plimmer students had paid by the school deadline. In each school there was only a small number of students who had not paid by the due date. Although it was undoubtedly time-consuming for staff to follow up these individual cases, there was nothing similar to the fees collection campaign observed at Tui College.

Guidance and discipline

At Tui College much emphasis was placed on pastoral issues because of the large proportion of students who presented serious social, motivational and behavioural problems:

Teacher: The pastoral system here is the main thing, it is the glue that holds everything together.

Teacher: [In] a school like ours, you are denying the facts if you ignore the pastoral side because kids won't learn if other things are not right. A lot of them are a long way back from sitting in a classroom saying, 'OK, let's get on with it, this is the role I play here.' So we spend a lot of time on pastoral things, meeting parents, getting kids to school. That of course is time taken away from subject preparation or whatever.

An important feature of the pastoral system at Tui College was that it was non-confrontational. Since students did not respond to aggressive disciplinary approaches, talking things through and applying gentle but continuing pressure was found to be a more effective, if time-consuming, approach:

Tui principal: And so you squeeze up the whole time. It's no good being stroppy, the kids just don't respond, they are used to that. So the only strategy is to constantly create an environment where kids feel good about themselves and are encouraged to give their best. It's an exhausting process essentially. You can never take anything for granted.

Pastoral issues took time not only because of the counselling approach required but because of the quantitative and qualitative scale of the difficulties. Guidance and disciplinary matters, often with a care and protection dimension, were the most pressing problem facing the staff and management at Tui College:

Tui DP: Let's take student A, who one month pinches some stuff in a pretty organized fashion, is suspended, comes back and in the space of two weeks manages to systematically rob two staff members, their wallets, keys and so on.[1] A practised criminal. Or student B, a girl who is totally out of control at home, sleeps rough in [the city], heavily into crime, Mum's been arrested, she's got a drug and alcohol problem, a father who is trying to claim custody but there's some sexual abuse history in the background, that sort of situation. That student, suspended for violence, back in school, picked up smoking hash. What do we do with that kid? There have been meetings with Social Welfare, Justice are involved but finally there is no place for that kid at school.

Tui AP: We have problem after problem after problem of the sort that are way beyond our skills to have any impact on. I'm talking about kids from dysfunctional families who by the age of 13 or 14 are involved in truancy and crime . . . So that's the big one for me, manifested in lots of ways, the kids who truant, the kids who go off their heads in the classroom, the kids who are depressed . . . There are probably ten kids who are so far out of control we can do nothing to fix it and their families can't either. Then there are a second raft of kids who are [also] serious . . . there is about 20 or 30 of them.

Not surprisingly, dealing with these cases was very time-consuming. The principal estimated that suspensions took 30 hours to process on average including meetings with the student, parents, outside agencies and the Board of Trustees.[2] Like the senior administrators, the guidance counsellor was also under enormous pressure and was thought by several staff to be completely swamped. He had a current caseload which included about 30 per cent of the school population and described the scale of need as a 'bottomless pit situation'. Many issues were poverty-related and involved liaison with government agencies.

The seriousness of the pastoral problems faced by the senior management team and guidance counsellor at Tui College meant that they had little time to deal with relatively less important disciplinary and pastoral issues. These were supposed to be addressed by a devolved pastoral system. Whereas many New Zealand secondary schools operate pastoral systems where form teachers are responsible to a year level dean who in turn is responsible to the senior management team, Tui College had developed a system of several 'Houses', each with its own head teacher who carried considerably more pastoral responsibility than deans normally would at other schools. Officially there

had been good reasons for developing this system,[3] but one of its unacknow-
ledged purposes was probably to prevent too many students ending up in the
principal's office too quickly:

House head: The House system makes things cyclical between the House
head and the form tutor. That circle might go around a bit then it goes up
[to the administration]. So there has been a lot of work before you get to
the point where you have to boot kids out.

Yet given the number of students that presented guidance and discipline
problems, the senior management team would have been completely overwhelmed if Tui College had not had a comprehensive pastoral system in place.
Some staff realized this:

Tui teacher: At [a nearby middle class school] problem children were sent up
the system very quickly 'cos there were so few of them. Whereas here if
they did that they would be swamped. I think the administration realizes
that and realizes, 'Hey, we really need to have the staff on side with us.'

Certainly the senior management team saw themselves as the court of last
resort:

Tui AP: I believe we should only be the end point of the system, when all
else is failed. So we are like the last stop.

The only misdemeanours which led to immediate suspension and 'last stop'
administration action at Tui College were starting a fight or carrying or using
drugs or alcohol. As a consequence the House heads further down the school
found themselves dealing with issues such as truancy and verbal abuse of
teachers. Some resented this:

House head: The House heads feel they are doing too much. They [senior
management team] pick up very little these days. Maybe a major fight
where parents come in . . . [The senior management team] are not very
receptive . . . it's like, don't hassle me, I've got enough hassles.

It was at the level of the form teachers – five or six in each House – that most
individual student problems were expected to be addressed. However, few
form teachers were able to deal effectively with the range of activities they
were expected to pick up:

House head: In terms of the [House] groups being self-actualizing, well, it
depends on the teachers in your group but the constraint is the time spent
on other issues . . . in form time there are too many administrative tasks
that need to be done, they don't have time for pastoral care.

One result of the demands placed on the guidance and discipline system at Tui
College was that little support was given to classroom teachers. They were
mostly expected to deal with their own discipline problems, but knowing they
had little backup, many teachers chose to avoid disciplinary issues, which
often led to unruly and disrupted classrooms.

Tui teacher: At Tui College, [students] don't go somewhere else. It's your problem, you deal with it. So it depends how much confrontation you are prepared to buy into.

Tui teacher: You are not really backed up over disciplinary issues. Swearing at staff is not really a big issue.

Another effect of the way in which the guidance and discipline system at Tui College at every level was either overwhelmed or ineffective was that some pastoral/guidance issues were not properly addressed. Trudy's case appears to be a good example of this. It will be recalled from Chapter 5 that Trudy left school towards the end of the year after being threatened with physical violence. However, the circumstances of Trudy's departure were not properly followed up by the school's pastoral system. Trudy had initially begun to truant single lessons, then whole days. The form teacher contacted home to find that Trudy's mother was in hospital and that Trudy was climbing out of her bedroom window at night to meet her 20-year-old boyfriend (who had recently been in court facing theft charges). She had also found out at this point that Trudy felt threatened at school. The House head and guidance counsellor were advised. The House head spoke briefly to Trudy about safe sex practices while the guidance counsellor reportedly told Trudy that her personal safety could be sorted out, and that it was not a good reason for not coming to school. Trudy's form teacher then put Trudy on an absence report but on the first day Trudy's father had written her a note: 'What Trudy does is my business.' The form teacher described how she had burst into tears at this response because she felt so frustrated. However, the next day, Trudy's father contacted the school and apologized, saying he had been in a bad mood on the morning Trudy had shown him the report.

Yet despite all this, Trudy's case was subsequently dropped by the school and, as some of her teachers noted, she was allowed to truant for the last six weeks of the school year:

Tui teacher 1: Trudy? She bombed out big time in the third term.
Tui teacher 2: Whose House was she in? Oh, I know.
Tui teacher 1: Nothing was ever followed up. And I even ran after her in [the local shopping centre] and I said, you know, 'What are you doing, why aren't you at school?' Oh, there was something about a kid got beaten up, no it wasn't a kid, it was a young adult got beaten up . . . and apparently she was involved and all these kids were going to beat her up at school or something. It's funny, she got on a report for wagging but she didn't wag Integrated Studies that much.

At the middle class schools things were entirely different. Here guidance and discipline difficulties on the scale experienced at Tui College were unheard of:

Victoria principal: We don't have, by and large, too much by the way of behavioural problems. When I went away from [a previous lower SES school] I knew I would go back to a crisis. Every day, every week. Here I

Table 7.2 Formal school suspensions (1994 school year)

Suspensions	Tui		Wakefield		Victoria		Plimmer	
	No.	%	No.	%	No.	%	No.	%
Whole school	52	9.5	11	1.8	30	3.2	19	2.7
Year 9	18	13.8	1	0.8	4	1.6	5	2.7

can go away, come back, things are handled . . . we can afford to be reasonably lax, that's not the word, we don't have to make law and order an issue, by and large.

None of the middle class schools suspended as many students as Tui College did (Table 7.2). However, this was because many more students were presenting serious problems at Tui College rather than because the middle class schools were less willing to suspend – in fact suspensions at these schools were for (relatively) minor offences such as smoking (cigarettes) and swearing:

Plimmer principal: It's an early step and it is also often the last. It's a way of saying to students, 'You are pissing your teachers off, you can have some time out.' The three more serious suspensions we would have had to have done this year, the parents could see the writing on the wall and took them out [permanently] voluntarily.

As a result of being under less pressure, the middle class schools were able to use strongly hierarchical referral systems which saw the small proportion of 'problem' students identified and passed quickly to deans and senior staff:

Wakefield dean (in staff meeting): So if you are having any problems just blue-slip them to us.

MPT: What about a student telling a teacher to 'fuck off'?
Victoria dean: Straight to [the DP] or [Principal]. Fast track. [The Principal] is hot on that.

There was little evidence that those in more senior positions were swamped with student problems as a result:

Victoria dean: I actually see the role of the dean as supporting the teacher . . . I intervene early.

Wakefield DP: Strictly speaking, by the time it gets to me it should be serious but in practice it doesn't really work that way. Kids bounce back between me and the deans and the form teachers like a fantail in a badminton match.

The middle class schools could impose strict disciplinary regimes because they had the support of most students and parents:

Wakefield dean: The kids who stand out are very few in number so they are easy to target. If this school was in [a working class suburb] the system wouldn't cope because your workload would increase, there would have to be a different way I suppose . . . Most [parents] have a nice, white, middle class value system so they say, 'Righto, I'll talk to young Johnny at home.' So in lots of cases we work very closely with parents, we couldn't do our job if we didn't have their backup . . . I have never been challenged yet – 'Why are you giving my kid a detention?'

Counselling was also an important activity at the middle class schools but the issues were different from those which arose at Tui College:

Victoria counsellor: There is not a lot of poverty-related stuff at this school. Redundancies yes, the emotional stuff, but not a lot of poverty stuff. Not a lot of physical abuse, that has a lot to do with socioeconomic levels, that goes for a lot of things . . . I don't have a lot of dealings with Social Welfare.

At the middle class schools staff were well supported and it was unlikely that individual students would have been overlooked as Trudy was. Rather these schools tended to use opportunities to 'nip in the bud' potential problems. For instance, when Vicky reclaimed a confiscated jacket by lying to school office staff, the action was considered serious enough to lead the dean to seek views of Vicky's behaviour and work from her teachers and to organize a meeting, also attended by the DP, with Vicky's mother.

Leadership and governance

Senior staff were clearly under a great deal of pressure at Tui College. Most of the pressure came from the kinds of instructional, pastoral and organizational issues already mentioned. However, there were also other less direct but important management problems generated by the intake. One of these was staffing. Although there was little evidence of a quicker staff turnover at Tui, the college typically received about half the number of applications for vacancies the middle class schools did. Moreover, there was difficulty in attracting good applicants. The principal was forced to make five new appointments long-term supply rather than permanent because he was not able to attract suitable applicants.

A related problem was that of monitoring staff performance. While all principals saw this as part of their job and had started competency procedures with some staff, the senior staff of Tui College had less scope for action if teachers were not performing well. Not only were they limited in the time they could spend on competency procedures, but they often struggled to find good staff in any case. This meant that although it is likely that Tui College students provided their own sorting mechanism in that teachers who were not coping often moved on, there were some who remained. Senior staff at Tui College were aware some staff were ineffectual but consoled themselves that such teachers were valuable to the school in other ways.

A third problem was trying to market a school for which middle class families had little respect. A phone survey of prospective parents in the area completed as part of the Smithfield Project (Waslander *et al.* 1994) indicated that middle class parents in the Tui College area were not intending to send their children there. Those whose children would be attending were working class parents who could either not afford to send their children elsewhere or saw no need to. The result was that the marketing efforts of Tui College got little response from middle class parents or even from parents of prospective students. Parent information night saw an almost empty hall. Related to this was the instability created by the school's declining roll. The school had to go through a redundancy process over several consecutive years. Apart from the damaging effects this process had on staff morale, it was also time-consuming and forced staff to teach some unfamiliar subjects.

Maintaining morale was also a trial in a school with so many problems. The Tui College principal used two main approaches. The first was to appeal to the concept of value-added education to show that the school was in fact being effective. The school had been involved in a quantitative school effectiveness study which suggested that the school was doing well in terms of increasing the achievement of most students. This was a real boost to the principal and something he stressed with staff, to parents in newsletters, and at the enrolment evening where he showed the graphs illustrating this. However, most staff seemed guarded about celebrating the results:

Teacher: I don't know about that report. Maybe kids here can make up more ground because they come from further behind.

Furthermore, despite the principal's evident desire to 'wean them [parents] off SC [School Certificate]', it was questionable whether the alternative value-added message was either understood by parents or acceptable to them:

Tui AP: Value-added education has been bandied around for a decade now, but I challenge you to go out and find five parents who know what it means.

Tui teacher: The gap between the parents' experience of education and what we do is large. It manifests itself in the number of kids who enrol in external examinations when we know they haven't got a ghost's chance of getting even above 40 per cent.

The second approach was simply to focus on the positives and refuse to acknowledge the difficulties. Consider the principal's end of year prizegiving speech:

This year we do not have to wait for examination results to come out to receive our ranking in the stakes. We have been CLASSIFIED.

> The league tables have been indelibly printed in the daily paper. Tui College is a [low-SES decile rating school] . . . What does that mean to you? Do you feel like giving up and saying, 'I told you we're no good – it's not worth trying any more. We can't be expected to do well. We are just the cannon fodder for the system. We just provide the dole queue of the future'? Or do you have a different response? For me, I have stopped talking to the press about social issues. I have no intention of going on feeding the prejudices of the wider public. I will only talk to them about positive, educational achievements [goes on to list the achievements of one student in Maths, several who have done well in sports].

The work of senior staff at the middle class schools was by no means easy either, but they were certainly under less pressure than those at Tui College. For instance, the Plimmer College's deputy principal was absent most of the year through illness, with little apparent effect on the school, the deputy principal of Wakefield College was able to complete a postgraduate degree while holding the position, and the principal of Victoria College was able to spend a lot of time away from the school, secure in the knowledge that things were being 'handled' in his absence.

The rolls of the middle class schools were well supported. Information evenings were all keenly attended by middle class parents 'shopping around', and the schools did not need to go through redundancy processes. It was also much easier both to motivate staff and to win parental support. There were more successes to celebrate and fewer problems. Newsletters at the middle class schools were full of student achievements, both sporting *and* academic, constituting powerful 'good news machines'. Those at Tui College were also positive but necessarily more circumspect. For instance, instead of proudly trumpeting exam results to parents as middle class schools could, Tui College focussed on other aspects. For example, from the first newsletter of the year:

> Examination Results: Congratulations to all students who did their very best. The overall School Certificate results are very difficult to interpret because exams are no longer scaled and national subject means varied from 46 per cent to 61 per cent. It is very pleasing to note from our results that the average mark for Maori students in English was the same as for European students. This is a most encouraging trend in the school.

There was also a sense that the Boards of Trustees of the middle class schools were more powerful than at Tui College and less likely to be intimidated by government agencies. One reason for this was that whereas the middle class schools all had Boards of Trustees whose members could bring legal, accounting and managerial skills to the position, the Tui College board members lacked these skills and required more help and guidance from the principal. It would probably be incorrect to overstress the value of having a more professional board composition because there was evidence that the principals of some of the middle class schools also found their boards were not especially useful because of their members' commitments elsewhere. Nevertheless,

Table 7.3 Government funding per student (1994)

	Tui	Wakefield	Victoria	Plimmer
Operational funding ($)	1135	905	717	830
Salaries funding ($)	3761	3429	2753	2991
Pupil–teacher ratio	15.2	15.7	18.3	17.2

Table 7.4 Mean funding ($) per student from sources other than Vote Education by school (1994)

Tui	Wakefield	Victoria	Plimmer
70	908	364	710

Table 7.5 Size of 'school donation'($) and proportion typically collected by school (1994)

	Tui	Wakefield	Victoria	Plimmer
'School donation' per student	50	60	60	100
Proportion collected (%)	60–70	85	85	72

there were times when the ability to get a free legal or accounting perspective was valuable or when Board members had useful contacts.

Finally, while Tui College received extra funding and staffing from the Ministry of Education, this was not considerable (Table 7.3). Moreover, Tui College attracted much less community funding than the middle class schools (Table 7.4). Although the ability and willingness of the latter to raise funds varied widely, all could raise much more local money than Tui College. Tui College did ask for a 'school donation' from each student but while this was smaller than any of the middle class schools and a smaller proportion was collected, this accounted for only a little of the differences between the schools (Table 7.5).[4] The middle class schools were able to raise more money from fundraising events, fee-paying students and business sponsorships than was possible at Tui College. For instance, raffles, entertainment evenings and phone company and supermarket sponsorships advantaged the middle class schools because parents there had higher discretionary spending power.[5]

Summary

This chapter has pointed to a range of organizational and management mechanisms for a school mix effect. Day-to-day routines were clearly much more difficult to carry out efficiently at Tui College. This school also had a much larger social welfare role than the middle class schools and it was not as well resourced in financial, material or staffing terms. Organizing and managing a school like Tui College therefore presented huge challenges for its teachers and senior team. A key point to bear in mind here is that the organizational and management advantages accrued by the middle class schools were also accompanied by the reference group advantages highlighted in Chapter 5 and the instructional advantages noted in Chapter 6. The position we have moved towards then is a view of a school mix effect as a cumulative phenomenon along the lines of the 'whole school' hypothesis. This and other conclusions and implications are discussed further in Part III.

 **PART III**

THEORY, PRACTICE, POLICY AND RESEARCH

 **8**

Understanding the impact of school mix

This chapter sets out to summarize and explain the impact of school mix and to look at its most immediate implications for schools. I begin by revisiting a number of key questions raised by the discussion in Part I to see how much light the Wellington study has shed on our understanding of the impact of school mix. These questions are:

- Does school mix have a genuine effect or is it a proxy for some other variable?
- If school mix does have an effect, how significant is it?
- If school mix does have an effect, how is it caused?
- If school mix does have an effect, to what extent is it modified by within-school segregation?

I will also ask:

- If school mix does have an effect, is it a universally optimal or zero-sum effect?

Finally, I examine what implications the study is likely to have for those in schools by asking:

- To what degree can school leaders and teachers promote 'effective' or 'successful' school characteristics irrespective of the mix of their school?

Each of these issues is discussed below.

A genuine effect?

It will be recalled that the Wellington study did not set out to demonstrate causal relationships between school mix, school processes and student achievement. What it has been able to show, however, is that numerous differences do exist in reference group, instructional, organizational and management processes which could plausibly explain how the effect could work. There is also considerable qualitative evidence to link these differences in processes to school composition. Indeed, in the light of the discussion, it is hard to see how a school mix effect would not occur. In this sense, the findings of the study have supported the idea of a school mix effect. Since conclusive evidence for or against a school mix effect is likely to remain elusive, these kinds of findings may be the best we can hope for.

A significant effect?

This study could not investigate the question of significance either, at least not in a statistical sense. However, it is difficult to see how years of exposure to working class reference groups, to less challenging and less engaged class-rooms and to a less smooth running and less disciplined school environment would not make a considerable difference to the achievement of ordinary working class kids at working class schools relative to those at middle class schools. Moreover, since there is a greater chance that students who attend working class schools will be more likely simply to drop out of the system (like Trudy) or be suspended, it could be argued that for some individuals the effect of school mix will be critical. It is also important to recall here that the differences among the case study schools in terms of their social class composition were not as wide as elsewhere in New Zealand. Had even higher and lower SES schools been included in the study, the process differences would have likely been even more marked. For instance, Hawk and Hill (1996) have carried out detailed research in eight very low-SES New Zealand schools. They paint a picture entirely consistent with that of Tui College, but even further removed from the middle class schools.

There are clear parallels here with process differences reported by qualitative researchers elsewhere who, while investigating somewhat different questions, have also compared schools of differing social class mix. Of particular relevance is research in the USA by Anyon (1981), Lareau (1989) and Metz (1990) as well as Connell *et al.*'s (1982) Australian study. Metz, for instance, reaches a very similar conclusion:

> For both individual students and individual teachers, the experience of life in school and the effectiveness of their academic efforts is deeply affected by the social class of the school in which they happen to find themselves . . . Neither a student nor a teacher would emerge from 4 years at any two of the schools with similar experiences, skills or attitudes. If these schools are at all typical, it is clear that teachers as well as students will have much more difficulty in developing their academic abilities at the lower-SES schools, and that teachers and students of

moderate ability will be helped to flourish in at least some directions in schools of higher SES.

(Metz 1990: 103)

What are the likely causes?

There are three levels at which we can now examine the question of causes. First, we can discuss *which* processes appear to be influenced by school mix to create the school mix effect. Second, we can examine *how* these processes might be influenced by school mix to create the effect and finally, we can consider how the school mix effect might fit *existing theories* of educational inequality.

The findings of this study support but move beyond previous reference group and instructional explanations for a school mix effect, to point to a whole-school explanation – one which involves reference group, instructional *and* organizational/management mechanisms. The school mix effect seems best understood as the *cumulative* outcome of numerous smaller effects resulting from differences in each of these areas among the schools, all of which were related in turn to their intake characteristics. The evidence points to there being clear advantages accrued by students who attend middle class schools. These are outlined below.

Reference group processes

Exposure to higher SES peers with:

- a wider range of curriculum-relevant experiences/social capital;
- higher levels of prior attainment;
- more school success;
- more regular school attendance;
- higher academic goals;
- higher SES occupational aspirations/expectations;
- less involvement in 'alienated' student subcultures;
- less violence and general conflict.

Instructional processes

Direct and indirect effects of:

- a more academic school programme;
- a wider range of extracurricular activities;
- more engaged, higher difficulty classes with:
  - more compliant/'able' students
  - more involved/motivated students
  - more classroom discussion/questioning
  - more demanding formal curriculum

- more demanding class and departmental use of texts and other resources;
- more demanding class, department and school assessment and reporting;
- peers with more personal classroom resources;
- being allowed to take texts home;
- better access to expensive video and computer resources;
- more qualified and higher SES teachers;
- more fulfilled/motivated teachers.

Organizational and management processes

Direct and indirect effects of:
- more efficient daily routines;
- less pressured guidance and discipline systems with:
  - higher levels of student compliance
  - fewer very difficult guidance/discipline cases
- less pressured school management with:
  - fewer student problems
  - fewer staffing problems
  - fewer morale problems
  - fewer marketing and promotion problems
  - fewer fundraising problems
  - more time to devote to monitoring performance
  - more time to devote to planning
- less pressured Boards of Trustees with:
  - more useful qualifications/contacts
- more financial resources.

The idea of a school mix effect resulting from *so many* smaller effects of these differences helps to explain why its importance has not been recognized by quantitative and qualitative researchers alike. If we look at these differences individually, each seems relatively insignificant. It is their *cumulative* effect however that may exercise a powerful influence on student achievement. In a sense this possibility comes close to Rutter's use of the notion of ethos. He and his colleagues argued that:

> the *cumulative* [his emphasis] effect of these various social factors was considerably greater than the effect of any of the individual factors on their own.
>
> (Rutter *et al.* 1979: 179)

But whereas in Rutter's analysis the notion of 'ethos' or 'climate' is disconnected from the social class context of the school, this study has explicitly pointed to two reasons *why* school processes could reflect school mix.

One concerns disparities in material and staffing resources, factors often cited as a cause of inequalities between schools. Although there were disparities among the Wellington schools, they were not dramatic enough on their own to explain the differences apparent between the schools. For instance, while it was true that Tui College collected much lower funding from non-government sources, this affected only the 'extras' (such as computers and musical instruments) available to its students. All schools were similarly resourced in terms of basics such as buildings and textbook allocations. Similarly, the staffing ratios at the schools were not markedly different.

Rather, this study has suggested that a more powerful explanation for the school mix effect revolves around the idea of school processes being both *negotiated* and a matter of *critical mass*. Negotiation is a term which has often been used by symbolic interactionists such as Delamont (1983) and Woods (1979). Curriculum theorists have also begun to study the ways in which curriculum and pedagogy is 'embedded' in the events that students and teachers jointly construct in classes (see Doyle (1992) for a summary). However, while research in both of these fields can be useful, neither gives much emphasis to social class. Here I want to link the notion of negotiation more explicitly to the social class characteristics of students (Jones 1991). It is likely that school policies and practices of many kinds must be negotiated with students on the basis of class-related levels of compliance, motivation and 'ability'. These in turn are related to students' views of schooling and their likely occupational futures (Brown 1987; Lauder *et al.* 1992). Metz makes a similar point:

> Teaching is an interactive endeavor; it requires making connection with students. If their attitudes and skills vary substantially, so must the content and style of teachers' work with them. Accordingly, the very nature of teachers' work varies with their students and so with the social class of the communities from which students come, even when teachers' own training or initial skills are similar.
>
> (Metz 1990: 99)

The Wellington study also points to the importance of critical mass. Many of the differences noted in the preceding discussion are best seen as issues of power, with the power relations between different social classes within schools being of central importance. This is because in a predominantly middle class school, the struggles of working class families and students are marginalized and can have relatively little effect on school organization and management. As a school becomes more working class, however, it can be predicted that the processes of the school will shift, despite resistance from middle class teachers and students, towards the culture of the increasingly sizeable working class group.

To explain further the impact of school mix at the most general level we need to look to the organic or inter-connected relationship between schools and middle class, rather than working class, families mentioned in Chapter 3 (Bourdieu and Passeron 1977; Connell *et al.* 1982; Lareau 1989; Metz 1990). In the case of school mix, these middle class/organic, working class/inorganic relations between home and school need to be seen played out at the school level as well as at the individual level. Schools develop processes that reflect their SES mix. Solidly middle class schools have strongly supportive student cultures which allow them to teach an academic, exam-based curriculum and to organize and manage themselves relatively smoothly. Working class schools will, in general, be quite the opposite. Consequently working class students who attend a working class school may often fail not only because of their own background but also because they are attending working class schools which cannot offer middle class types of school resources and processes necessary for academic success. Conversely working class students who attend a middle class school are more likely to succeed because they are exposed, despite their individual class backgrounds, to the contextual benefits of a middle class school mix. Yet a deficit approach to working class culture is not intended here. Rather the Wellington study highlights the extent to which school effectiveness in an academic sense not only reflects the middle class bias of schooling in capitalist societies but also appears to rest upon the cultural resources and responses of students from middle class families.

The idea of middle class/organic, working class/inorganic relationships may also be specifically linked to instructional processes through the notion of the *negotiated curriculum*. While some writers have viewed curriculum negotiation largely as a voluntary activity which can be used to improve student learning (Boomer and Lester 1992) others have argued, as I do, that teachers are more or less required to respond to the needs and desires of the groups of students they teach (Delamont 1983; Powell *et al.* 1985; Metz 1990; Jones 1991; Grant and Sleeter 1996). Teachers (and schools) must respond to the social class characteristics of their students because to ignore these characteristics, even if it were possible, would be to teach 'inappropriately' and generate student resistance. The group that must be responded to is likely to be the *predominant* SES group within a class or a school. This is the group which is most likely to determine instruction because, as Delamont points out:

> Pupil power is . . . group power. A pupil's strength [in the classroom] is directly related to the number of classmates who . . . share the same definition of the situation.
>
> (Delamont 1983: 77)

The most numerous group of students will therefore usually determine the teacher's approach to the curriculum. As one teacher at Plimmer College put it: 'You go to the middle don't you and if the middle is high or low, that's going to affect learning isn't it?'

It is also important to stress that the curriculum is negotiated with middle class as well as working class students. Following Bernstein it might be thought that the curriculum could be negotiated only where there is weak framing (and classification) in an attempt to cater for working class students. Bernstein notes:

> Knowledge . . . tends to be transmitted, particularly to elite pupils at the secondary level, through strong frames which control the selecting, organisation, pacing and timing of the knowledge. When this frame is relaxed to include everyday realities, it is often, and sometimes validly,

not simply for the transmission of educational knowledge but for purposes of social control . . . the weakening of this frame occurs usually with the less 'able' students whom we have given up educating.

(Bernstein 1975: 98–9)

However Jones's (1991) study and this one suggest that middle class students may also facilitate their teachers' attempts to teach a more tightly classified and framed examination curriculum. This is because for middle class students 'real' knowledge is not necessarily 'relevant' knowledge – it can also be the more abstract knowledge which will lead to exam success. Thus what is negotiable here is not the tightly framed and classified examination curriculum itself, but the extent to which teachers focus on and teach it. It is in this sense that curriculum can be seen to be the subject of negotiation in schools between both working and middle class students and their teachers.

What is the impact of within-school segregation?

The case study of Victoria College suggests that the school mix effect can be significant despite tracking, and helps to explain why Lauder and Hughes (1990b) found a school mix effect despite many of their schools being banded. Most obviously, school organization and management processes appear to be more demanding and efficient in middle class schools irrespective of tracking at the classroom level. However, reference group and instructional processes could also cause a school mix effect despite tracking. This is because it appears what may be more important than whether a student is in a tracked or mixed-'ability' class is the SES characteristics of that class. A student in a low track in a high-SES school may still benefit more from having higher SES classmates and friends and more demanding instructional processes than a similar student in a low-SES but untracked school.

Two caveats need to be entered here. One is that the particular nature of tracking will be important in determining its effect – Victoria College was only partially banded. The other is that this conclusion should not be seen as any kind of argument for within-school segregation. Rather I am arguing the need to see within-school practices in the deeper context of differences among schools. The numerous studies over the last two decades of the effects of within-school segregation on student achievement need to be joined by more studies which simultaneously examine the effects of segregation within *and* among schools.

A universally optimal or zero-sum effect?

Lauder and Hughes (1990a) and other writers[1] have claimed that while (generally middle class) strong achievers may lose to some degree by mixing with (largely working class) low achievers, the gains of the weaker students will far outweigh the loss of the stronger. Walford and Pring (1997) also point to the 'levelling up' of working class student achievement rather than a 'levelling' down of middle class attainment. Benn further stresses the universal benefits of a social mix:

> We found evidence over and over again that having a mix – both in terms of attainment and social intake – made a big difference to schools, whether you looked at academic results, or whether you looked at figures related to attendance or indicators like staying on. Again and again having a mix did not end up halfway between the best and worst results or highest and lowest scores of whatever was being measured, as might be assumed, but always towards the higher end.
>
> (Benn 1997: 128)

On the other hand, policies which attempt to balance school intakes in order to improve working class achievement might have a negative effect on present levels of middle class achievement. This is suggested by Willms (1986) and Heath and Blakey (1992) who argue that school composition is more likely to be a zero-sum game – that all students achieve better at higher SES schools. For instance, the latter suggest:

> Contextual effects operate across the board: even less able students in a socially advantaged school will tend to have better than expected performance while the more able pupils in a socially disadvantaged school will tend to have worse than expected performance.
>
> (Heath and Blakey 1992: 128–9)

The Wellington study did not examine the effect of school mix on middle class individuals but the evidence does point more to the school mix effect being a zero-sum game than being universally optimal. This is because it is difficult to see why middle class students would not be affected by many of the reference group, instructional, and organizational/management differences discussed here in a similar way to working class students. Middle class students who attend relatively working class schools will also experience processes that will not be as beneficial in terms of academic outcomes as those experienced by students attending middle class schools.

It is feasible, as Lauder and Hughes (1990a) argue, that because of their cultural capital, middle class students will not 'lose' by being schooled in a working class setting to the same extent as working class students will 'gain' by being schooled in a middle class setting. However, this is quite another thing to arguing that balancing school mix can benefit all students. Instead the Wellington study implies that policies which set out to address school mix in order to benefit low-SES families will inevitably involve *some* cost in terms of middle class advantage. Thus balancing school mix is at heart a political and moral issue of power sharing, rather than simply a 'win–win' solution to inequality. This is because high-SES schooling is a positional good used to gain relative advantage in a class society, a point to which we return in the next chapter.

It is also important to note here that the experiences of the matched students at Plimmer College suggests that if there is too much of a gulf between individuals and the culture of schools, the advantageous effects of a high-SES mix may be partially lost. This will be the case for instance where teachers are so preoccupied with the needs of high-SES students that they fail to notice and help those whose class or ethnic culture does not fit as comfortably with that of the school (Wells 1996). However, this needs to be weighed up against the numerous advantages which also come from attending a high-SES school.

To what extent can school leaders and teachers promote 'effective' or 'successful' school characteristics irrespective of the mix of their schools?

A central issue raised by the Wellington study is the question of how we should understand the differences between schools. For instance, all kinds of descriptive typologies of school characteristics are often drawn up with little indication as to why the different kinds of processes described have developed.[2] The apparent blindness of these discussions to the possibility that the nature of student intake may explain many differences seems strange when read alongside powerful accounts of the effects of class and ethnic inequalities in educational provision, such as in Kozol (1991). Even 'sensitivity to context' studies which claim to be looking at contextual issues fail to appreciate the effects of school mix. For instance, Evans and Teddlie report a finding that effective low-SES schools have 'initiating' principals (concerned with reform) whereas effective middle-SES schools have 'managerial' principals (concerned with the maintenance of the status quo). However, they cannot explain this quantitative finding and call for 'rich qualitative answers'. They ask:

> Why is it that initiators are very common in effective low SES schools but much less so in effective middle SES schools? Do they violate norms of teacher autonomy at the middle SES schools? Does the community find their approach overbearing?
>
> (Evans and Teddlie 1995: 18)

In terms of the findings of this study the answer seems clear. There is, in general, relatively little to change at most middle class schools – they are seen to 'work' by students, staff and parents alike. What call is there for reforming principals in such schools? At working class schools on the other hand, problems are frequently persistent and substantial. Innovators are more than welcome in such schools, indeed it may be argued that most educational innovation is found in working class schools precisely because of this search for solutions. Furthermore, whereas a middle class school principal is able to delegate many responsibilities, a working class school principal appears to need a more 'hands on' approach if she or he wants policies carried through in the context of myriad and incessant daily demands.

This study has pointed directly to school mix as a potentially powerful explanation for many differences among schools across numerous facets of school life. Particular processes appear to 'fit' working class and middle class schools and cumulatively form distinctive school cultures. This is because school policies and practices often have to be negotiated with students rather than simply laid on them. However, most E&I proponents assume students passively allow the principal's or teacher's will to prevail. They rarely acknowledge the possibility that student characteristics might influence teacher practices as well as the other way around. Instead there persists an uncritical faith in the ability of schools 'to make a difference'. Yet the belief that schools and teachers can 'make the difference' by teaching what they choose in the ways they choose is not supported by this or earlier qualitative studies which have looked at schools and classrooms in depth.

But the Wellington study does suggest that teachers and school leaders can make *some* difference over mix. For instance, Victoria and Wakefield had 'pushing' policies that were probably maximizing their ability to make a difference over mix, whereas Plimmer College appeared to be resting largely on the characteristics of its mostly 'able' and compliant students.[3] It seems likely that where a school/teacher has 'pushing' policies, the effects of mix on achievement will be somewhat diminished. Where this is not the case, it will be somewhat larger.

These findings tend to support the SER claim about the importance of effective policies and practices. It reminds us that it would be 'inappropriate to conclude that social class alone determines the experience of students and teachers in schools and that nothing can be changed, or that schools do not make a difference' (Metz 1990: 92). At the same time it is also hard to get excited about the possibilities when the study has also pointed to school processes being so powerfully bounded by the SES mix of a school and the power relations and resources generated by that particular mix. This was illustrated by the general similarity between the middle class schools and their differences from Tui College. It was also shown by the analysis of student engagement and academic difficulty across the schools in Chapter 6 which indicated that while there was variation within all the schools, the middle class schools generally had more highly engaged and academically challenging classes.

The findings clearly have important implications for understanding and evaluating school effectiveness. They suggest that many factors which have been identified as contributing to achievement may indeed be school *based* but nonetheless not school *caused*. They relate to family background effects and will therefore not be easily modified by the kinds of recipes for success that SER proponents typically advocate. For example, in terms of the findings of this study, most of what Mortimore *et al.* (1988), Sammons *et al.* (1995) or Reynolds *et al.* (1996) have identified as features of school effectiveness could clearly also be viewed as related to school mix. For instance, none of the following should probably be seen independently of the influence of school mix: the nature of the school environment, the amount of time on-task, the nature of tasks, the level of staff expectations, the style of leadership, or the degree of parental involvement in a school.

There will also be important limits to which working class schools can promote those academic, orderly characteristics of higher SES schools usually regarded as 'successful' or 'effective'. For instance, although Tui College had teachers who might have been teaching better, even if all the teachers at Tui taught as well as its best teachers (in terms of student engagement and academic difficulty), the school still could not offer what the middle class schools did. In any case, this kind of comparison is quite unrealistic because across the Wellington schools what it meant to be a successful teacher varied by school mix.

At Tui College, the most successful teachers were those who took a highly structured role which could create controlled classroom environments where learning, even if at a relatively low academic level, could take place. In this sense they were 'trainers'. An emphasis on motivation/discipline and structured learning tasks seemed to be necessary. To take a more directly curriculum-orientated approach without putting sufficient emphasis on classroom control and organization led to classes that were at best un-focussed, at worst chaotic. In complete contrast, at Plimmer College the most successful teachers were those who took a low-key role by providing the necessary stimulus material or discussion starters that allowed students to learn independently. They were, as the AP said, 'facilitators'. Teachers at this school had flexible programmes that allowed student choice and en-couraged creativity through projects and assignments. Successful teachers at Victoria and Wakefield colleges came somewhere between the Tui/Plimmer extremes but somewhat closer to the Plimmer College model. At Victoria and Wakefield colleges successful teachers tended to be the traditional 'up front' 'talk and chalk' teachers rather than trainers or facilitators. With their relatively mixed clientele, structure and routine were more important and valued here than at Plimmer College but not as much as at Tui College. This allowed these teachers to give much more formal academic instruction as well as incorporating aspects of both the Tui and Plimmer approaches at times.

However, although 'good' teachers at any of the middle class schools could probably have fitted easily in to the other middle class schools, their style would have caused difficulties at Tui College where the disjunction between the academic curriculum and working class students was far greater. For instance, as several Tui College teachers stressed, it was simply not feasible to focus primarily on academic content at Tui when student pastoral needs were so pressing. Nor was it possible to expect classes with large numbers of students with low prior achievement to work concertedly towards academic exams. Teachers at Tui College needed to praise students for making personal progress despite the fact that their successes were seldom of the same order as students in the middle class schools. The priorities and strategies of successful

Tui College teachers were necessarily very different from their colleagues in the middle class schools.

However, an alternative interpretation of the findings of the Wellington study could be that teachers at the middle class schools had higher expectations of their students and so were more demanding. This was probably correct in a sense, but nevertheless it is unlikely that teachers at Tui could have easily maintained higher expectations, nor would this have necessarily helped. Instead the study highlights the likelihood that teacher expectations are themselves context bound, that they will be largely generated in response to the dominant characteristics of the student body. In this respect, teacher expectations will be not so much high or low, as appropriate or inappropriate. They will also be self-correcting in that where they are too far away from their students' expectations, resistance will modify them.

Research has been done which is not inconsistent with this view. For instance, Good and Brophy (1994) argue that, while well-publicized experimental studies have often pointed to teacher prejudices creating inappropriate expectations, studies conducted under more natural conditions suggest that, in general, teachers' expectations of their students' achievements are quite accurate, 'sometimes even more accurate than predictions based on test data' (p. 94). Nevertheless the emphasis of most research has been on how teacher expectations impact on students rather than on why teachers form the expectations they do. Moreover this literature invariably concludes that teachers are ultimately responsible for their levels of expectation. For instance, Good and Brophy conclude:

A particular danger is that low expectations combined with an attitude of futility will be communicated to certain students, leading to an erosion of their confidence and motivation for school learning . . . Therefore learn to control your attitudes and expectations, don't let them control you!

(Good and Brophy 1994: 114)

Nevertheless, further research is required to determine the extent to which teachers develop particular levels of expectation in response to the characteristics of the students they teach. This is not to suggest that teachers are always correct in their views of their students and what is appropriate classroom practice for them. However, they are probably a lot more realistic than many researchers and policy makers believe. McLaughlin and Talbot (1993) make a useful distinction between the objective realities faced by teachers and the subjective constructions developed by teachers. However, the strength of their analysis of teacher expectations is that it is couched within a 'bottom up', negotiated understanding of teacher practices which they contrast with the 'top down' view of most researchers:

[The] teacher perspective of students as context has not received a great deal of attention in the literature on teaching or educational research on schools and instruction. In process–product models of teaching and input–output models of school effects, students are conceived as the objects of educational treatments rather than contexts that shape teaching practice. This distinction between student as product and student as context of teaching matters enormously to our understanding of classrooms. Viewing the students as product directs attention to how students perform and away from what teachers do in response to the attitudes, behaviour, competencies, and circumstances that students bring with them to the classroom.

(McLaughlin and Talbot 1993: 221)

Approaches to school-wide problems also seem likely to represent a practical and philosophical/ideological response to the specific nature of problems presented by a school's particular mix. Pastoral care as it was practised in the Wellington schools provides a good example. Tui College had taken what might be regarded as a 'devolved semi-counselling approach' to pastoral matters. Staff were generally forced to recognize the school had large numbers of students with serious pastoral and learning needs and in this respect many took what Johnson *et al.* (1994) would probably call a 'socially critical' orientation to pastoral issues. That is, they realized students were not simply being 'naughty', rather that there was 'the impact of situational factors on student behaviour' (p. 272) making it necessary to be more flexible.

There was, in any case, little point in taking a straight punishment-based disciplinary approach at Tui College because such confrontation often would not work with students in the absence of middle class parental support. Instead, as the principal of Tui College put it, it was necessary to 'squeeze up' despite this being an 'exhausting process'. However, we saw that the scale of such problems meant pastoral management had to be devolved to avoid senior staff being swamped. This had the useful effect of delaying the suspension of students creating problems, yet it also meant that teachers had to be relatively tolerant of non-compliance from these students as the school tried various approaches to 'fix' their problems. Once those dealing with the offending had finally run out of patience and energy, many students were suspended, with much senior staff time taken up.

By comparison, Wakefield and Victoria colleges took more centralized disciplinary approaches to pastoral care, having fewer students with serious problems in or out of school. While these schools did have guidance counsellors, in most instances students here were viewed as misbehaving rather than having guidance problems. These schools took more 'traditional' orientations to school discipline which

call for strict adherence to class and school rules, a range of escalating punishments for rule breakers and a discipline regime in which the authority of teachers and school leaders is largely unquestioned.

(Johnson *et al.* 1994: 265)

With strong parental support, these schools were able to be relatively intolerant of student non-compliance. Both schools had strong hierarchical disciplinary systems which coped well with individuals or groups – 'problem' students quickly came to the attention of senior management and were suspended if they didn't conform. Because the numbers of such students were manageable, senior staff had the time and energy to intervene early. Classroom teachers did not have the discipline responsibilities of Tui College teachers.

Finally, Plimmer College had developed a mixed semi-counselling approach to pastoral care. Students here were counselled to take responsibility for their own behaviour in a way that was perhaps closest to Johnson's 'liberal progressive' orientation to school discipline. This highly individualized approach was possible because numbers were not great and staff had the time. This type of counselling was also what the liberal, well-educated parents of students expected. In theory, difficulties were expected to be dealt with first by staff, but in practice many teachers quickly sent misbehaving students to the deans, AP or guidance counsellor. Any serious difficulties appeared to be handled on an *ad hoc* basis, by teachers or senior staff. The principal gave the impression the school would like to 'wash its hands' completely of the few students who did misbehave in more serious ways. Needless to say, this would hardly have been possible at Tui College.

This example again points to decontextualized models of school characteristics being quite inadequate. The central lesson for teachers and school leaders must be that many so-called 'successful' school characteristics will probably only develop when there is a reasonable proportion of middle class students. Conversely, the true effectiveness of low-SES schools like Tui College can only be properly understood in the context of the cumulative and often overwhelming demands presented by their student bodies. The example of collecting exam fees suggests that any particular organizational or management goal could be attainable with sufficient effort. But the problem is that teachers in schools like Tui College have far too many balls to juggle to devote the required time and energy:

Tui House head: Form teachers have a lot to do and they get knocked back a lot, told off a lot. But they are being expected to, you know, check log books, check uniform, check absences, check seniors have paid their fees . . .

Senior staff at Tui College acknowledged this problem but felt powerless to do much about it because they were overwhelmed too. As the Tui DP who had recently had some contact with a middle class school summed up:

You can't do everything, you can't, you can't . . . Our management structures are probably not as good as they should be but that probably reflects the pressure we are all constantly under. You do not get time, the school does not allow you time, to sit back and reflect. I cannot believe the people I'm meeting at [a middle class college]. I cannot believe the, not laid back, but just open, friendly, unflurried way the staff relate to each other. It is extraordinary. And [that school] is working quite efficiently. But people don't have that kind of gaunt, drawn, lunatic look about them that you constantly see around here.

We should note however that all the discussion has so far assumed school resources remaining at much the same level as at present. An alternative way to think about what is achievable in a school like Tui College is to think in terms of what could be achieved given significant extra resources, such as staffing and funding. These would allow many of the extra difficulties noted at Tui College to be overcome. Nevertheless, the middle class schools still had inherent advantages including reference group processes and a richer environment of classroom questioning and discussion. Only by actually changing the mix of the school could these be replicated.

In any case, Tui College and schools like it are unlikely to get extra resources or be helped by measures to balance school intakes because both go entirely against the tenor of the current movement to reform schools through choice, devolution and accountability. In the next chapter I further examine the relationship of school mix to these kinds of policies.

9

Social class segregation and the politics of polarization and blame

When we begin to think about the relevance of school mix to current debate over markets in education, it is important to remember that markets are often unleashing longstanding class dynamics in education, rather than creating entirely new trends. Consequently, I begin this chapter by considering the enduring problem of social class segregation and the role of high-SES schools in providing positional advantage. This leads into a discussion of the politics of polarization where I explore both the likely implications of school mix for student achievement in schools which are increasingly differentiated by markets and the feasibility of self-management in low-SES schools. The following section is concerned with the politics of blame, particularly the way neo-liberals think about school failure in educational markets as well as the forms of managerial accountability used by governments to scrutinize schools. In particular I examine ERO's 'context independent' inspections in New Zealand, Ofsted and 'failing schools' legislation in the UK, and educational performance indicators in the UK and USA. Finally, I look at the evaluation of teachers as well as considering why the politics of blame might gain the support of a significant number of teachers and school leaders.

Are middle class schools better?

Schools in capitalist societies differ widely in their social class composition because of the effects of residential segregation, school selection, and the popular belief that socially elite schools are better. As Jencks *et al.* (1972) have observed, 'many people define a good school not as one with fancy facilities or highly paid teachers but as one with the "right" kinds of students', a view in which 'the quality of a school depends on its exclusiveness' (p. 29).

That this is a common view among parents is supported by studies which have investigated the process of school choice. These have tended to reveal that 'a significant influence in choosing a school is who else chooses it' (Hirsch 1997). Some studies have directly reported parents' concerns about sending their children to low-SES schools. Fowler (1993: 108) quotes middle class parents in New Zealand complaining about schools being in a 'low socioeconomic area' and having 'undesirable young people', 'racial groups' and a 'rough element'. In Scotland, Echols and Willms (1995) found that lower SES parents who deliberately chose to send their children away from their designated school were even more concerned with 'social and reputational' factors and 'disciplinary climate' than higher SES parents. In the US, Wells (1996) found that even African–American students who had returned to low-SES, all-black urban schools from white, middle class suburban schools thought the latter were better schools for reasons related to the higher status and cultural capital of their student bodies. Gewirtz *et al.* also argue with respect to a group of English parents they call 'privileged/skilled choosers':

> What is important is with whom your child goes to school. We are not arguing that this is the only factor in choice, but that it is a decisive constituent of choice-making. For some parents it is of crucial importance; it is less so for others, but it is rarely unimportant.
>
> (Gewirtz *et al.* 1995: 34)

Although these studies often illustrate that there is nothing simple about choice and school mix, it does seem that after proximity (also often related to SES because of residential segregation), intake composition is a key consideration of most parents, although this may often be indirectly expressed through references to school 'safety', 'standards', 'quality' and 'feeling'.[1] For the Smithfield Project study we asked over 500 parents which secondary school they had chosen for their child for the following year. We found that initially, irrespective of SES, most parents said that they would prefer their child to attend (named) high-SES schools. Yet in the same breath, many working class parents discounted the possibility that their child could attend these schools. Our research also showed that over time the aspirations of other low-SES families became progressively 'cooled out' as they came up against the difficulties of getting their children into the high-SES schools. Although 68 per cent of low-SES parents initially identified a high-SES school as their ideal choice, in practice only 18 per cent enrolled in these schools (Hughes *et al.* 1999). It would seem that when families – including working class families – send their children to low-SES schools this is less often because they don't regard high-SES schools as better schools but because they are unwilling or unable to send their children to those schools for a variety of class-related reasons (Reay and Ball 1997; Hughes *et al.* 1999).

A second indication of the greater popularity of high-SES schools is that they tend to be oversubscribed while low-SES schools struggle to maintain rolls. For instance, among the Smithfield schools the highest SES schools had long waiting lists whereas the schools with low-SES intakes had generally experienced a marked decline in enrolments after the removal of zoning through the loss of their more affluent students (Waslander and Thrupp 1995; Hughes *et al.* 1999). Although the decline of low-SES schools has sometimes been seen primarily as an issue of 'white flight' (Corbett 1994), our findings suggested that middle class Maori and Pacific Islands parents were also avoiding low-SES schools.

All of this indicates that many parents, regardless of class or ethnic group, believe that their children will be advantaged by attending high-SES schools, even if their children do not attend such schools themselves. (Having said this, it also seems that once choices have been made, necessity often becomes a virtue.) Central to our understanding of this is the critical importance of high-SES education as a means of both social closure and social mobility. By keeping out the children of the working class and ethnic minorities, high-SES schools serve parents seeking relative advantage (Ball 1997a). Put another way, high-SES schooling needs to be seen as a *positional good*. Marginson (1997: 38) defines positional goods in education as 'places in education which provide students with relative advantage in the competition for jobs, income, social standing and prestige'. They are hierarchical, scarce in absolute terms and have a zero-sum character:

> With a fixed number of positional goods at each level of advantage one person gains position only at another's expense. 'Positional competition in the language of game theory, is a zero sum game: what winners win, losers lose.'
>
> (Marginson 1997: 40 citing Hirsch 1976: 52)

The fact that high-SES schools may offer positional advantage helps to explain why these schools are always more popular than low-SES schools which have little positional value.

Marginson also notes that whether or not schools with high positional value offer real advantages in terms of achievement is unknown:

> Whether positional goods actually add value to the prior social advantages of students is a complex question. Research has failed to conclusively separate schools' effects on student achievement from the effects of home background.
>
> (Marginson 1997: 39)

Other accounts reflect this uncertainty. Taylor *et al.* (1997: 92) refer only to attendance at private schools 'being assumed' to provide positional advantage. Similarly Whitty *et al.* (1998: 119) regard high-SES schools as only 'seeming to offer the best chance of academic success'. Marginson (1997: 39) suggests this issue may be a moot point anyway since positional goods in education probably ultimately depend as much on perception as on reality: 'What matters is that positional goods, such as places in elite schools are *generally recognised* to constitute relative advantage' (his emphasis).

Nevertheless a school mix effect is important here because it suggests that there may be some real benefits to be gained from attending high-SES schools other than those which eventually come with the 'old school tie'. By noting the advantages that accrued to the matched students at the middle class schools over those at Tui College, it appears that parents *can* enhance their children's academic achievement through attendance at higher SES schools. Other things being equal, most students probably will achieve better in a middle class school than a working class school. It therefore seems that the class intuition of parents seeking positional advantage may have more substance than many have thought. The findings also help to explain the appeal of elite private schools (Edwards and Whitty 1997). These benefit not only from having students with very high-SES backgrounds but also gain contextual advantages from bringing them together.

Yet although the SES segregation of schools is likely to advantage some families considerably over others, it only rarely becomes a matter of public debate. The reasons for this appear to vary somewhat from nation to nation. New Zealanders have long drawn on a bucolic ideology of egalitarianism to ignore the considerable social class differences between their (mostly state) schools, at least in public. The prevailing official view has been that, by virtue of its youth, scattered geographical settlement and outlook, New Zealand is a fairly egalitarian society with fairly similar schools. Nonetheless, even a cursory examination of the history of school enrolments in New Zealand suggests this has been a myth (McCullouch 1991).[2] Unsurprisingly this view has begun to break down under recent market reforms. These have unleashed 'rich seams of competitiveness and envy' (Hirsch 1997: 159), to the extent that there is now something of a 'middle class education panic' over the increasingly apparent social class disparities between New Zealand schools (Brett 1998).

In contrast, social class disparities between schools in the UK have been not so much ignored as accepted as part of the natural order (Hirsch 1997). For instance, although the comprehensive school movement did partly represent an attempt to reduce class segregation, it was motivated as much by the desire of many post-war middle class British parents to obtain a grammar school-type education for their children (Walford and Pring 1997). Power (1997: 447) suggests the comprehensive movement may be seen as 'a minor blip in the longstanding preservation of differentiation and hierarchy'. There has also been continuing social polarization of schools within the comprehensive sector (Benn 1997). Comprehensivization also left entirely untouched the highly privileged role of the substantial British public (private) school sector. Benn comments:

In the UK there was . . . merely a process of introducing more and more schools named comprehensive into a system that continued to accept selection and still does, and which continued to accept that it is natural for the wealthy and influential to be educated entirely apart from every-one else, as it still does. We have tried in the past to examine that balance between what some call freedom of choice and others call provision of privilege that detracts from majority rights . . . we act nationally as if the issue has been settled. Yet we know it is not.

(Benn 1997: 126)

Disparities of wealth and power are also an everyday fact of life in the USA. As Aronowitz (1997: 190) points out, they are considered acceptable in a society which is often seen as 'the great exception to the rule that social class is destiny' and where the dominant paradigm is one of 'virtually unlimited possibility'. The existence of elite private schools is also rarely questioned in a society dominated by private institutions oriented to the market. In the USA social class segregation has also been overshadowed by the more politically pressing concerns about racial segregation raised by *Brown v. Board of Education* which led to desegregation orders and bussing during the 1960s and 1970s. More recently, as the idea of separate schools for different ethnic groups has gained favour, the same emphasis on ethnicity over class has allowed between-school SES inequality to be overlooked (Orfield *et al.* 1996). This is a problem I return to in Chapter 11.

Overall, whatever the national ideologies that allow SES segregation, the likelihood of school mix having a significant impact on achievement points to it being highly inequitable. More immediately, school mix helps us to understand the social limits of educational markets.

Student achievement in schools with increasingly polarized intakes

Although SES segregation between schools has been longstanding, recent 'choice' policies such as 'open enrolment' have been widely predicted to intensify it.[3] As already noted, in the 'lived market' working class families are often not able or willing to exercise choice in the ways theorized by neoliberals. This is because of financial or practical reasons, class-based beliefs, or lack of knowledge and power to access higher SES schools. Consequently, working class students are most likely to be left behind in 'sink' schools with increasingly poor intakes as higher SES families choose more popular schools for positional advantage. At the same time there is little evidence of the preexisting social hierarchy of schools reducing through the promised *diversity* of types of school provision (Glatter *et al.* 1997), an argument which in any case ignores the positional value of traditional, high-SES education.

This is the general argument, but the detail and context of choice policies will also influence the extent to which they will have polarizing effects (Elmore and Fuller 1996). It is also hard to gather firm evidence of the extent of SES changes following market reforms because of the confounding effects of residential segregation and selection prior to the introduction of market reforms. Nevertheless, polarization resulting from the reforms does often appear to have become a reality. Whitty *et al.* conclude:

[T]here is a growing body of empirical evidence that . . . the emphasis on parental choice and school autonomy is . . . increasing the differences between popular and less popular schools on a linear scale . . .

(Whitty *et al.* 1998: 42)

Certainly the Smithfield study of enrolment patterns before and after dezoning found that 'socioeconomic segregation between schools has been exacerbated more than would be predicted simply on the basis of residential segregation' (Waslander and Thrupp 1995: 22). Generalized socioeconomic shifts across the market were small but there were noticeable effects on individual 'sink' schools. For example, 'Kauri College' dropped from a very low 5.3 on the Elley–Irving scale to an even lower 5.7 after the removal of zoning. This appears to be a continuing process. A later phase of the study points to a domino effect, with students moving from the lowest SES schools to higher SES schools, followed by the highest SES students in these schools then moving on to even higher SES schools and so on (Hughes *et al.* 1996, 1999).

Discussions which take the next step of linking this polarization of intakes to the polarization of school processes and achievement outcomes have been understandably more tentative. Nevertheless, Walford (1997: 63) argues that 'Much of the present [British] government's educational policy . . . will lead to a system of unequally funded schools which will provide very different educational experiences for children of different abilities, social classes and ethnic groups.' Whitty *et al.* (1998: 119) also suggest that while market reforms in Britain 'may be enhancing the educational performance of some children, and certainly that of those schools in which the more advantaged children are concentrated, they seem to be further disadvantaging many of those very groups who were disadvantaged by the previous system'. Gewirtz *et al.* argue:

Across schools we appear to be seeing an intensification of status hierarchies, provisional differentiation and segregation within the state system. Working class children and particularly children with SEN [special educational needs], are likely to be increasingly 'ghettoized' in underresourced and understaffed low status schools. The effects of school 'context' on pupil achievement, together with the underresourcing and understaffing of such schools, are likely to significantly impair the learning achievements of the children attending them . . . ethnic-minority children . . . are likely also to be disproportionately represented in the underresourced and understaffed schools.

(Gewirtz *et al.* 1995: 188)

In the USA Elmore and Fuller also suggest that

it seems plausible to expect that, other things being equal, increasing parental choice will accelerate both the social stratification of schools and the gap in student performance between schools enrolling high concentrations of poor and working class students versus those with predominantly working class students.

(Elmore and Fuller 1996: 191)

The Wellington study is again relevant here because it supports the view that the polarization of school intakes will heighten disparities in achievement outcomes. In today's 'sink' schools, and perhaps in others if polarization continues over time, academic achievement is likely to deteriorate as a result of a low-SES school mix. Conversely, mean levels of attainment in schools which are able to attract higher SES students will probably rise. This implies that market policies will create more disparate educational outcomes and, ultimately, life chances. The Wellington study also provides some explanation of why this might be the case.

Other aspects of the polarization of school intakes are also relevant here. One is the use of overt and covert means of selection and suspension (exclusion) by oversubscribed schools as a way of reinforcing and improving their market dominance (Ball 1993a). Schools which are able to shut out working class students in one way or another will indeed accrue advantages. Not only will teaching be easier, but the mean achievement level of students will probably rise, further boosting the position of such schools in the academic league table and their subsequent reputations. However, unpopular schools which are forced to take the (usually working class) students will experience greater problems. This was probably also the case at Tui College. One teacher there argued that the school was letting in 'too many difficult kids'. Another complained that more popular schools gave away their 'bruised kiwifruit' but kept the 'export grade'.

The Wellington study also suggests that many working class students who have been 'plucked from the ashes' to attend private schools through voucher schemes such as the UK's now abandoned Assisted Places Scheme or New Zealand's continuing version, the Targeted Individual Entitlement scheme, may well be advantaged in terms of their achievement if it means they are attending higher SES schools. This has to be weighed against the token nature of these schemes – taking in too many working class students would remove the advantaged processes of the high-SES host schools which provide their initial attraction. Nor should we ignore the evidence that most of those who gain entry to these schemes do not appear to be from especially low-SES backgrounds anyway (Edwards *et al.* 1989).

The feasibility of self-management and school improvement

From a critical perspective, self-management is often seen to be about the state retaining power over education while discharging responsibility for funding and providing it (Smyth 1993; Whitty *et al.* 1998). A number of studies have also indicated that self-management is more difficult to achieve in working class schools due to disparities in material and staffing resources, as well as in the professional contacts and management skills of those on governing bodies (Gordon 1994; Wylie 1997; Whitty *et al.* 1998) and class-based differences in parental involvement in schools (Lareau 1989; Hannaway 1995; Lareau and Shumar 1996). The Wellington study supports these findings but also points to the intense pressures on teachers and school leaders generated by students in low-SES schools. These should not be underestimated:

Tui principal: The proportions of time I spend on things vary because you can be sailing along and suddenly get hit by a crisis that can absorb days of work for the senior admin. The AP and DP pick up most of that but there are times when I realize that the people pressure, the kid pressure, needs to be spread a bit so I pick up the basic pupil stuff.

Tui AP: I just put out fires basically, try and put out little fires before they spring up as bushfires.

Tui DP: You take the standard issue of the knock on the door, 'Mr —, I've just discovered so and so smoking dope in the toilet' . . . you are interviewing all day. Basically if there is a knock on my door at 9.30am and that sort of thing has happened, that's the day gone.

While self-management appears to create more work for all teachers and school leaders, these intake-related pressures mean that time and energy required to implement demands from central agencies will be especially scarce in low-SES schools. For instance, the middle class schools in Wellington were able to give much more attention to recent curriculum and assessment reforms. At Victoria College the demands of accreditation for the New Zealand Qualifications Authority (NZQA)[4] were being met in a systematic fashion with considerable consultation and use of outside 'experts'. On the other hand, Tui College's principal wrote the accreditation document during a week of his summer break. Although the school was ostensibly keeping up, this was only achieved by taking shortcuts – by observing only the letter of what was required rather than the spirit. It is dubious whether this approach would have translated into much real change:

Tui teacher: What you have is that if anyone came in from outside the school and looked at our policies, it looks really good. But when you look at staff and what's happening in classrooms and what's not happening in classrooms, no one wants to get in there and start scratching around too much because they are going to find there is lots of stuff happening that's just crap. And lots of stuff happening that is really good too. But it's all unstructured, its not tight at all.

School improvement may also be much harder to carry out for those who struggle to see the wood for the trees. Yet, as noted earlier, a 'hands on' approach by principals may be less a matter of choice than necessity in working class schools:

Tui principal: I'd like to think you don't need to be [as directly involved], that I could go somewhere else and be a different sort of principal because a lot of the 'hands on' drive would not be necessary. It would come from the community and from the teachers who would have that much more time to have more wide-ranging thoughts and projects themselves. I think it is hell of a hard here to get your mind on the broad canvas when you are locked into the day-to-day.

These pressures are overlooked in nearly all contemporary discussions of school devolution or self-management. The difficulties are ignored by neo-liberals who simply blame principals of low-SES schools if they don't gain sufficient market share (see the next section). Some brands of managerialism, for example those espoused by ERO and Ofsted discussed shortly, also hold school staff heavily responsible for school failure. Even 'warmer' versions of managerialist discourse tend to be quite unrealistic about the ability of principals and teachers to bring about improved achievement in low-SES settings. For instance, the New Zealand Ministry of Education would no doubt claim that it has taken steps to identify low-SES schools and has made extra funding or staffing available to them. To a degree this is true, but the assistance made available is not only limited, it is usually made available only on a contested or short-term basis or as a one-off, 'kick start' grant and also often involves heavy reporting requirements. One problem with such approaches is the sheer amount of time, energy and knowledge required to access the extra resources (Hawk and Hill 1996). Another problem is that while this type of assistance often assumes that there will not be any continuing funding need, this is seldom the case. Problems don't just go away, at least not without a change of student intake.

Poor performers or just plain poor?

The preceding choice and self-management problems come together in the politics of blame employed by neo-liberals for whom the popularity of schools is directly linked to their performance. Principals of unpopular schools are held accountable for the spiral of decline because they have not improved their schools sufficiently to boost their schools' reputations and hence student intakes. The eventual failure of some schools can therefore be seen simply as the price to be paid for a quality education system. Chubb and Moe are frank about this 'natural selection' agenda:

> Schools that fail to satisfy a sufficiently large clientele will go out of business . . . Of the schools that survive, those that do a better job of satisfying consumers will be more likely to prosper and proliferate.
>
> (Chubb and Moe 1990: 33)

In New Zealand, the argument has also been put clearly by Douglas:

> With choice, performance would matter. Good schools would prosper and expand: badly performing schools would shrink and die if they didn't change. Poor educational practices would be weeded out and good practices exposed.
>
> (Douglas 1993: 94)

However, a serious problem with the neo-liberal account is that, as already pointed out, schools in decline in the marketplace are invariably those with low-SES intakes. If, given a choice, most parents prefer middle class schools over low-SES schools for reasons related to positional advantage, this is hardly a problem for which the principals of the latter can be held to account. The positional nature of educational markets means that school success and failure is much more complex than neo-liberals assume. Marginson points out that only at the lower end of the market does competition really work (because higher SES schools are typically insulated by their positional advantage). However, it is also here that schools cannot compete:

> It is only in the bottom segment of the market, where positional values are relatively low, that competition operates in the orthodox manner. The market is contestable (albeit at the expense of stability) and institutions striving to fill their places do compete on the basis of efficiency and consumer focus. But they are constantly being undermined by the flight of higher achieving students to more prestigious establishments; and real improvements in learning tend to be underrecognised because, in positional terms, these institutions have a low status that is regardless of their educational efforts.
>
> (Marginson 1997: 45)

The findings of the Wellington study illustrate how much greater the demands on staff are at low-SES schools like Tui College than at middle class schools. This means that, even when low-SES schools are able to gain some kind of market share, they will be unable to deliver similar academic programmes. Overall it seems likely that most low-SES schools are not so much ineffective as *overwhelmed*. To cope with their difficulties quite different policy responses are needed from those suggested by neo-liberals.

A further problem with the neo-liberal account is that schools in a spiral of decline do not necessarily close. Astin (1992) points out that because popular schools have no incentive to expand and all students have to go to school somewhere, schools in decline rarely go out of business regardless of the quality of the education students are receiving. Student demographics are also an important consideration. In the mid-1990s there was discussion of closing some New Zealand secondary schools with declining rolls (Clifton 1995). However, substantial increases in the school-age population now make this improbable in most areas. A more likely consequence of market reform for the foreseeable future is the continuing existence of a heavily polarized system of provision.

ERO and 'context independent' school inspection

Managerialist notions of accountability in education also reflect the politics of blame because of the way school evaluation agencies attempt to construct school failure as the clear responsibility of schools themselves. They often demonstrate an uncompromising stance on school performance in which the quality of student achievement is seen as the result of school policies and practices and any reference to broader socio-political factors is ruled out as an excuse for poor performance. Indeed, it is the capacity of these agencies to hold that schools are failing and that school staff are responsible for the decline which provides their ideological power as agents of accountability. Acknowledgement that the social and political context may create problems for schools would clearly 'muddy the waters' in a way which would make the work of these agencies much more difficult and lead to greater resource demands on the state. At the same time, many educators are not convinced that school staff should be held fully responsible for school failure. As a result the blaming approaches taken by school evaluation agencies have often been contested.

New Zealand's ERO provides a particularly clear example of the politics of blame and its contestation. Consistent with the managerialist doctrine of external accountability to prevent 'provider capture' and improve effectiveness, ERO's emphasis is on 'external' rather than 'friendly' inspection. Its Chief Review Officer, Judith Aitken, has publicly identified with the neo-liberal critics of education and has talked frankly of the place of ERO within a neo-liberal economy (Aitken 1994). Most significantly in terms of its ideological role of 'turning up the heat' of market reform, ERO has vigorously pursued 'failing' schools and 'incompetent' teachers. There has been a degree of support for this approach from some teachers and school leaders but there have also been numerous complaints that ERO is misguided and unfair in its school evaluations. Teacher unions have threatened to boycott reviews (inspections) altogether.

Since 1993 ERO has carried out 'assurance audits' and 'effectiveness reviews' to check compliance with regulations and to indicate teacher and school performance.[5] However, these take little account of the social or political context of schools (Robertson *et al.* 1997). For 'effectiveness reviews' ERO asks schools to prepare an 'achievement statement' which identifies what they count as achievement for their students and purports to take this statement into account when assessing school performance. This approach could be seen as a weak form of contextualizing assessments, yet ERO's claims to be able to compare the relative quality of New Zealand schools are obviously questionable without a stronger indicator of their social context. There is a measure freely available – the Ministry of Education has developed a reasonably sophisticated system of SES deciles based on census data which it uses for informing policy and distributing funding. To date, however, ERO has shown little interest in using these decile ratings for value-added purposes.

The likely impact of social and political contexts on school performance is also mostly absent from national ERO documents and in public statements by the Chief Review Officer. Two ERO publications which do explicitly address socio-political issues are those concerned with 'barriers to learning' (ERO 1995; ERO 1996a). Although frequently couched in a deficit discourse, these reports acknowledge obstacles 'beyond the control of schools . . . created by their interface with the broader social context' (1996a: 6).

> Some barriers to learning [include] the home environment of the student in terms of parental stress, family instability and unemployment . . . Teachers cannot ignore the plight of students who are sick, abused, using alcohol or drugs or those who are the victims of parental neglect.
>
> (Education Review Office 1996a: 9)

Schools are unable to escape this social reality or the considerable resource and time demands it entails, yet ERO's view is that this kind of work is not part of the 'core business' of schools and they must not let it preoccupy them:

> These factors do not however absolve teachers of their responsibility to deliver high quality programmes . . . barriers to student learning remain unidentified and unaddressed if teachers see deficits in the social and economic circumstances of their students as an excuse or a reason for low levels of achievement . . .
>
> (*ibid.*: 10)

> By identifying a student's home circumstances as a barrier to learning, the school belittles its professional ability and responsibility to effect change.
>
> (1995: 7)

If ERO's procedures and statements at the national level can be seen to emphasize the responsibility of schools for their own success or failure, its ideological work has been even more intensely played out at the local level where refuting the contextual claim has become an important activity. Reviewers are required by ERO to sell the message to staff in 'failing' low-SES schools that much higher quality practices are possible irrespective of context. This claim has met with considerable scepticism from those who struggle daily with the manifestations of poverty and prejudice. ERO's response has been to enlist political support for its judgement that schools are failing rather than overwhelmed.

The debate surrounding an ERO report, *Improving Schooling in Mangere and Otara* (ERO 1996b), provides a good example. Mangere and Otara are two of New Zealand's most entrenched areas of urban socioeconomic disadvantage and white/middle class flight (Department of Statistics 1992; Corbett 1994). Ramsay *et al.* (1981) found that, while some schools in these South Auckland suburbs did appear more effective than others, they nevertheless had low levels of student attainment and serious problems related to student turnover, truancy, pastoral needs, and teacher recruitment and morale when compared to schools in less disadvantaged areas. As elsewhere in New Zealand (Gordon 1997; Hughes *et al.* 1999), the policies of choice have led to intensified socioeconomic flight from many schools into others with generally higher SES intakes and better reputations either within or beyond Mangere and Otara.

Yet consistent with the technicist approach to inspection noted above, ERO's reports on Mangere and Otara schools have never discussed these problems. During the mid-1990s ERO reports became increasingly disparaging of local schools in a way which eventually generated considerable media headlines (*New Zealand Herald* 1996a). In response, some schools banded together to run newspaper advertisements to counter what they claimed was ERO's 'misinformation' (*New Zealand Herald* 1996b). In addition, a lobby group made up mostly of local principals, the At-Risk Committee, argued that problems in the area were mostly those of social inequality. Difficulties caused by the indifferent performance of some local teachers and principals were seen by this group as the exception rather than the rule. Consequently it did not accept ERO's assertion that the problems of schools in the area could be mostly addressed by improving management and staff performance. Instead it argued:

> [Our Committee believes that] ERO's work must be documented within a social context and that data on deciles and additional funding are pieces of baseline information . . . for the first page of [ERO] reports.
>
> (Dunphy 1996: 4)

ERO's announcement in 1996 that it was planning a 'wide-ranging review' of educational problems in the area reflected a continuing standoff between many local educators and ERO. An ERO-appointed inquiry group eventually produced a report which largely confirmed ERO's own interpretation of the situation. Yet the report (ERO 1996b) is flawed in several ways. To begin with, it contains little analysis of 'the problem'. The introduction moves directly to argue that the issue in Mangere and Otara schools is primarily one of poor performance. It provides the remarkable statistic that '42 per cent [of Mangere and Otara schools] are performing very poorly or are underperforming' (p. 3). This bald figure is apparently derived from an analysis of whether schools have had good or bad reviews and whether a follow-up review has been deemed necessary. However, nowhere is there any discussion of review methodology to support or qualify the claim. Instead the report simply states: 'Through external evaluation of all schools over the past seven years, ERO has gained an overview of relative school performance nationally' (p. 3). Yet this surely amounts to little more than a self-referential assertion that 'we have looked at lots of schools so we know what we are doing'.

The report also tries to argue that the problem is one of poor performance by dismissing the contextual claim. For instance, the work of Ramsay *et al.* (1981) is cited as showing longstanding 'educational disadvantage' in Mangere and Otara (p. 3). But this is only half the story – Ramsay's discussion linked many educational problems in the area to socioeconomic factors. The introduction also claims that compensatory funding and advisory support given to schools in the area over recent decades to address 'ineffective schooling' (not the effects of poverty?) did not succeed, yet there is no attempt to demonstrate or explain this.

The report also attempts deliberately to dismiss SES as a cause of 'the problem':

It is commonly asserted that there is a strong link between school failure and the degree of disadvantage in a socioeconomic setting. There are, however, some 20 per cent of the schools in these two districts that provide an effective education for their students. Their boards, principals and teachers have, with varying degrees of success, met the challenges of their students' backgrounds and concentrated on teaching and learning to the benefit of their students.

(Education Review Office 1996b: 4)

Yet the claim that there are some low-SES schools in the area which show others up is also dubious. We (again) cannot be sure that these 20 per cent of schools really are more effective than the other 80 per cent because of ERO's weak methodology. Moreover, while some Mangere and Otara schools might perform a little better than others, it is most unlikely that they will be performing *much* better. As we saw in Chapter 2, the notion that there are exemplary schools in low-SES areas which perform considerably better than others was very popular in the first generation of American effective schools research. Yet it was not long before researchers were pointing out that the performance of students in exemplary ghetto schools was still a far cry from that of students in schools in middle class suburbs (Purkey and Smith 1983).

The Ministry of Education was asked to respond to ERO's Mangere and Otara report. Fortunately their response reflected a 'warmer' version of managerialism. It noted the presence of 'contextual factors' which it defined as

the communities within which the schools operate, including factors such as poor health, household crowding, single parent families, low income and high benefit dependency, high unemployment, low educational qualifications and high crime rates.

(Ministry of Education 1997a: 1)

This response has formed the basis of a school improvement initiative for the area which looks set to provide some additional resources to Mangere and Otara schools rather than simply punishing them for not measuring up (Hotere 1998).

The ERO appraisal of Mangere and Otara schools therefore represents one in which the failure to take account of the social and political context of low-SES schools has led to schools being *harshly* judged. Another scenario to consider is that where school reviewers are not encouraged to consider the relationship between school processes and school mix, the problems of low-SES schools may also be *glossed over*. Hawk and Hill (1996) point to this defect of some ERO reviews and it also seemed to occur at Tui College. This school had an assurance audit and an effectiveness review close to the time the Wellington study was undertaken and in both cases ERO gave glowing reports. Yet comparison of the reports with my observations suggested that ERO picked up few of the important features of Tui College, particularly the intractable difficulties posed by the nature of the student intake and the sense of powerlessness staff felt in dealing with these. Indeed the ERO reports seem to be about a different school from the one I was studying. For instance, the ERO reviewers judged that:

- the school had a strong sense of direction and commitment at all levels from the teaching staff to the management and board;
- school goals were well set, implemented and assessed;
- all was well with the management and resourcing of curriculum with individual students well supported;
- there was strong pastoral support for students via the devolved pastoral care system, a clear school response to student misbehaviour and well-managed detentions and suspensions;
- systems were in place to support 'able' students;
- quality teaching and learning were evident;
- teachers were effective at establishing and reinforcing classroom routines;
- the school offered many extracurricular activities;
- since policy is evolving, school practice was close to policy.

However, the Wellington study does not support these findings.[6] They paint a picture which, although supportive in one sense, is also quite erroneous. So why did ERO end up with such a rose-tinted view of what was happening at Tui College? Recent interviews we carried out for research on ERO suggested the principal and staff saw it as a fair game to focus on the school's best side because the ERO process was unfair anyway:

Tui principal: It's how you help. Does ERO have any role in actually helping schools who do have their backs to the wall through external factors or whatever without kicking them when they are down? That's the challenge . . . You see . . . ERO was also supposed to signal clearly to the Minister issues that were of concern to schools that are preventing schools from operating. Now that side has just got totally lost. But you see, what they try to do is wrap it into the report on the school as if it is the school's fault. But you really need to write the report back to schools on their internal effectiveness in these current conditions and then you need to write another report . . . so that part of their job should be to record barriers to learning from outside forces. But what tends to happen is a single report and you shoot the messenger. That's what happens in [Mangere and Otara] and places.

Robertson *et al.* 1997: 100)

The predictability and superficiality of the ERO review process which focusses primarily on school policy rather than practice made it easy for Tui College to do well in their inspections:

MPT: (talking about the documentation sent to ERO): So it was all pretty well laid out for them?
Principal: It was absolutely laid out.
Teacher: And then when they were here, they were just sort of pointed

around, I guess, I mean not only was the documentation there . . . they were shown to where the evidence would be of what was on the paper.
Principal: Basically you have got to come up with information for them which is good enough for them to accept at face value.

(Robertson *et al.* 1997: 101)

While pleased to get a favourable review, those interviewed were doubtful that it represented a good picture of the school:

MPT: So how happy were you that it [the review] was an accurate picture of the school?
Teacher: Well we were very satisfied with the report itself but I don't know that the framework within which they operate would give any more of a detailed or specific picture really . . . The reports themselves are very – well, they are very generic sort of overview type statements really, rather than specifics. They are just a cameo I guess.

(Robertson *et al.* 1997: 102)

What seems likely is that in the absence of any procedural channels to properly recognize and compensate for a school's social context, ERO reviewers often do so informally when they write their reports. After all, they can hardly help but notice contextual differences between working class and middle class schools. Yet because review procedures do not permit reviewers to acknowledge or explore this issue properly, they are essentially forced to guess at how critical to be of particular schools. In the case of Mangere and Otara they were 'too tough'. At Tui College, the attempt to be context independent has covered up deep-seated issues related to school mix and rendered many problems invisible. Although this may be preferable to unfairly blaming schools, it does little or nothing to help them address their deep-seated difficulties.

Ofsted, E&I research and failing schools legislation

The Ofsted in England adopts a similar politics of blame strategy. Its Chief Inspector, Chris Woodhead, was described by the *Times Educational Supplement* in 1996 as the nearest thing English education has to a 'pantomime villain' (9 February 1996: 18). However, an important difference is that while most New Zealand academics have been critical of ERO's politics and methods – even likening ERO's approach to that of the medieval inquisition (O'Neill 1996) – there has been a more favourable relationship between Ofsted and British academics who endorse E&I research. This can be seen in the relatively uncritical nature of most British research literature on Ofsted, for instance the edited collections of Brighouse and Moon (1995), Gray and Wilcox (1995a) and Ouston *et al.* (1996). Most authors in these collections have been content either to describe Ofsted's approach or to point to specific problems in its methodologies rather than subject it to more searching criticisms (Thrupp 1998). No doubt related to this, while it has been rare for ERO to refer to academic research, Ofsted has often used E&I arguments to justify criticisms of schools. For instance, Tomlinson notes that the Ofsted's deputy director has used value-added arguments to blame schools for poor performance:

> The mix of socioeconomic background of pupils in LEA-maintained [Local Education Authority] schools is not widely different across all schools, poor schools cannot parade this as an excuse for low standards.
>
> (Cited in Tomlinson 1997: 14)

Neverthless this relationship has been double-edged for both parties. On the one hand, since E&I research does provide some legitimacy for the politics of blame, Ofsted appears to have done much more to enable value-added SER researchers to take its inspection methods seriously compared with ERO – which has had a quite naked agenda of ruling out the contextual claim. For instance, a Pre Inspection Context and School Indicator (PICSI) has been used by Ofsted to build up a background picture against which to contextualize judgements about a school's performance. The Ofsted inspection handbook suggested that this contained

> key performance data about the school from earlier years to enable trends to be identified; information about the social and economic character-istics of the area in which the school is situated; and comparative data to help inspectors to set the school data in a national context.
>
> (Ofsted 1995: 20)

On the other hand Ofsted has back-tracked in places to avoid the contextual claim which is also at least partly supported by value-added research. For instance, Ofsted did explore a more systematic approach to assessing value-added by commissioning a pilot study from school effectiveness researchers at the London Institute of Education (Sammons *et al.* 1994). All seemed to be going well when the *Times Educational Supplement* (1996) carried the front page headline 'Inspectors to Take Account of Deprivation'. The story announced that following the pilot study 'inspectors would be instructed to take into account the social background of pupils and compare like with like in the interests of reaching fairer judgements'. The PICSI would now include factors such as 'the number of children eligible for free meals, those with special educational needs and the educational level of the local population'. The editorial of the same issue asked 'Has Chris Woodhead been caught secretly acting on the side of the angels?'

However, in a letter to the *Times Educational Supplement* the following week, Chris Woodhead refuted the story, stating that no final decision had yet been taken (Woodhead 1996). The reasons given for not proceeding with a contextualized approach were that the methodology might not be accurate enough and that 'it is essential that Ofsted does nothing to encourage the use of pupils' backgrounds as an excuse for poor performance' (p. 23). This rather public backing out of the use of more rigorous assessments was obviously a matter of concern to some E&I researchers (see Gray in the next chapter), but is entirely predictable. As the OECD comments, the British government has always been unwilling to 'discount for social class' in league tables and was unlikely to accept Ofsted's assessments being 'watered down':

> Value added measures that relate schools' results to 'what might be expected' of their pupils raises the delicate issue of whether less should be expected of deprived children than of privileged ones. The present administration has always argued that low expectations are likely to become self-fulfilling and there is no excuse for low standards.
>
> (OECD 1995: 59)

A second important difference between ERO and Ofsted is that the latter forms just part of the policy package which reflects the politics of blame in England. In particular, after a school is designated as 'failing' by Ofsted, 'special measures' introduced in the Education Act of 1993 can be invoked by the LEA or by an Education Association (an appointed group of commissioners).[7] According to Stark, a policy maker involved with the special measures legislation, the intention of the special measures policy is that within two years a 'failing' school should have either been 'restored to health; making substantial progress towards leaving special measures; or in some cases, heading for closure' (1998: 35). Although 12 schools had already been closed through special measures by the end of 1996, Stark (*ibid.*: 43) concludes that 'most schools have not been destroyed by special measures: in most cases they have been revived by them . . . recovery, or in some cases substantial progress towards it, within two years or so seems to be the general rule'.

This optimistic view of 'special measures' presents several problems. First, it paints a rather too benign picture of the intent of the policies. Tomlinson argues that the failing schools legislation was primarily a means used by the Tory government to undermine Labour-dominated LEAs and to push along the privatization of education by countering the reluctance of schools to 'opt out'. It was also intended to put pressure on 'poor' schools to close:

> The failing schools legislation of 1993 was designed to kill several birds with one stone. Since schools with low levels of achievement were largely located in Labour controlled, disadvantaged, innercity areas, legislation could be designed to remove schools from the LEA, further weakening their influence. It could also boost the grant-maintained figures without any parental ballot. The Education Association, as pp. 50–52 of the White Paper (DFE 1992) explained, was the chosen instrument to effect all this.
>
> (Tomlinson 1997: 8–9)

Second, Tomlinson also indicates that it is schools initially misdiagnosed as 'failing' by Ofsted, in a similar way to ERO, which are then being shut down by 'special measures' which do not begin to address the real social and political roots of school failure. Her analysis of Hackney Downs, a school shut down by the first Education Association appointed under the failing school legislation, indicates that this school was initially overwhelmed (Tomlinson 1997, 1998). 'Special measures' then intensified rather than relieved the plight of the school:

> (Hackney Downs) school, whose decline can only be understood within a macro-context of historical, social, economic and political factors, and the interplay of vested interests, was villified at the micro-level and closed on the advice of an Educational Association in 1995. The acting head and teachers who had the misfortune to be in post in 1995 were blamed for circumstances and situations absolutely and completely beyond their control.
>
> (Tomlinson 1997: 16)

Third, it is hard to see the failing school policies succeeding to the degree that Stark suggests.[8] The negative effects of 'naming and shaming' on school reputation and staff morale and recruitment need to be considered and claims about raised teacher expectations and improvements in teaching must be questioned. For instance Stark (1998: 38) suggests: 'The evidence available to Ofsted and the DfEE suggests that expectations are rising particularly rapidly in schools under special measures.' However, the impact of school mix suggests that although cheerful whistling may be evident in 'special measures' schools, in reality, levels of expectation are unlikely to have changed much. In a similar way, if classroom processes are linked to school mix it is hard to see how the quality of what is offered in classrooms will have 'rapidly and substantially improved' as Stark claims. Where 'special measures' *have* turned schools around, intake changes and the injection of additional resources are likely to be the cause. However, Slee notes:

> systematic population cleansing such as was the case with the Ridings School and large injections of funding previously not delivered to the school is not dwelt upon by those chronicling the new histories of schools which are 'turned around'.
>
> (Slee 1998: 107)

What is clear in any case is that the actual closure of schools raises the stakes of the politics of blame in the UK, despite an inspection system which appears to make some efforts to contextualize its findings. Nor do things seem to be getting any better. While, as Gibson and Asthana (1998) point out, the White Paper *Excellence in Schools* (DfEE 1997) published by the incoming Labour government contains a rhetoric of concern about contextual issues, the Labour government nevertheless immediately named and shamed 18 'failing' schools. A year later, in May 1998, it was announced that a new Bill, the *School Standards and Framework Bill*, would be introduced to give Ministers the power to directly close schools which are not seen as responding to special measures, rather than having to go through LEAs as has previously been the case. At the same time it is proposed to set up 100 Education Action Zones to tackle underachievement in the UK's most disadvantaged areas. The impact of these remains to be seen but Gibson and Asthana (1998: 205–6) note that this initiative stands alone as a direct response to underachievement in areas of serious disadvantage, that it is targeting only the schools in greatest difficulties and that it emphasizes school-based initiatives rather than external intervention.

Value-added performance indicator systems: are they good enough?

Like inspection, indicator systems are widely used to scrutinize school performance (OECD 1995). These also vary in the extent to which they acknowledge the SES context of schools and uphold the politics of blame. There are broadly three levels of indicator quality with respect to SES context:

- the use of raw indicators which completely fail to take value-added into account;
- QAD (quick and dirty) approaches which only partly consider value-added; and
- supposedly 'good' value-added approaches which claim to take context 'properly' into account.

An obvious British example of the first approach can be found in the 'league tables' of school examination results in newspapers which followed the publication of a 'Parents' Charter' in 1991. In the USA the approach can also be seen in school test results which have been collected by most states and are reported locally. It is also reflected in the famous 'wall chart' which began to compare the educational performance of American states following the publication of *A Nation at Risk* (US National Commission on Excellence in Education 1983). At all levels, the publication of this sort of performance data remains controversial because it is not at all contextualized. Nevertheless there is a considerable degree of public and political support for the publication of raw data on performance, no doubt because in many cases it so clearly signals the positional value of schools. There is also support from some E&I researchers who, while acknowledging the approach is not fair, still see the use of raw data as a useful way of putting schools under pressure to perform (see Barber in the next chapter). Despite its limitations, raw performance data is often the basis of policy discourse. For example, league tables have been used by the British government and media to support self-managing grant maintained schools over LEA schools. However Whitty *et al.* (1998) point out that grant maintained schools should achieve higher results because most are selective and have higher SES intakes.

The second, 'quick and dirty' (QAD) approach[9] acknowledges that performance indicator data require contextualizing but does this only weakly because of a lack of resources and technical expertise and/or a lack of political will to take the issue seriously. Some examples of a QAD approach include providing SES data alongside raw performance data for rough comparative purposes or comparing school performance in groups of schools with broadly similar characteristics. This is the approach apparently used by Ofsted and it can also be seen in data provided annually to Parliament by the New Zealand Ministry of Education which give school SES deciles alongside their examination results. It is an approach also widely used in the USA. For instance, California releases a school 'report card' on each school which includes SES data alongside test results and other outcome data (Selden 1994). In some states a similar approach is also being used to distribute incentives or sanctions to districts and schools. In South Carolina, for example, districts which do not measure up to the typical performance indicators of districts with broadly similar population profiles are considered 'seriously impaired' and face action similar to 'special measures' (OECD 1995).

Given the evident limitations of both the preceding approaches, there have been some recent attempts to develop better value-added indicator systems. Yet since those doing this work are generally SER researchers drawing on the usual quantitative tools, even today's 'good' performance indicator systems may underestimate the impact of school mix in the same way that the SER literature has typically done. For instance, Fitz-Gibbon has been an enthusiastic advocate of a value-added indicator system in the UK and clearly sees this as a preferable alternative to Ofsted inspections (Fitz-Gibbon 1996, 1997; Fitz-Gibbon and Stephenson 1996). However, her own findings on compositional effects in relation to school performance in the 'Value Added National Project' are, as usual in Hierarchical Linear Modelling analyses, small and inconsistent. This leads Fitz-Gibbon to suggest that they can probably be overlooked because the expense of taking them into account in a value-added indicator system would not pay off (Fitz-Gibbon 1997). Fitz-Gibbon in any case regards the view that there is a strong relationship between SES and school performance as the mistaken consequence of using aggregated data (Fitz-Gibbon 1996). This argument is disputed by Gibson and Asthana (1998) who make a case for school-level data and stress that the kind of value-added approach used by Fitz-Gibbon 'is inadequate precisely because patterns of segregation between schools serve to amplify the impact of socio-economic factors on school performance' (p. 201).

What all this suggests is that while performance indicators may also support the politics of blame, they will do this to varying extents depending on the indicator system used. Raw indicators are completely inadequate but this is at least widely recognized in education circles (Lodge 1998). The use of QAD performance data may therefore actually be more problematic because it may be considered contextualized, while still being wide of the mark – a case of a little knowledge being a dangerous thing. Finally, even relatively sophisticated value-added indicator systems such as the one being developed by Fitz-Gibbon are still likely to underestimate the impact of school mix. If this is the case, we could expect that low-SES schools will usually be regarded as underperforming and middle class schools assessed too favourably in relation to what is really going on.

Assessing teacher competence and improving the practice of teachers

As well as increased pressure on schools as a whole, there have been numerous attempts in recent times to define good or competent teachers, usually in relation to some kind of initiative to evaluate their performance.[10] But as with the literature on teacher quality discussed in the next chapter, these lists tend to be concerned only with generalizable features of good teaching. Moreover there are different emphases even within these generalizable lists. This state of affairs is obviously irksome to some. A recent Ministry discussion paper on teacher education in New Zealand notes for instance:

> The main problem is that there is no nationally consistent means of defining or identifying quality teaching . . . This lack of nationally consistent standards of quality makes it difficult for those responsible for employing teachers to make well informed decisions . . . different sets of standards or criteria for a range of purposes can lead to both confusion and inefficiencies.
>
> (Ministry of Education 1997b: 25)

This paper goes on to propose a structure of nationally agreed professional standards. Yet one of the implications of the argument that good teaching is highly context bound is that a nationally consistent list of attributes of quality or competent teachers is likely to remain elusive. Rather, contextual differences related to student composition will have to be carefully considered if we are at all serious about assessing teachers fairly. This is because even if a value-added approach which takes account of *individual* differences between students is used, if teachers in low-SES schools are judged against the academic effectiveness of those in high-SES schools they will inevitably appear inferior because of additional difficulties related to the *group* characteristics of their students. The negotiated nature of teaching also suggests that pressure on teachers from above by way of managerial accountability will do little to improve the quality of academic teaching and learning in working class schools because of the way school mix appears to constrain and enable teachers.

Taking a wider perspective on this point, the impact of school mix also helps to explain the general failure of attempts to change teaching practice through top down reforms, whether they be changes to management, curricula or assessment. Elmore *et al.* (1996: 237) conclude that 'the relationship between changes in formal structure and changes in teaching practice is necessarily weak, problematic and indirect'. They point out that while people both within and outside schools like to focus on changing school structures because it provides a sense that schools are 'doing something', actually changing the practice of teachers is much harder to achieve. 'The one is highly visible and sexy; the other is more difficult and indeterminate' (*ibid.*: 238). The Wellington study clearly suggests that one reason it is so difficult to bring about teaching practice changes relates to the negotiated nature of teaching.

However, this is unlikely to be a popular message with policy makers as it once again means that teachers can't simply be held responsible. Nevertheless it is essential that policy makers consider the implications of school mix. Metz comments:

> To the degree that the educational reform movement sets aside class differences as unimportant, it brackets and overlooks one of the major influences on schools. It consequently relies for all of its impact on attempting to change patterns that exert much weaker influence. To ignore the most forceful influences in a situation is rarely a prescription for effective reform.
>
> (Metz 1990: 100)

The support of teachers and school leaders for the politics of blame

In part the success of the politics of blame has stemmed from its ability to capture the hearts and minds of many practitioners. For instance, there appear to be many school leaders who, if not exactly avid fans of Ofsted and ERO, do at least think the approach of these agencies is necessary to keep up standards (Riley and Rowles 1997; Robertson *et al.* 1997). This points to the problem that even if many educators have preferred to quietly send their own children to higher SES schools, their professional discourses have often tended to revolve around the belief that all schools are much the same. To some extent this belief has broken down under market competition in recent years, but not entirely. For instance, one New Zealand principal, concerned about schools competing with each other for students, recently argued that 'principals had to believe' that all schools were successful and publicly state that belief'.[11] Similarly Walford (1994) has argued that during the 1960s and 1970s there was a conspiracy of 'official' silence over the possibility of differences between UK comprehensive schools.

The argument that all schools are much the same ignores the positional value of high-SES education and has frequently left progressive educators unprepared for the politics of polarization and blame. In New Zealand the ideology may reflect the long-cherished egalitarian myth noted previously. Because it has tended to obscure disparities between schools, this myth has probably helped ERO's ideological cause by encouraging teachers to think of all students and schools as fairly similar and therefore to accept the idea that differences in student performance may be largely the responsibility of teachers.[12] However the same could surely not be said for either the UK or the USA. With histories of more overt social differentiation and more self-conscious interventions towards equity (such as the Plowden report, the comprehensive movement, the civil rights movement and 'bussing'), teachers in these countries are likely to be much more aware of the impact of disadvantage.

What is more likely to be behind the support of teachers and school leaders for the politics of blame in these countries is a concern to avoid a deficit stance towards working class or minority students. But how far can this be realistically taken? It is certainly important not to judge individuals because of their backgrounds but when this stance is used to hold teachers or school leaders responsible for the achievement or lack thereof of students from disadvantaged backgrounds, they become unfairly hoist by their own petard. While it should be possible to make school staff aware both of the risks of taking a deficit stance *and* what they can and can't be held responsible for, E&I research has served the Right by doing only the former. We have already seen that indifference to social class and school mix has been heavily promoted within the SER literature. As we shall see in the next chapter, it is an important feature of the 'improvement' literature as well.

 **10**

Improvement research: how realistic?

In this chapter I consider the treatment of social and political issues in what I broadly classify as *improvement* research. My main focus will be on school improvement literature but I shall also touch on the associated fields of school restructuring, school change, school leadership, school management, school development, teacher quality and teacher development. The discussion will therefore have a broader and somewhat different focus from Chapter 2's review of SER, but it is required for two reasons.

One is the central methodological difference between effectiveness and improvement studies. The latter, while owing 'at least part of their intellectual heritage to school effects research' (Stringfield and Herman 1996: 163), and often citing SER findings, tend to be less quantitative and value-added in orientation, relying more on case studies of school change. As a result of these differences, we should probably not see the improvement literature as just the 'operational branch' of SER in the way that Slee and Weiner (1998: 1) suggest. The same differences imply we should not simply read the improvement perspective on school mix from the SER literature.

The other factor to be considered is that the improvement literature has become a force to be reckoned with, one which in many respects has overtaken SER because of its perceived advantages. As Hargreaves puts it, 'faith in generalised and scientifically known principles of school effectiveness has begun to be superseded by commitments to more ongoing, provisional and contextually sensitive processes of school improvement' (1994: 59) But just how 'contextually sensitive' is improvement research? That Hopkins and colleagues (1994) consider SER the most rigorous of the E&I fields should make us think twice. Given the problems with SER already discussed, what does this imply about the rest of the literature? Several issues need to be explored here:

- To the extent that improvement writers lean on value-added school effectiveness work, is there a critical edge to their use of it? In particular, are
improvement writers at all questioning of the SER assertion that policy and
practice are largely independent of mix or do they simply carry this over as
an unquestioned assumption into improvement work?
- If the latter is the case or, alternatively, if there is no reference to value-
added approaches, how do improvement writers deal with the social limits
of educational reform, if at all? Does this issue enter into the models and
concepts they employ? Do they acknowledge 'savage inequalities' between
schools? If so, what do they see as the implications of these?
- Is there any evidence of support from improvement writers for the politics
of polarization and blame?

These are the key questions but addressing them poses a formidable challenge.
Not only is the sheer quantity of improvement literature overwhelming, but
there are important differences in the researched quality of this literature.
Works derived from general management models are a particular problem.
These indicate little real willingness to engage with the actual difficulties of
educational reform, social or otherwise. They epitomize the kind of school
improvement texts Evans complains about which have an answer '[n]o
matter how complex the problem, or how dismal the history of previous
efforts to treat it . . . Indeed, it often seems that the greater the dilemma, the
greater their expectations for change' (1996: 3).

Texts on Total Quality Management (TQM) in education (Bonstingl 1992;
Glasser 1992; Greenwood and Gaunt 1994; Arcaro 1995; Shaw 1995) provide
an excellent example. Arcaro, for instance, asserts that 'Quality works as well
in education as it does in business. It is a revolution' (Arcaro 1995: xi). He
suggests TQM will require a 'paradigm shift' but it is one which appears to fit
rather well with the agenda of the Right:

> Schools must learn to work with fewer resources. Education professions
> must help students to develop the skills they need to compete in a global
> economy . . . Money is not the key to improving the quality of education.
> The quality of education will improve when administrators, teachers,
> staff and school board members develop new attitudes . . .
>
> (*ibid.*: 2)

This sort of approach contrasts greatly with improvement work which has
researched the day-to-day problems faced by schools, and is often discounted
by 'serious' improvers. Sergiovanni (1996: 15) regards TQM as 'a metaphor for
theories and management schemes that we have indiscriminately imported to
education' while Cuttance (1997: 107) suggests 'it would be odd if we were
to take up a strategy that had been developed outside of education if we
cannot provide a clear argument as to why it is to be more relevant than the
educationally derived alternatives'. Nevertheless TQM and other generic
management models do get taken up by many schools. As Ball (1997b) well
illustrates, we should not underestimate their likely impact.

There are also important international variations in the context and focus of improvement research. For instance, whereas 'school improvement' is in vogue in the UK, researchers in the USA usually refer to 'school restructuring'. This is a catch-all phrase for numerous reform aspirations and programmes but it carries the connotation of fundamental change – the view that 'simply improving parts of schools as we know them isn't enough' (Newmann and Wehlage 1995: 1). The USA has seen much greater corporate involvement in its reform efforts than has the UK, and ethnicity issues are also more to the fore in the USA. Moreover there are significant political differences such as the Civil Rights legislation of the 1960s and the equity guarantees 'hardwired' into the American Constitution. As Boyd (1996: 81) has noted, these mean that 'Tory ministers pursue their objectives with an unhampered zeal that American congressmen can only envy.'

Given all of these considerations and limited space, I have chosen here to discuss the work of just six British and North American improvement writers who have achieved a high international profile – Michael Barber, David Hopkins, Michael Fullan, Sam Stringfield, Louise Stoll and John Gray. All have contributed books to the Cassell or Teachers College Press series on school development/reform or are on the editorial board of *School Effectiveness and School Improvement*. They have been chosen (as many others might have been) because their work illustrates a spectrum of improvement perspectives and emphases with respect to the questions raised above, moving from least (Barber) to most (Stoll and Gray) contextually sensitive. Focussing on a small number of individuals like this provides a better sense of how various improvement discourses are being packaged. At the same time it is a small group so I shall also refer to the work of a number of other improvement writers in a concluding discussion.

Barber

The work of Barber (1995, 1996a, 1996b, 1998) is at one extreme of the spectrum of those considered here because it provides such a clear example of both the refutation of the social limits of reform and the links between improvement literature and neo-liberal and managerial politics. For instance, in his well-known TES-Greenwich address he claims that:

- 'the government's insistence on shifting both autonomy and accountability to school level is a step forward';
- 'Ofsted and government – are there to create a context in which schools are enabled and encouraged to improve themselves';
- 'the Ofsted framework . . . is laced through with an understanding of school effectiveness';
- various (named) politicians have a good grasp of school effectiveness and school improvement issues;

- 'the school effectiveness literature . . . provides a rock on which to build a [teaching] profession for the future';
- there is a culture of low educational expectations amongst the British public;
- '[Ofsted] has changed the educational landscape for the better';
- 'the primary responsibility for promoting success and avoiding failure lies with the school';
- a high reliability approach [see Stringfield below] should be taken to educational provision;
- 'failure as defined today can be reduced and ultimately eliminated';
- critics have no alternatives.

(Barber 1995 in Barber 1998: 17–32)

In a recent postscript Barber explains that he gave this speech partly to refute teachers' use of 'submarxist language' to justify student underperformance (Barber 1998). He also claims that the British government's policy on school failure has proved 'a tremendous success' and adds that as a result of the speech he was given the 'poisoned chalice' (this didn't stop him drinking it!) of shutting down Hackney Downs School. Barber admits that his emphasis on failure may have had a demoralizing effect on British teachers but concludes that the issues needed to be raised.

Since *The Learning Game* (Barber 1996a) begins with the plight of homeless people, it seems to hold more promise of a thoughtful discussion of the impact of social disparities on schools. However this is not the case. As Dale notes:

The book is full of breezy pragmatism and appealing platitudes that stand in for vigorous analysis . . . Barber is as likely to quote a conversation overheard in a café or a discussion in a pub as he is to refer to academic research.

(Dale 1997: 452)

The lack of real analysis underlying Barber's arguments is well illustrated by his discussion of school failure and success. He plays off the failure of Hackney Downs School against the 'intoxicating' atmosphere of Hayward High, a school he previously researched (National Commission on Education, 1996). Barber justifies the closure of Hackney Downs School by pointing to poor teaching, a weak organizational culture, 'the militancy of union extremists' (which feature a lot in his account) and 'changing social circumstances' (about which much less is said). However, his account contrasts markedly with Tomlinson's (1997, 1998) detailed analyses of Hackney Downs School which point to the devastating impact of poverty, market forces and the 'special measures' policies on the school's fortunes. Barber's discussion of the extent and causes of the success of Hayward High is also less than convincing.[1] The success of that school is seen to hinge largely on the qualities of the principal who set off a spiral of improvement. No doubt the principal was very good, but was this all there was to it? What about external factors? Where did this school stack up against others in the local market? To what extent did social conditions among the families which made up the intake really worsen over time as claimed by staff? Isn't it odd that teachers' judgements at Hayward High were not disputed while those at Hackney Downs most certainly were?

Barber's use of school effectiveness literature in *The Learning Game* lacks a critical edge:

> The research on school effectiveness has . . . contributed to a fundamental and wholly welcome change of climate . . . The research allows us to quantify just how much difference schools can make . . . The most brilliant study in this field is *School Matters* . . .

> The effectiveness research requires teachers to face up to their own importance . . . Whereas under the old order there was a tendency to blame the system, society, the class structure – anyone other than schools themselves – for underperformance, now there is no escape.
>
> (Barber 1996a: 128, 131)

Barber also stresses the 'generalisability' of the characteristics of effective schools developed by Sammons and colleagues for Ofsted (Sammons *et al.*: 1995). He makes no mention of any 'sensitivity to context' findings and he glosses over the limitations of Ofsted inspections, league tables, choice and markets. Consider, for instance, his perspective on the publication of raw exam results. Having just pointed out the importance of considering 'value added' he then suggests:

> Nevertheless the published tables – in spite of their inadequacies – do put schools in the public eye. Schools that appear very low in the tables do experience pressure, and many have striven to improve themselves. Some headteachers claim the whole process is demoralising since, however much they try, they cannot progress all that far up the table. In public, this is what most headteachers say. In private however, they sometimes say something different. They say that appearing at the bottom of the table has had a galvanising effect. They say that it has enabled them to demand change from their staff and they often say that it has opened their eyes to the fact that they were indeed doing much less well than they should have been, compared to other schools in similar circumstances.
>
> (1996a: 125)

Barber is clearly prepared to support what he accepts is an unjust method of judging school quality if it brings pressure to bear on schools. This 'ends justify the means' approach is part and parcel of the politics of blame but is likely to be counterproductive when, as the Wellington study indicates, means do matter. Neither a heightened awareness of failure nor simply demanding change from the staff of low-SES schools is going to help when teachers face powerful contextual constraints.

Barber (1996b) contains more critique of the school effectiveness literature but it is along the usual school improvement lines, saying it has limitations for use in improving schools, rather than anything more fundamental. Barber's support for self-management and accountability via Ofsted as ways of putting pressure on schools to perform is also slightly more qualified in this book than those already mentioned, and he does suggest some useful ideas about how best to support schools. But overall there is little analysis – his decontextualized approach persists.

Overall, because many of Barber's arguments seem more like those of a politician than an academic, it comes as little surprise to find that Barber was seconded from his university post in 1997 to head the DfEE Standards and Effectiveness unit for a government which campaigned under the educational slogan 'Zero Tolerance'.

Hopkins

If Barber overtly supports markets and managerialism, Hopkins does so less directly through his 'neutral' technicist approach. Over the last decade Hopkins has been a prolific writer in the areas of school improvement (Hopkins 1987, 1996; Hopkins *et al.* 1994) as well as on related areas such as teacher quality (OECD 1994a), and teacher and school development (Hargreaves and Hopkins 1991, 1994; Hopkins *et al.* 1994). Hopkins is at his best when summarizing research but his work is marked by an uncritical use of SER findings, a decontextualized approach to improvement issues and a rather diffident stance to the politics of reform.

Many of these shortcomings are illustrated in *School Improvement in an Era of Change* (Hopkins *et al.* 1994). As noted earlier, this provides a glowing account of SER. In it Hopkins argues that this literature is 'amongst the most robust that we have in our quest for educational reform,' that it is 'empirically the most valid in the whole area of educational change' and that 'it must therefore be taken seriously' (pp. 42–3). What follows, in Hopkins's own words, is 'an account which respects the conventional wisdom in the area' (p. 42). The same approach permeates the entire book including discussion of models of school change and school culture. It seems that Hopkins has little difficulty with any E&I work – he is happy to 'embrace multiple perspectives' on change. Even when he describes Caldwell and Spinks's (1988) account of the 'self-managing school' as 'mechanistic' (which it is), Hopkins is quick to add that this is meant 'not in a pejorative but in a technical sense' (p. 74).

Hopkins's improvement work employs only generalized models and concepts which rarely acknowledge any impact of SES on school processes. For instance, although Hopkins (*ibid.*: 20) argues that the school improvement agenda is about changing the culture of schools, his discussion concentrates on organizational notions of culture (after Schein 1985) rather than making any mention of social class culture and its impact on schools. Even his discussion of the importance of pupil and parent involvement in schools makes no mention of the impact of social class. When 'context' is discussed it is never SES context (or gender or ethnic context for that matter) but other more general contexts such as the classroom (p. 118) or the 'size, shape and location' of schools (p. 151). The same problem appears to be common to all of Hopkins's work. For instance, 'quality teachers' have only generalized attributes in his writing rather than attributes which may vary according to school mix (OECD 1994a). Nor does his work on development planning (Hargreaves and Hopkins 1991, 1994) or his attempts to 'theorise' school improvement (Hopkins 1996) refer to SES context. As Ball (1993b: 67) notes, the discourse is 'technically-oriented, rational and apolitical', a case of 'management in the best of all possible schools'.

Hopkins does sometimes discuss the politics of reform but he prevaricates. For instance, in Hopkins *et al.* (1994: 12) he argues, 'We have no evidence to suggest that accountability and increased competition, as strategies for improving the quality of education for all, actually work'. He also comments: 'We appear to be living in an Alice in Wonderland world of educational reform where the sole rationale for many policies is the public support for them by a small group of ideologically commited politicians' (p. 18). On the other hand he does not cite any of the numerous critics of recent British education policy and talks of working with schools 'within the framework of the national reform agenda' (p. 2). Mostly however, he seems to prefer to hedge his bets as to the outcomes of reform. We are told, 'Whatever one thinks of our national reforms . . . The jury is still out' and 'Whatever one's position . . . there are lessons to be learned . . .' (pp. 5–6).

Hopkins seems to believe that schools can and should meet their own aspirations for their students in spite of the central policy agenda. He notes that policy does not travel far into schools and that this allows some autonomy for schools to engage in their own processes of improvement. However, this approach is likely to underestimate the impact of both markets and accountability measures on schools. For instance, school development planning could be seen as a means of driving the policies of central agencies into schools (Taylor *et al.* 1997). Moreover, while Hopkins argues for a high degree of external support for schools, he also argues for a high degree of pressure on them in a way which may support the politics of blame (p. 83).

Fullan

Fullan's books on the 'meaning of educational change' (Fullan 1982, 1991) have become key school improvement texts but he also takes a technicist, organizational approach to social and political matters. According to Huberman, Fullan has worked towards a complex 'social technology' of school improvement which involves evolutionary 'rolling' models of change and which uses phenomenological approaches which consider how those involved are actually viewing change (Huberman in Fullan 1992). Although Fullan's analysis of change processes in schools is certainly detailed and sophisticated in an organizational sense, he seems mostly to overlook or ignore contextual limits to change. Fullan (1991) includes a section on 'Why Planning Fails' which notes:

> [L]et us admit the hypothetical possibility that some social problems . . . contain innumerable interacting causes that cannot be fully understood. Nor can we necessarily change those factors that we do understand as causes. Further there is such an overload of problems that it is not possible to solve very many of them with the time, energy and resources at our disposal.
>
> (Fullan 1991: 98)

He goes on to argue:

> Recognising the limitations of planning is not the same thing as concluding that effective change is not attainable. But in order to conclude that planned educational change is possible . . . we would need to find examples of where a setting has been *deliberately transformed* [his emphasis] from a previous state to a new one that represents clear improvement.
>
> (*ibid.*: 100)

Nevertheless among the various case studies which follow, the most 'compelling' evidence for change that Fullan is able to point to is Mortimore *et al.* (1988) which he uses to argue that 'successful change is possible in the real world, even under difficult conditions. And most of the reasons for the achievements can be pinpointed' (Fullan 1991: 101). In short, underlying Fullan's argument that 'positive results on a massive scale' (p. 354) can be achieved, there is once again nothing better than the same SER findings discussed earlier.

Fullan's analysis, although interesting, rarely provides much sense of SES differences between schools. Student body characteristics are left out of his 'factors influencing implementation' (1991: Chapter 5). General community characteristics are considered but class is barely mentioned. Fullan (1992) contains a very detailed case study chapter on the problems of introducing computers into schools in Ontario. However, the ability of low-SES communities to raise funds for the purchase of computer hardware and support seems largely assumed. For the most part Fullan and Hargreaves (1992) also present nothing more than a generalized discussion of the difficulties facing teachers and schools. Only briefly in a section on the 'context of teaching' are SES differences mentioned:

> The belief that because some schools are successful at making particular improvements and therefore any school can be just as successful is a false and dangerous one. For instance, the existence of exemplary models of staff collegiality in some schools should not be interpreted as meaning that norms of collegiality can be established just as easily in other schools. Reviews of existing research in this field, in fact, suggest that collegiality tends to prosper in middle class environments where resources are better, working environments more congenial, staff more carefully selected, and

a sense of hope and possibility more strong . . . the challenge of collegiality in working class multi-cultural schools is likely to be different and probably greater than in those exemplary instances of good practice that are held up as beacons for the rest of us to follow.

(Fullan and Hargreaves 1992: 45–6)

However, such acknowledgement of the reality of low-SES schools is rare in Fullan's work. Fullan (1993) notes that during the 1980s 'societal problems worsened [and] the education system was tinkering' (p. 2) but this is also mostly another account which, preoccupied with overcoming the organizational limits to change, gives only fleeting consideration to wider social limits.

Fullan also fails to provide a strong critique of neo-liberalism or managerialism. He appears to regard educational reformers as essentially well-meaning but requiring better models of implementation. His discussion of 'the fundamental problems of educational change' includes:

(1) the growing and deepening alienation amongst teachers; (2) the balkanisation and burnout of passionate reform-minded teachers; and (3) the overwhelming multiplicity of unconnected, fragmented change initiatives.

(Fullan 1997: 217)

Certainly these are all huge problems but surely they are symptoms rather than cause?

One of Fullan's most frequently cited suggestions is the need for governments both to support and to put pressure on schools. This is probably a useful idea but one which is sometimes misused (for instance by Barber) to justify tough accountability measures.

Stringfield

Stringfield's work sometimes recognizes the social limits of reform but he also appears to believe that it is quite feasible to engineer schools to prevent student failure. One of Stringfield's more circumspect moments can be found in an overview of school effectiveness and restructuring efforts in the USA when he talks about 'continued over-promising':

As members of a scholarly community, it is our obligation to promise no more than we can deliver. The credibility of the US school effects field has been called into serious question in the last ten years. We believe that the primary cause of this questioning has been the overpromising of dramatic results from a still narrow and young research base. When Edmonds (1979) stated that, 'we can, when ever and where ever we choose, successfully teach all children whose schooling was of interest to us', he was partially correct. We know enough to do that on a limited set of children in a school reasonably free of strife, if the faculty are willing to make a concerted, multi-year effort to achieve that one goal. We have yet not demonstrated that we know enough to achieve that goal for all students in an entire city, or state, and certainly not a country. While we are making progress, we should promise no more than we can deliver.

(Stringfield and Herman 1996: 175–6)

This is an important admission, not only because it is rare for improvers to acknowledge that Edmonds may have overstated his claims, but because it is relatively modest about what has been achieved and what may be achievable. But most of Stringfield's other work has a more upbeat tenor. For instance, much of his recent work (Stringfield 1995, 1997, 1998; Reynolds and String-field 1996) appears to be premised on the possibility of creating 'failure-free' schooling. Indeed Stringfield claims:

While the maps must be improved, and while ever better routes must be explored and developed, we can look forward with a great deal of optimism knowing enough seriously to take on the historically un-imaginable tasks of eradicating functional illiteracy and inadequate mathematical skills from virtually all school children, regardless of back-ground. We can do this in our lifetimes.

(Stringfield 1998: 219–20)

So what are the bases of this claim? Stringfield (1998) lists three: the findings of the Louisiana School Effectiveness Study (LSES) (Teddlie and Stringfield 1993), the findings of the Special Strategies Studies (Stringfield *et al.* 1997b), and the notion of schools as High Reliability Organisations (HROs) (Stringfield 1995, 1997). None of these are without problems.

The LSES findings claim that demographically matched outlier schools varied substantially in their effectiveness and that their degree of effectiveness was linked to school characteristics such as the pace of instruction, the extent of planning, use of school time and so on. However, whether or not this analysis of effectiveness is accepted depends on how much weight the reader chooses to give to Teddlie and Stringfield's methods. An examination suggests rough measures of SES, crude categorization of schools as low- or middle-SES and as 'more effective', 'typical' and 'less effective', and only limited school observation. For instance Stringfield (1998: 211) informs us, as if it were a strength of the study, that 'the [outlier] schools were observed by two person teams for at least three days per school on four separate occasions over six years'. Yet this equates to just 24 researcher days in each school over a six year period. In some years each school would not have been visited at all! Can this really be adequate for understanding how a school works? No wonder it took a matter of years for observers to realise that one school's library was only neat and tidy because it was kept locked (*ibid.*: 214)! If getting this information took so long, how could observers be expected to identify more complex school processes such as those to do with classroom instruction?

What Teddlie and Stringfield have done is not unacceptable in quantita-tive SER terms – indeed from this perspective the LSES study is probably

exemplary. But from a broader reading their approach leaves many unanswered questions. What is also troubling is that so many features of
Stringfield's so-called ineffective schools as well as of the Special Strategies
Studies schools which failed in their improvement efforts (Stringfield *et al.*
1997b) appear to be those which are also often associated with low-SES
schools. In the case of LSES these included more classroom interruptions,
more discipline problems, less student time on-task, less awareness of the
significance of the work being covered, failure to cover the required curriculum, lack of rigorous intellectual classroom discussion or debate, interruptions to the school programme, problems with recruiting and monitoring
teachers and so on. According to Stringfield, the failing Special Strategies
Studies schools had ten destabilizing elements. Some of these – leadership
crises and management, communications and scheduling problems – might
be expected to occur in any SES context, but many are difficulties which
might be particularly expected in low-SES settings such as funding problems,
staffing, curriculum alignment, teacher commitment, public image, and poor
physical facilities. In short, where Stringfield concludes that 'the ten de-
stabilising elements are, almost by definition, more prevalent in ineffective
schools' (1998: 217), I would want to add that many of them are likely to be
more prevalent in low-SES schools too.

All of this raises the question: whatever happened to Teddlie and Stringfield's (1993) argument that 'school [SES] context is important'? It certainly
doesn't feature much in Stringfield's recent work which rarely refers to the
SES characteristics of the schools he is talking about. However, this was
always a rather limited claim in any case. The argument was never that low-
SES schools were by nature likely to be less effective than high-SES schools
but rather that they required 'different strategies for success' (*ibid.*: 42). The
notion that school 'effectiveness' could follow from school mix rather than be
independent of it was itself apparently never countenanced.

We also need to ask of Stringfield's recent work whether any schools, let
alone low-SES schools, could, or indeed should, be expected to become HROs
like air traffic control and 'certain responsibilities on nuclear aircraft carriers'
(Stringfield 1997). Such a suggestion can be interpreted (to paraphrase Stoll
and Myers 1998: 207) as 'merely [a] metaphor [which] helps us . . . to
understand the consequence if schools are not successful for all pupils'. A less
charitable view would be that the notion of schools as HROs is a case of
rampant technicism. What is apparent in any case is that it would be much
easier for schools in high-SES settings to have higher reliability because of the
kinds of resources available. For instance, Stringfield (1997: 149) points to
the way in which schools that operate like HROs 'make sure that things
work'. He cites the example of a school 'securing assistance through non
traditional routes' when the local district could not quickly provide a tech-
nician to fix an air conditioning system. Yet this is clearly an instance where a
wealthier school could probably throw money at the problem and a poorer
school could not (although something breaking down doesn't seem very
HROish anyway!). In a similar way low-SES schools usually have less

professional parental expertise on their governing bodies, less experienced staff, less compliant and 'able' students and so on. It is therefore hard to see how such schools could run as HROs. But none of this is acknowledged in Stringfield's account – instead we are given the impression that with the right leadership and training, all schools would be equally capable of becoming HROs.

No doubt part of Stringfield's upbeat approach will have been conditioned by his need to 'sell' restructuring programmes to government and corporate sponsors. For instance, Stringfield is heavily involved in the Memphis Re-structuring Initiative which he describes as a 'multi-site, multi-model, multi-method, longitudinal study of top-down support for diverse bottom-up restructuring efforts' (Stringfield *et al.* 1997a: 4). This massive initiative offers a veritable smorgasbord of 'break the mould' restructuring programmes to Memphis schools. Most are funded by foundations and corporations as part of the New American Schools (NAS) Development Corporation initiative which was in turn set up by the Federal Goals 2000 programme in 1991. In order to secure the NAS funding, school districts and states commit themselves to 'achieving a critical mass (30%) of transformed schools within five years' (Kearns and Anderson 1996). In short, this is a high-stakes funding environment which would leave little room for diffidence in any discussion about the ability to achieve reform. Nevertheless there is already early evidence from Memphis that school intake characteristics including SES, prior achievement and student mobility have 'a significant impact' on the implementation of restructuring programmes (Smith *et al.* 1997).

Finally, Stringfield provides yet again an uncritical view of the politics of reform. For instance, he attributes the recent attention being given to school ineffectiveness to 'increasing confidence' within the improvement field but makes no mention of the politics of blame which could also foster this development (Stringfield 1998: 210). He also appears to accept at face value the argument that unemployment or underemployment is due to lack of job skills. He suggests that unemployment has 'created a problem, not just for the poor, but for the affluent who do not wish to be obligated permanently to supporting the poor' (*ibid.*). Implicit in this point appears to be a conservative notion of welfare dependency, of the wealthy being burdened by the problems of the poor. There is no suggestion that their poverty may be the outcome of policies which have favoured the affluent.

Stoll

In many respects Stoll's work is more contextually aware than any of the preceding authors but she still offers rather mixed messages (Stoll and Fink 1996, 1998; Stoll and Reynolds 1997; Stoll and Myers 1998). On the positive side, *No Quick Fixes* makes some thoughtful points about the limits of school effectiveness, the importance of school context and the need to avoid the politics of blame:

School effectiveness research has demonstrated that . . . school can make a difference. In taking up these important research findings, some policy makers, however, have construed this to mean that the school is responsible for the success or otherwise of its pupils. There is some truth in this, but only to a limited extent . . . It remains important, however, to recognise that schools exist within a wider social context . . . It seems clear that education policies related to improving schools in difficulty are most likely to succeed when taking the wider national and community interest into full account. . . .

(Stoll and Myers 1998: 10)

If we look at other OECD countries, we find a distinct difference between those who emphasise *failure of pupils* (most countries) and the few, including England and Wales, who talk in terms of *school failure* . . . When failure of the school is emphasised, the external contest is not considered. Indeed it is believed anyone who suggests the context may contribute to the school's problems is complacent and has low expectations of the pupils.

(*ibid*.: 9, Stoll and Myers's emphasis)

and

In our view, *every* child has a right to the best possible education. For this to occur, attention must be paid to the contextual causes of failure that lie outside the remit of the school as well as what occurs within it.

(*ibid*.: 16, Stoll and Myers's emphasis)

This goes right to the heart of the matter and there is more – Stoll and Myers also express concerns about politicians' use of language such as 'zero tolerance' (they dispute Barber's claim that this is the same as 'success for all'), the misuse of value-added SER findings, the importance of the impact of social conditions on student achievement, the need for low-SES schools to receive additional financial resources and management support, and the negative impact of Ofsted.

On the other hand, some of Stoll's other recent work suggests that only limited weight is being given to the impact of the social context of schooling. For instance, notions of school culture outlined in Stoll and Fink (1998) in the same collection make some links to school mix but remain very much within an organizational perspective. A 'sinking' school is described as follows:

A sinking school is a failing school. It is not only ineffective: the staff, whether through apathy or ignorance, are not prepared or able to change. It is a school in which isolation, self-reliance, blame and loss of faith are dominating norms, and powerfully inhibit improvement. It will often, although not always, be in socially disadvantaged areas where parents are undemanding and teachers explain away failure by blaming inadequate parenting or unprepared children.

(Stoll and Fink 1998: 192)

The view here appears to be that while 'sinking' schools are often in low-SES settings, their 'ineffectiveness' is a matter of expectations rather than being more systematically related to the impact of school mix on school processes. (This is also a perspective which seems less than sympathetic to the problems of teachers in low-SES settings). Similarly, a 'cruising school' is a school which is 'perceived as effective' but 'is usually located in a more affluent area where pupils achieve in spite of teaching quality' (Stoll and Fink 1998: 193). This is an attractive concept but one which fails to consider the multiple advantages that *any* school with a higher SES intake is likely to enjoy. Indeed, in terms of the school mix argument, there is a sense in which all higher SES schools are likely to be 'cruising' because the processes which support academic work are so much easier to carry out there than in low-SES settings.

A limited view of the impact of school mix is also presented by Stoll and Reynolds (1997) account which points out that there are problems generalizing SER and improvement findings across SES contexts:

> For school improvement to occur, more is required than the notion of what works across context in the average school or data on the relationships between school processes and outcomes for all schools. What is needed is knowledge of specific factors that will generate improvement in particular schools in particular socioeconomic and cultural contexts. Since only a small amount of our school effectiveness data-base is analysed by context, the delineation of the precise variables that school improvement needs to target to affect outcomes is currently impossible.
>
> (Stoll and Reynolds 1997: 31)

The acknowledgement of context here is clearly useful but what also seems to be emerging is a perspective similar to that taken by Teddlie and Stringfield (1993). Stoll and Reynolds do not seem to be acknowledging that low-SES schools may actually be harder to improve but arguing that a *different* approach will be required. This is how Stoll and Fink (1996) also appear to interpret Brown *et al.*'s (1996a) findings as well because they cite their study to support the idea that 'different improvement strategies are necessary in low-SES and high-SES schools' (Stoll and Fink 1996: 58). However, since this approach fails to question the primacy of pedagogy and management over school mix it may still end up supporting the politics of blame, even as it accepts that context is important.

Gray

Like Stringfield and Stoll, Gray brings an extensive background in SER to his improvement work. His analyses tend to be more careful than most. For instance in *Good School, Bad School* Gray approaches previous case studies of school improvement with a healthy scepticism:

> Most case studies of improving schools report that some improvement

(eventually) occurred. In our view such studies, biased as they tend to be towards the change efforts that worked, probably give too rosy an impression of how much change can take place over relatively short periods of time.

(Gray and Wilcox 1995b: 244)

Gray reminds the reader that Lightfoot (1983) said of her 'excellent' Carver High School that 'the school had a long way to go before it could claim that most of its students were receiving a good education' (pp. 312–13). He also raises numerous questions about Ofsted's case study of Newall Green High School, a school which was supposed to have improved markedly over a year (Ofsted 1994). He concludes:

> The purpose of this critique is not to suggest that there were no important changes at Newall Green over the period between the two inspections. We doubt, however, whether the school's experience was typical of improvement efforts in similar schools. A sense of realism about what schools can be expected to achieve over periods as short as a year is required. If a failing school's fate is to be judged simply by the distance the most successful have travelled then most will be damned.
>
> (Gray and Wilcox 1995b: 249)

Nevertheless Gray does keep faith with the claim that substantial school improvement is possible. For instance, he suggests:

> It is hard to keep momentum going and rather too easy to help an initiative change direction and fade away. We must expect to plough our way through numerous cases which claim to have been successful to *find those which probably have.*
>
> (Gray and Wilcox 1995b: 257, my emphasis)

Gray is also prepared to countenance some 'cautious' and 'heuristic' discussion of closing and reopening schools. This matter also provides a taste of the research-centred manner in which Gray typically responds to issues of policy:

> Although there is much interest amongst policymakers in the problem of closing 'ineffective' schools, there is not much prospect of them doing so as a direct response to the problems posed by research on school improvement. 'School closure' will, doubtless, continue to be a last resort when all other efforts have failed – a long, drawn out and painful experience for all concerned.
>
> (*ibid.*: 254)

Like many school improvers, Gray's preferred role is that of the 'neutral' researcher providing 'objective' findings for policy makers. This is a perspective from which 'bad' policy is created mostly by misinformed policy makers who can, however, be reasoned with. He suggests: 'The current range of initiatives, programmes and sanctions being utilised with "failing" schools would strongly suggest that educational policies need the silent voice and truths of research knowledge more than ever before' (Gray *et al.* 1996: xi). But some of his own work also illustrates the limitations of expecting a reasoned response from politicians and policy makers. For instance, over the last few years Gray has repeatedly expressed reservations about Ofsted's attempts to acknowledge the effects of context. Pointing to his earlier research with HMI inspectors, which suggested their attempts to contextualize school exam performance were seriously flawed (Gray and Hannon 1986), Gray suggested in 1995 that little may have changed:

> Since that time, judgements appear to have become more consistent but not necessarily more appropriate. Some distinct breaks with practice in the recent past may be required.
>
> (Gray and Wilcox 1995c: 138)

Gray was one of those who hoped that the work on value-added being done for Ofsted by Sammons *et al.* (1994) might represent a step forward:

> There are indications that steps are being taken to assist inspectors by providing evidence on performance levels for schools of different types, where school type is taken to include schools serving different socioeconomic communities. How prominent such contextualised data will become in inspectors' reports remains to be seen.
>
> (Gray and Wilcox 1995c: 138)

When, as mentioned in the last chapter, Woodhead subsequently announced that Ofsted would not proceed with a contextualized approach Gray was clearly disappointed. He argued (1997: 18) the benefits of a contextualized approach and questioned how Woodhead had been able to single out 'star' schools as claimed in his recent annual report. In response to Woodhead's argument that 'it is essential that Ofsted does nothing to encourage the use of pupils' backgrounds as an excuse for poor performance' (Woodhead 1996), Gray argued:

> This is a familiar argument but not one which can be held by someone who professes 'the importance of comparing like with like' and who draws attention to the 'gulf in achievement between schools in similar circumstances'.
>
> (Gray 1997: 19)

Nevertheless, as noted in the last chapter, Ofsted's backing out of the use of more rigorous assessments was also entirely predictable given the prevailing ideology.

Recently Gray has become involved in the development of Ofstin (Office for Standards in Inspection), a pressure group set up to monitor Ofsted. A recent Ofstin report contains numerous references expressing concern that Ofsted methods might unfairly discriminate against low-socioeconomic schools (Boothroyd *et al.* 1997).

Discussion

The overall picture painted by the preceding improvement writers is not very clear about the social limits of reform or the likely impact of neo-liberal and managerial policies. If they fairly represent the range of what is available (and more examples below suggest they do), most improvement literature appears to perceive few limitations in school effectiveness work and is often contextually just as wanting. Gray's work and Stoll and Myer's (1998) collection are among the most searching but neither emphasizes SES context enough. Much of the literature also seems to offer direct or indirect support to the politics of polarization and blame. Even more disturbing is the way some improvement researchers, like Barber, have become actively involved in these politics.

The uncritical use of SER findings

Gray understands the possibility of SER findings being confounded by school mix and there are others who also indicate a healthy concern about school and teacher effectiveness findings (Elmore *et al.* 1996; Newmann and associates 1996). Yet among most improvers, this kind of questioning is rare. Although few offer as much praise as Hopkins, most appear to accept generalized SER findings at face value. For example, Sammons's 11 generalized school effectiveness factors (Sammons *et al.* 1995) are frequently cited in recent improvement work. School improvement writers who criticize SER complain that it is too abstract or 'thin' to guide school improvement strategies. They do not offer a more fundamental critique of its claims, its methods or its politics. As many improvers have also been involved in SER, this may be considered unsurprising. The above range of views suggests however that those closest to the SER literature will often be the most aware of its contextual vulnerability.

The marginalization of social class

Issues of social class are often marginalized in improvement research which tends to concentrate on organizational or instructional problems or only give limited weight to the social dimensions of schooling. This occurs in a variety of ways – one is by sampling. As in the SER literature, research into schools undertaking improvement work has rarely included a diverse range of SES contexts. Most researchers follow Louis and Miles (1990) in concentrating on schools in low-SES urban settings which are more often thought to need improvement. Huberman and Miles (1984), in contrast, surveyed 12 school improvement projects but only one was in a 'lower class' school.

Even where school samples are apparently chosen for SES diversity, it is common for improvement studies to ignore the SES dimensions of schooling in subsequent discussion (e.g. Chapman *et al.* 1996; Rudduck *et al.* 1996). Like SER, improvement literature tends to favour generalized rather than context-specific discussion. This is seldom made explicit – it is more the case that the literature is vague about what sort of students, classrooms or schools are actually under discussion. The reader is therefore encouraged to take the view that schools' problems and solutions are essentially the same regardless of their social setting. For instance, Lieberman and Miller (1992) offer an interesting chapter on 'The Social Realities of Teaching' but make no mention of social class context. Sometimes the focus is on individual psychological constructs rather than the impact of social structures. In Slavin's (1996) model of instruction and student achievement the student 'inputs' are 'aptitude' and 'motivation' rather than class, ethnicity or gender.

A particularly good example of a decontextualized improvement is provided by the literature on teacher 'quality'. As in Hopkins's work, research on teacher quality tends to focus on features of good teaching which, in a similar way to recipes for effective schools, are generalizable across teachers in all SES settings. However, this level of generalization means that the research is hardly enlightening. Ramsay and Oliver (1995) point to quality teachers being intelligent, warm and compassionate, determined and having a sense of humour. All of this is well and good but rather self-evident, particularly when the apparent *differences* between what constitutes a successful teacher in the four Wellington schools suggest approaches to teaching are likely to be heavily influenced by context.

The school leadership literature also tends to suffer from the problem of using an overgeneralized conception of schools rather than acknowledging SES differences. The problem can be seen for instance in the well-known work of Sergiovanni (1990, 1994, 1996). To give a rather obvious example where a decontextualized approach falls down, Sergiovanni (1990: 1) begins by stressing the importance of 'gambare' ('to persevere, to do one's best, to be persistent, to stick to one's purpose, to never give up until the job is done and done well'). In this spirit he cites a 'successful principal' in Los Angeles who, having installed some gardens in huge flowerpots around the school, replanted the pots 15 times after they were vandalized. This is admirable of course but what is left out of discussion here is that in many schools such perseverance in the face of adversity will never be called upon. Nor will this kind of unproductive activity have to use up so much time.

When social class matters are raised, improvers often don't seem to know how to respond. We saw that Stoll and Fink (1996) interpreted the work of Brown *et al.* (1996a) not as suggesting that low-SES schools may be harder to improve but simply that different approaches will be required. Reynolds *et al.* (1996: 137) cite the same research as an example of 'work at the school effectiveness/special educational needs interface, studying how schools vary in their definitions, labelling practices and teacher/pupil interactions with such children'. This seems to miss the significance of the findings altogether.

Decontextualized notions of school and teacher culture

One of the most significant ways that the impact of school mix is marginalized in improvement research is through notions of school culture which emphasize the organizational, management and instructional dimensions of schooling at the expense of the culture of students and the community. This is a central limitation in all the improvement literature surveyed here and appears to be a problem common to improvement literature in general. As a result we get school and teacher cultures which are 'stuck' and 'moving' (Rosenholtz 1989); 'individualist', 'collaborative', 'contrived' or 'balkanised' (Fullan and Hargreaves 1992; A. Hargreaves 1994); 'wandering', 'moving', 'stuck' and 'promenading' (Hopkins *et al.* 1994); 'formal', 'welfarist', 'hot-house', 'survivalist', 'traditional' and 'collegial' (Hargreaves 1995); and 'moving,' 'cruising', 'strolling', 'struggling' and 'sinking' (Stoll and Fink 1996, 1998). What we don't get, however (except in passing as we saw earlier with Stoll and Fink's work), are ways in which these various models of culture relate to middle class schools and working class schools, white schools and minority/indigenous schools and so on. Hargreaves (1995: 38) probably comes as close as any improver to the problem when he says that 'whilst there is a general question of whether school effectiveness correlates with school culture, there is an equally important question of whether some cultures are more effective with certain kinds of teacher and certain kind of student'.

This is not to argue that the various attempts by improvers to sum up different types of school and teacher culture might not be useful in some respects. However, they fail to consider the impact of students and their cultures, either individually or collectively, on school organization and management and instruction. As a result they do not acknowledge the reciprocal, negotiated nature of schooling and therefore tend to attribute school processes to staff rather than students. Hargreaves (1995) recognizes the problem when he points out that in recent times staff cultures have been highlighted rather than student cultures, as in earlier research. He omits to point out that discussion of class was also lost in this shift in emphasis. In response to Schein's argument, often cited by Hopkins, that possibly 'the only thing of real importance that leaders do is create and manage culture' (Schein 1985: 2), I would add the important rider that school leaders will have to respond to powerful student cultures also.

Research support for the politics of polarization and blame

Given that research can help to create climates of opinion which may either underpin or undermine particular policy directions, the question of whether the improvement literature provides research support for the neo-liberal and managerial agenda in education is an important one. Although none appear to provide the kind of fundamental critiques of the New Right to be found among researchers outside the E&I movement, the above examples suggest that perspectives taken by improvers do vary markedly. Writers like Barber seem to have embraced the New Right agenda in education. Reynolds (1996) is another who has argued that 'on balance, devolution to schools will be a positive development'. He claims that education policy research is 'full of enthusiasm for the positive results for devolution of power to schools' (p. 133), but in doing so he has completely ignored the considerable body of literature which has not viewed decentralization in such glowing terms (such as Bowe *et al.* 1992; Smyth 1993; Angus 1994).

At the other end of the spectrum, researchers like Stoll and Gray express much more concern about the politics of polarization and blame. Others whose work reflects similar concerns include Elmore *et al.* (1996), Newmann and associates (1996), Townsend (1997) and Myers and Goldstein (1998). Some of these are particularly worried about the co-option by policy makers of simplistic versions of their craft. Others are tapping into policy literatures which are more critical of reform.

Most frequently, however, improvement writers are located somewhere in the middle with Hopkins, Fullan and Stringfield – not so much supporting the agenda of the Right in their writings but not taking enough account of it either. It is often difficult to determine what they actually think about the politics of reform. They frequently seem to accept market-based arguments about the value of reform, or aspects of them, at face value and they usually acknowledge equity concerns only in passing. Often these problems occur together. For instance, Murphy (1991: 8) suggests on the one hand, 'Perhaps for the first time in our history, economic forces and equity issues, or quality and equity values/goals, are being conjoined in the service of improved education for all students.' On the other hand, buried near the back of his book, he provides a discussion of the 'potential disequalising effects' of restructuring (p. 77).

Improvers also support the politics of polarization and blame when they emphasize the most optimistic readings of their findings over more cautious ones which better reflect what is generally known about the pervasive impact of class on achievement. This problem can be seen to a greater or lesser extent in almost all of the work above and also mars a number of otherwise more critical accounts. The School Restructuring Study (Newmann and associates 1996) is one such study which gives its findings an excessively optimistic gloss. It claims that 'in spite of much scepticism and many obstacles, American public schools are capable of sophisticated teaching that produces achievement of high quality for students *regardless of social background* (my emphasis) . . .' (p. 14). However this bold claim, based on HLM analysis, is hard to square with some of the authors' other arguments. For instance, Newmann puts the success or otherwise of authentic pedagogy down to two factors – an emphasis on 'intellectual quality' and 'strong professional community'. These in turn are seen to depend on a variety of 'cultural' (i.e. organizational/ pedagogical) and 'structural' (i.e. organizational) conditions. What isn't at all clear, however, is how any of these can be sustained in the face of the cumulative constraints on working class schools.[2]

Improvers further support the politics of polarization and blame when they assume that special initiatives will be carried out on a wider basis. When the political will to provide funding on a broader basis is not forthcoming, school reform efforts too often turn out like fireflies, 'flickering brightly but soon fading' (Tyack and Cuban 1995). For instance, Slavin's 'Success for All' and 'Roots and Wings' programmes have probably succeeded because of the huge input of resources, including individual tutoring, they have brought to schools (Slavin 1996). It seems unlikely, however, that governments would be willing to provide the same level of resourcing on more generalized basis. Slavin (1996: 261–2) also discusses his 'Vision 2020' plan to create a school system in which schools would be 'routinely able to place a high floor under the achievement of all students while ensuring that all meet their full potential'. He acknowledges that such a plan would require district, state and national support but he does not discuss the likelihood or otherwise of this being forthcoming.

Part of the problem is that school improvers – American writers in particular – often seem to write for an audience of potential funders where the rhetoric is one of success rather than a possible lack of it. We should not underestimate the pressure on improvers to talk up the outcomes of their programmes in order to get a share of the private or state funding which is available for new initiatives. Timeframes can also become entirely unrealistic when politicians want results within electoral cycles. Yet when reforms aim at basic institutional changes or the eradication of deep social injustices, the appropriate period for evaluation may be a generation or more (Tyack and Cuban 1995). And even that may be being optimistic!

It is also often difficult to know how much any of what researchers say or do has an impact on policy because the 'takeup' of research by policy makers is rarely obvious. Nevertheless, as we saw with Ofsted and ERO in the last chapter, there are examples where policy makers on the Right *have* clearly used the arguments of improvement writers for their own ends.

Direct involvement in the politics of polarization and blame

Barber's involvement in the closure of Hackney Downs School and his secondment to head the DfEE Standards and Effectiveness unit raises the important issue of the propriety of improvers becoming heavily involved in implementing the agendas of neo-liberal/managerial governments. There are numerous examples of improvers – and E&I proponents generally – becoming caught up in New Right political initiatives around the globe. To give a couple of New Zealand examples, Ramsay (New Zealand's representative on the editorial board of *School Effectiveness and School Improvement*) was a member of the Picot taskforce which became the vehicle for introducing markets and managerialism into New Zealand schools (Taskforce to Review Education Administration 1988). Edwards, another prominent New Zealand improver, was the academic member of the government taskforce which recently reviewed the Education Review Office and recommended little change (State Services Commission 1997).

That E&I researchers are asked to take up such roles is unsurprising because their problem-solving approaches are likely to appeal to policy makers in Right-wing governments. No doubt many would respond that they should be involved in creating public policy. For instance, Sammons and Reynolds argue in response to Elliott's (1996) criticism of this kind of political involvement:

> We are very much in favour of research attempting to influence policy, in line with the expressed policy of the British Educational Research Association, and we believe that the virtue of research needs to be asserted and that educational researchers have a 'social responsibility' to disseminate their findings to a wide audience . . .
>
> (Sammons and Reynolds 1997: 125)

They go on to absolve themselves of the outcome of their involvement by arguing that in any case 'political expediency' has often taken precedence over their advice (*ibid.*). This is probably quite correct and it is not hard to have sympathy for researchers whose good intentions are abused when they move into the political arena. Nevertheless, even where researchers argue in hindsight that their involvement has had only a partial influence on policy, it has also already given that policy, including unsupported aspects, status and legitimacy. The current environment is one in which there are certainly status and financial rewards to be gained by researchers prepared to support neo-liberal and managerial initiatives. Nevertheless, if E&I proponents have any concern with just educational provision, such activity has to remain highly problematic, despite protests to the contrary.

 **11**

Conclusion: let's be realistic!

Two general conclusions can be drawn from the Wellington study. One is that while schools may make *some* difference to student achievement, this is likely to be smaller than typically assumed by E&I literature because of the way school mix affects school processes. A second conclusion must be the consequent need to re-emphasize the social limits of school reform in research, policy and practice. These views may seem rather discouraging when compared to the upbeat tenor of the E&I literature. Yet if we are honest, the findings of the Wellington study will serve to remind us that school reform has frequently failed in the past because educators and policy makers have been reluctant to acknowledge the deep-seated nature of many educational problems and too ready to accept partial and inadequate answers.

At one level this lack of caution may be due to the common belief that there must be a ready solution for every problem. Sarason has noted:

> Too many people have to believe that in the societal arena we are dealing with problems which have 'solutions' in the sense that four divided by two is a solution. In that arena we are always dealing with problems we have to solve again and again. That fact is hard for the American psyche to take because we have been schooled to believe that with a deep and sincere national resolve, plus the right amount of money and resources, no problem is intractable, no problem is unamenable to foreseeable eradication.
>
> (Sarason 1995: 87)

We should also bear in mind that being optimistic about school reform may also have helped avoid dealing with tough questions about the impact on education of social inequalities of power and resources. Tyack and Cuban argue:

[T]he utopian tradition of social reform through schooling has often diverted attention from more costly, politically controversial and difficult societal reforms. It's easier to provide vocational education than to remedy inequities in employment and gross disparities in wealth and income.

(Tyack and Cuban 1995: 3–4)

It is precisely because the issue of school mix highlights powerful social inequalities in the provision of schooling that developing a realistic response will not be easy. For policy makers it will mean grappling with the possibility that technical solutions will never be enough, that schools and teachers in low-SES settings may only be held partly responsible for addressing poor achievement, and that educational quality in low-SES settings will not be able to be substantially improved without redistributive policies of various kinds. For teachers and school leaders in low-SES schools, a more realistic view of the social limits of reform could provide welcome defence against the politics of blame but it also imposes a difficult balancing act. While understanding that there are powerful constraints on the ability of their schools to be 'just as good' as those more advantaged, teachers still need to strive to do their best by the students in their care. Finally, for families and communities it will mean dealing with the issue of why, on the grounds of justice and equity, it may not be acceptable to educate our children in highly segregated school settings.

Despite these problems, there are at least three good reasons for moving towards a more realistic position on school mix and the social limits of reform. Most important is the pressing need to improve the lot of students in low-SES schools. Current market-led reforms appear to be largely bankrupt when it comes to this task – indeed the evidence points to devolution, choice and tough forms of accountability only making matters worse by polarizing school intakes and school quality. A second concern must be that the politics of blame are also unfair on teachers and school leaders in low-SES schools. What Tomlinson (1997) refers to as the 'blood sport' of hunting down failing low-SES schools and their staff appears too often a shameful case of punishing the victim. A third reason for being more realistic is that over-optimism will be a recipe for further public disillusionment about state-funded education. Tyack and Cuban (1995: 132) ask, 'What will happen to public confidence in leaders – and in public schools – when . . . impossible goals are *not* met in the millennial year 2000?' One flippant answer might be that the target date for 'failure free' schooling will simply be moved back a decade or two, as with Slavin's (1996) 'Vision 2020'. But how long can unrealistic policies be pursued without losing the support of policy makers, educators, parents and the general public entirely?

No easy answers

In seeking solutions to the problems caused by school mix, it would be easy to replace one set of unrealistic policy goals with another. To begin with, class-based resistance to measures designed to bring about greater equality from families advantaged by current policies should not be underestimated. In practice in an unequal society, most people probably want their own children to compete successfully for an advantaged social and economic position even if they claim they want to be fair to all children. This problem will be especially important if, as I have argued, the school mix effect represents something of a zero-sum rather than a win–win situation as is often portrayed.

This class-based resistance means only the collective power of the state could bring about real change by acting to temper the aspirations of the powerful and protect those who are less influential and well-resourced. However, even some on the Left have questioned whether state intervention is desirable any longer. For instance Hatcher (1996: 55) warns against a 'social democratic statist model which serves fatally to depoliticise and demobilise those popular energies which alone are capable of effectively challenging the reproduction of social class inequality in education'. Hatcher is right on many educational issues, but when it comes to reducing between-school segregation it is difficult to see how strong state intervention can be avoided. Improving the position of those who are currently disadvantaged will inevitably reduce opportunities for those who are currently favoured.

Yet strong intervention in education on the grounds of reducing inequality is currently unlikely because governments on the Right are so hostile to such equity measures. Many governments around the world are instead hell-bent on redefining and reducing their educational responsibilities, often as a prelude to privatizing them, at least partially. Two decades of this kind of activity leads Whitty *et al.* (1998) to question whether state intervention remains feasible even if it is desirable. This remains to be seen. All hope should not be lost while the electorate retains some democratic power and in many instances a growing ability to question the rhetoric of the Right. At the same time there is no possibility of any simple return to the past. Marginson is correct when he argues that 'the road to something better must pass through the marketised systems and will be affected by their evolution and implosion' (1997: 280).

We also need to remember that education alone will not hold all the answers. As Anyon has argued in the American context:

> The structural basis for failure in inner city schools – and the failure of educational reform there – is political, economic and cultural, and must be changed before meaningful school improvement projects can be successfully implemented. Thus, I think the only solution to educational resignation and failure in the inner city is the ultimate elimination of poverty and racial degradation.
>
> (Anyon 1995: 8)

Effective educational reform therefore needs to take place in conjunction with other redistributive policies to address social and economic inequality through taxation, social welfare, employment, health and housing policies. But in all of these areas the state is again under attack from the pervasive ideologies of the Right. In New Zealand, for instance, poverty has become redefined as 'welfare dependency', unemployment signals a 'flexible labour market', health for the poor has become a matter of waiting lists and government-provided housing has either been sold off or is rented at market rates.

All of this implies that, while it is possible to suggest a number of solutions to the problems created by school mix, they will often not be tenable in today's political climate. Nevertheless long-term solutions are important to consider because they point to what would be required to make a difference if it did become politically feasible. In a sense such goals represent the inverse of what is currently on offer from E&I researchers and policy makers. While that tends to be ideologically acceptable to the Right but contextually blinkered, what is offered below is contextually more realistic but unlikely to find much favour on the Right.

Long-term solutions

Reducing SES segregation

The key solution to the effects of school mix will be to reduce between-school social class segregation. This is essential because the negotiated nature of school processes means that many of the advantageous processes of middle class schools would be impossible to replicate in working class schools without actually changing the mix of the schools. These include reference group processes and the richer environment of classroom questioning and discussion generated within middle class classrooms. Intervention in the market to reduce the SES segregation of school intakes would have the effect of both sharing the problems of poverty more evenly around schools and moving middle class cultural and economic resources into (presently) low-SES schools. Thus Whitty *et al.* (1998: 131) suggest that 'instead of transposing organisational characteristics, one might think about transposing some of the socioeconomic features of "successful" schools'.

The question is how best to reduce SES segregation. One way would be to lessen the effects of residential segregation ('selection by mortgage') either through policies which try to 'break rather than strengthen the relationships between schools and their communities' (*ibid.*) or, in new housing areas, by attempts to reduce residential segregation through town planning (Benn 1997). However, either approach would require reconsidering the use of residential segregation as the basis of school enrolment. For instance, Hirsch (1997: 164) points to the unthinking acceptance in Britain of the primacy of residence in allocating school places. He asks, 'Where there is competition for access to school places, must we accept a situation where residential elites form through the clustering of families around the best schools, reinforced by the common judgement by parents of schools with privileged intakes to be, prima facie, "good"?' In the USA where issues of class and ethnicity are powerfully linked, it would also be necessary to move past the simple judgement that desegregation failed, and instead reconsider the reasons why it may have failed as well its successes (Orfield *et al.* 1996).

One way to reduce selection by mortgage would be to use zoning creatively to ensure that schools have a reasonable mix of students. As the history of USA desegregation efforts illustrate, this will work more effectively in smaller urban areas where differing SES groups live closer to each other. School places could also be put to the ballot. This was done in New Zealand when choice was first introduced and our evidence suggests that, even though the random effects of balloting only applied to 'out of zone' enrolments, it was able to cut through the effects of residential segregation and create schools which were less segregated than the neighbourhoods they drew from (Waslander and Thrupp 1995).

Another way to reduce SES segregation would be to prevent high-SES schools from enrolling only desirable, high-SES students who have been 'cream skimmed' from less prestigious schools. In a sense schools can hardly be blamed for such 'social cleansing' when high-SES students enhance their positional value, but it does not help to reduce SES segregation and its effects. A voucher scheme in which vouchers have a greater value for disadvantaged students has sometimes been mooted as a solution to this issue (Moe 1995). However, there would clearly be a limit to the number of working class students that high-SES schools would consider taking before they began to lose positional advantage. The power to accept or decline students therefore needs to be taken out of the hands of individual schools and given over to a more impartial process such as the balloting or zoning approaches mentioned above. Benn (1997) suggests that admissions systems for all schools need to be based on the same principle and overseen by the same democratic process for all schools alike, accountable to the community as a whole.

A third approach to reducing segregation would be to try to make the process of choice more equitable by providing public transport for school children or giving all parents more information about the available schools (Adler 1993). However, it is hard to see how such measures would prevent the systematic 'cooling out' of the aspirations of working class parents (Hughes *et al.* 1999). A further, important, possibility may be a 'controlled choice' approach which offers parents some choice of school while also intervening in the process of choice to ensure that school intakes are as well balanced as possible. Although this might seem like a case of having one's cake and eating it, the idea of balancing school intakes is not entirely incompatible with the notion of choice. This kind of intervention would allow (and indeed require) parents to choose from a small group of specified schools (including provision for single sex, coeducational, religious schooling and so on) but would intervene in the choice process to prevent SES segregation.

Ironically, asking all parents to choose from a limited number of schools but intervening to provide some balance to their intakes may actually work to reduce the significance of choice in three ways. First, by ensuring that all schools have reasonably mixed intakes, parents may be less concerned about the school their child ends up attending. As Hirsch (1997: 164) argues, 'admissions policies that encourage a mixing of abilities, classes and races might ultimately help to ensure that more preferences are met by reducing the perceived differences among schools based on their intakes'. Second, because their child could end up in any one of several schools, parents would also have more interest in making sure that all local schools are viable and well resourced. Walford (1997: 63) talks about 'harnessing the legitimate desires of those parents who are concerned about the schooling of their own children, such that they demand high quality education for all children and not just their own'. Third, intervening in school intakes will also help school staff to feel that they are getting a fairer deal. Thus Benn points out:

> Once schools and colleges . . . are confident that polarisation is being checked and that equity in operations can be demonstrated to them in practice, they will gain that confidence which comes from the assurance that they have the best there is and can look upon their area and its intake as being just as capable of doing well as any other.
>
> (Benn 1997: 129)

A controlled choice scheme has operated in Boston where, as Walford (1994: 159) notes, it has been at least partly successful: 'it is still very limited in its overall effect, but for most children it probably represents a move towards greater equity by using a method which is more acceptable to most groups'. However, Walford also warns that middle class resistance to the Boston scheme highlights 'the considerable difficulties inherent in trying to bring about equity' (*ibid.*). The problem is that many parents will not be content with a similar education to everyone else and will still often employ any means, legal or otherwise, to provide positional advantage for their child.

A quite different kind of challenge to reducing SES segregation will come from those who see it threatening moves towards greater ethnic autonomy in education, either through regular schools which have become dominated by a minority ethnic group as a result of white flight (such as all-black ghetto schools in the USA) or through schools which have been specifically set up to foster a particular minority or indigenous language and culture (such as New Zealand's Kura Kaupapa Maori). These need to be seen as quite different situations – one is autonomy by default, the other autonomy by choice.

In the first instance, it is because ethnic divisions tend to run along class lines that efforts to reduce SES segregation in regular school systems would bring together students from dominant and minority ethnic cultures. That this could have damaging assimilatory effects is accepted but it also under-estimates the importance of social class alongside ethnicity in schooling. At the heart of this issue is the problem of competing paradigms. Much of the academic discourse around ethnicity in education does not sufficiently acknowledge the existence of social class and vice versa (Aronowitz 1997). It seems clear however that the costs or benefits of segregation/autonomy cannot be adequately explored without consideration of both.

The issues have been well captured in the USA in an exchange in *Educational Theory* between Foster (1993) and Kozol (1993). Foster argues that the ideology underlying integration policies

> unwittingly reinforces the inherently racist, classist belief, one rejected by a large segment of the Black community, that poor Black children are incapable of excelling academically unless they are sitting next to more advantaged white children.
>
> (Foster 1993: 32)

Yet Kozol responds that Foster 'passes by very quickly, as if it were a marginal point, the fact that segregated schools have tended to be unequal schools' (Kozol 1993: 60). His book *Savage Inequalities* (Kozol 1991, the subject of the above exchange) makes it clear that white flight in the USA is not only a matter of ethnicity, it also represents middle class families avoiding working class schools and withdrawing resources from them. Orfield *et al.* take the same view:

> In contemporary debates, desegregation plans are often ridiculed as reflecting a belief that there is 'something magic about sitting next to whites'. In fact, however, a student moving from a segregated African American or Latino school to a white school is usually moving from a school with concentrated poverty with many social and educational shortcomings to a school with fewer burdens and better resources to prepare students for college or jobs . . . Black disenchantment is most likely when the desegregation plan is not able to provide access to strong middle class schools for black children, a particular problem in plans in older central cities with few remaining middle class families . . .
>
> (Orfield *et al.* 1996: 54)

In New Zealand many Maori educators also stress that because a regular school is predominantly Maori as a result of white flight, this doesn't automatically make it a 'bad' school. Nevertheless our Smithfield research suggested that high-SES Maori and Pacific Islands families are just as likely to avoid low-SES, predominantly Maori and Pacific Islands schools as Pakeha/European families. We concluded that 'choice of non-local school is primarily dependent on the socioeconomic background of students with the relatively better off families, regardless of ethnicity, sending their children out of local schools' (Waslander and Thrupp 1995: 8–9).

The Wellington study helps to explain why some Maori parents might want to keep their children out of low-SES schools in the regular school system even if it means putting them into predominantly Pakeha schools. While none of the 13 students selected for the study were Maori, it is hard to see why Maori students would not have been similarly affected. In particular, there was little evidence that Maori students were being advantaged by being at Tui College despite an outward appearance of having more emphasis on things Maori – more Maori staff, larger bilingual and Taha Maori programmes and so on.[1] On the other hand, the study pointed to important advantages for Maori students at the middle class schools over those who attended Tui College. For instance, the middle class schools often had stronger Maori language programmes than Tui College despite having fewer Maori staff, classes or students.

This is where the distinction between autonomy by default and autonomy by choice is important. Perhaps it is a perfectly reasonable position for indigenous and minority groups to reject the former but support the latter. For instance, many Maori see Kura Kaupapa Maori as the preferred option for young Maori. But surely if that is not feasible or not wanted, the next best thing would be a high-quality education in a regular school. The Wellington study suggests that for a variety of reasons this will be less likely to occur in low-SES schools. As a result, despite assimilatory effects, some of which may be able to be addressed by thoughtful policies and practices at the school level, Maori and other indigenous and minority groups are generally likely to benefit from policies which reduce segregation in regular school settings.

When it comes to autonomy by choice there are different issues to consider. The Wellington study suggests that academic success will be more likely in middle class contexts. This raises important questions about the success of low-SES autonomous schools for ethnic minorities. Will school mix have an effect in these schools as well and if so, how much? Will the advantages which apparently accrue to minority students from being in such schools be able to outweigh the disadvantages of being schooled in a low-SES setting? If the advantages of ethnic autonomy do not outweigh the disadvantages of a low-SES mix, are minority or indigenous students in low-SES autonomous schools being set up to fail like their counterparts in low-SES schools in the regular school system? Finally, if autonomous schools for ethnic minorities replicate the class segregation of the mainstream system because of unequal resourcing, will this disparity be acceptable to members of ethnic minority groups? Or will it simply replace one form of injustice with another?

This debate also raises the question of the role and funding of private schools in a pluralistic society. In this matter it is necessary to be both tolerant and uncompromising. While, within reason, any religious or ethnic groups *should* be entitled to set up their own school, the growth of SES elites needs to be discouraged regardless of any claim to 'special character'. State funding of private schools should be very much tied to the SES characteristics of their intakes, with high-SES private schools receiving no funding. This is because while it is sometimes argued that such schools take pressure off the public school system, they also deprive it of cultural and financial resources. Unfortunately the trend in New Zealand and elsewhere has been towards increasing the state funding of high-SES private schools as part of the growing privatization of education in general.

Resourcing schools

A measure to address the impact of school mix which would not threaten middle class interests so directly as reducing segregation would be to provide substantial additional resources to low-SES schools. Yet it is commonly argued by neo-liberals that giving more resources to low-SES schools is not the answer. For instance, Chubb and Moe (1990: 194) argue, 'In our view the performance problems of the public schools have little or nothing to do with inadequate funding and they cannot be corrected by digging deeper into the public purse.' However, Kozol (1991) rightly points out that many of those who make this claim send their own children to highly resourced schools. His account and many others already mentioned make it difficult to see how considerably lower student–teacher ratios along with more guidance and management staff and funding could not make some difference to the achievement of students in low-SES school settings. Greatly increased staffing seems to have sometimes been involved in attempts to turn around English 'special measures' schools (e.g. Whatford 1998).

There may also be a case for paying teachers and principals more in low-SES schools as well as increasing their time for preparation and professional development and reducing contact time with students. This would not only provide more incentive to teach in such schools but also recognize that teaching there is more demanding and stressful. While there is a risk this kind of measure will have a divisive effect on the teaching workforce, it is also the case that recent calls to re-empower teachers often overlook the very different realities faced by teachers in high- and low-SES settings (e.g. Hargreaves 1997b). Just as high-SES schools have been insulated from the worst effects of educational markets, so to some extent have their teachers. The real crisis is likely to be amongst those teaching in low-SES settings who have carried a disproportionate share of the fallout from reform.

It is imperative that, if low-SES schools are to be assisted, *substantial* additional resources must be provided. Too often additional resources – money, time, materials – provided to low-SES schools constitute what one New Zealand principal has described as 'real Oliver Twist stuff: they put a bit in the bottom of my bowl and I've got to be grateful for that, but, fair go, it is not a meal' (Hubbard 1995: 22). It is also important that improved resourcing not be seen as a temporary measure or involve heavy reporting demands – such approaches tend to be counterproductive when the aim is to take pressure off schools. Nor should the supply of resources be subject to proof of outcomes because the gains made will often be very difficult to quantify in the short term. Indeed an argument can be made that irrespective of whether achievement gains become evident, resources to low-SES schools need to be increased simply because they should be decent and safe places for students to come to each day (Noddings 1993).

The curriculum

Because of the negotiated nature of teaching, reducing SES segregation would itself have an important effect on the kind of curriculum teachers offer in schools. Additional resources will also help, but there are further curriculum issues which will also need to be addressed to overcome further the social limits of schooling. At an immediate level, policies which encourage teachers to move freely between schools (for instance by higher pay and guarantees of stable employment at lower SES schools) would at least help to give all students the opportunity to be taught by staff who have familiarity with teaching an academic exam-oriented curriculum. 'Mixed ability' classes and teaching methods also need to be encouraged over tracking, particularly at a time when within-school differentiation appears to be becoming more popular as a means of marketing lower SES schools to middle class parents.

All of this also needs to be coupled with approaches which reduce conflict between students from very different backgrounds as well as addressing the social and academic concerns and difficulties of students (of whatever class or ethnic group) who find themselves in a minority situation as a result of attempts to address school mix (Brantlinger 1993; Wells 1996). Those who have genuinely tried to work within the spirit of comprehensivization or desegregation will be able to share a host of experience about what does and does not work (Clarke 1997; Fine *et al.* 1997).

These approaches will be useful but will do little to resolve the fundamental tensions between working class students and an academic curriculum which reflects mostly white, middle class culture. Hatcher suggests that

> the comprehensive principle needs to be reaffirmed. But on its own that is not enough. Thirty years of experience of comprehensive schools have demonstrated that they continue, as do primary schools, to be sites of social reproduction of inequality.
>
> (Hatcher 1996: 52)

Since comprehensivization has only ever been partial and limited, this is perhaps a little unfair. However, Hatcher is right to call for a curriculum which would reflect the culture of all groups in society rather than just that of the dominant – Connell (1994) refers to this as 'curricular justice'.

Fairer methods of ensuring accountability

Governments also need to take a more balanced policy approach than is usual at present to assessing school performance and making them accountable. For even when students' individual characteristics are taken into account in a value-added analysis, all schools should still not be expected to perform at the same level unless the contextual effects of their group characteristics are also taken into account. Rather, good policy will acknowledge that schools can be more or less effective, but will also be realistic about ways in which the nature of student intakes and related resource disparities and market positioning can create important constraints and possibilities. This policy would need to move away from the approaches signalled in Chapter 9 and draw on the kind of contextualized research discussed below which could allow policy makers to gain a more realistic view of what the goals should be and where performance might be lifted. Unfortunately, at a time when policy makers appear reluctant to discard even the use of raw exam results (Gray 1997) and tend to favour the

'rigorous' findings of quantitative research, the chances of differential constraints related to SES being taken properly into account seem slim. To do so
would bring unwelcome complexity to models of the educational marketplace.

Challenging the politics of polarization and blame

For political reasons none of the preceding solutions are likely to come about
in a hurry or perhaps even in the foreseeable future. However, Marginson
(1997: 281) points out that '[t]he question of who benefits from markets can
be opened for scrutiny, well before the breakdown of market organisation has
been reached'. This possibility highlights the importance of developing a
counter-ideological critique of the politics of polarization and blame as a
more immediate response to the problem of school mix. The challenge must
be to present alternative contextual perspectives wherever possible. Researchers and teacher educators as well as concerned individuals and groups in and
beyond schools can do useful work here.

Research

In so far as E&I research fails to acknowledge adequately the social and
political context of schooling, it clearly remains as much a part of the problem
as of any solution. This has been an important message of this book and an
issue which is also well canvassed by Slee *et al.* (1998). A general lesson to be
learnt from this literature is the critical importance of the politics of research.
Today's E&I researchers need to consider the worst possible outcomes of their
work and act accordingly. In some cases this may involve turning down
funding for projects which are tied to potentially dubious ends. Too often
researchers appear to have expected a sympathetic response from policy
makers. At present this is probably a good recipe for supporting the politics of
polarization and blame. Researchers like Tomlinson (1997) who have been
involved in E&I research in the past but who have shifted position in response
to today's political climate deserve much respect.

We also clearly need more research which takes better account of school
mix and educational markets. Lauder *et al.* (1998: 63) propose a contextual
model of 'effective schools' research which would 'be concerned with the link
between capacities, potentials and limits within specific social contexts and
within specific positions within an educational market'. Research within the
contextual model would ask four questions: 'what impact does a school's
community and intake have on its performance; what impact does the
educational market have on its performance; under what conditions could
schools perform better, and how are we to develop contextual criteria for
holding schools accountable?' (*ibid.*).

As Lauder *et al.* go on to point out, this approach would also be more open
theoretically and methodologically than current SER. Rather than simply

assuming that schools can mediate external factors, research within the contextual model would seek to document the conditions under which school processes may or may not be 'relatively autonomous' (i.e. able to be independent of their social and political context). A contextual model of research would therefore put aside the E&I literature's premise that schools 'can make a difference' and begin to take seriously the possibility that in important ways they may not be able to. Genuine openness to qualitative research approaches and the use of social theory is also required.

A particular need will be to recentre social class in E&I research. There is enough evidence from this and other studies to illustrate the importance of social class and the limitations of generic models when considering E&I matters. However, recentring class has to be a challenge taken up not only by E&I researchers but by other educational researchers as well. While post-modernist and post-structuralist theories have offered numerous insights over the past two decades they have also led to the wholesale neglect of class. As a result, Apple (1996: 140) notes that 'while a focus on identity politics is growing, it is much harder to find work on the best of recent theories of class'. Yet as Apple has also recently argued, class has not gone away and it would be a serious error to deny its power because it can't explain everything (Apple 1997). Fresh theorizing about what social class has come to mean today is therefore required, along with supporting empirical research.

Teacher education

Earlier it was noted that many practitioners do not challenge the politics of polarization and blame. This is probably true also of many teacher educators, even those with reservations about the growth of neo-liberalism and mana-gerialism in education. The rather too benign view of Ofsted inspections offered by Hackett (1996) is just one example of this too-ready acceptance. It returns us to the issue that the professional discourses of educators have rarely given much weight to socioeconomic differences between schools.

Teacher educators, drawing on contextualized research, can help their students to understand what teachers may or may not reasonably be held responsible for in various school settings. This cannot be left only to those who teach the sociology or politics of education, particularly at a time when these areas of study have often been removed from teacher education courses or are under threat. Indeed, since an awareness of the social limits of reform will help to deflect the politics of blame, it might prove to be one of the most crucial understandings teacher education students carry away from their training.

At the same time, finding the right balance in discussion of the politics of blame will require much sensitivity. On the one hand it is important to avoid a deficit approach. On the other, students need to understand there *are* external social and political factors which impinge unequally on schools and which are rarely acknowledged by those committed to markets in education. Students have to realize that the reluctance of teachers to be judgemental about student backgrounds is often a good thing but may also sometimes be taken advantage of for political ends. A good way to approach this will be to analyse the debates which have occurred around the closure of so-called failing schools such as Hackney Downs.

Teachers and school leaders

Teachers and school leaders must also publicly reject the politics of polarization and blame. Those in high-SES schools can do this whenever they are honest in their public statements about the way in which their schools gain advantage from their high-SES intakes. It is always refreshing to hear the headteachers or principals of middle class schools publicly comment, as they occasionally do, that 'yes, our students did do well in such and such an exam/ scholarship/competition but you would expect that with our intake'. In this way teachers and school leaders at advantaged schools can refuse to buy into the view that less popular schools are 'bad' schools. They can also help by building co-operative rather than competitive relationships with other schools, by ensuring that their own practices are the least selective or exclusionary possible, as well as by supporting any moves to provide additional resources to schools which need them most. All easier said than done perhaps, particularly when community preferences are so powerful, but the ability of practising teachers and school leaders to influence community opinion is often considerable.

In low-SES schools, teachers and principals may be able to do less about the politics of polarization and blame except to strive to do their best by the students in their schools. Keeping a record of various day-to-day problems and the successful and less successful efforts of staff to overcome them may help to retain a balance between accepting powerful limitations on change and doing the best possible job. It could also supply evidence to counter claims of ineffectiveness. Staff in low-SES schools can take heart from knowing that what they are doing is of genuine importance, and that they are probably doing it as well as can reasonably be expected given the circumstances. They should not be afraid at times to make good use of the gulf between official policy and classroom practice in the service of their students. For instance, when schools are often being asked to impose inappropriate or damaging curriculum or assessment innovations, paying only lip service to what is required may be entirely justifiable.

Those in low-SES settings who want to be 'just as good' as middle class schools may perceive this as a 'negative' or 'defeatist' approach. Their own intentions, like that of the E&I movement, are often admirable, but it must be realized that over-optimism at the school level will also have its costs. Not only is it a recipe for personal disillusionment, but it will prevent careful analysis of problems, lead to a poor return on the expenditure of staff energies and help to feed the politics of blame. It can also lead to low-SES schools and school districts being run by what Orfield *et al.* (1996) refer to as a 'well paid parade of illusionists'. Similarly, teachers and school leaders should resist the urge to draw inspiration from media accounts of heroic teachers and principals winning against the odds in 'tough' schools. Closer inspection invariably finds the reality is not as impressive as the story. Test scores turn out to be improved but still low. Impoverished suburbs turn out to be gentrifying in a way that has brought a quite different school intake.

Parents and communities

It would be neither reasonable nor realistic to ask middle class families to exercise individual responsibility for reducing SES segregation by moving their children from very high- to very low-SES schools to reduce SES segregation. In practice, however, many choice decisions faced by middle class parents are not of the magnitude of having to choose between high- and low-SES schools: they are about choosing between very high-SES schools and somewhat more mixed schools. Given this, some middle class parents may think twice about trying to get their children into the most socially elite schools they reasonably can. But when it comes to the crunch most probably won't.

What does need to occur in any case is more public debate about the social costs of a schooling system which is highly segregated. This could help to create a climate of public opinion which might support the state acting to balance school intakes in a way that would mean there was less at stake for individual middle class families because so many others would be similarly affected. For this to occur we need to move to a position where the implications of school mix are better understood. In order to exert pressure for change, working class families need to be aware that while low-SES schools may not be as good at promoting academic achievement, this is not so much a social judgement on their own lives as a reflection of the class bias of schooling. On the other hand, middle class families need to acknowledge that school choice is not value-free: enrolling one's own child in a high-SES school has direct implications for the schooling and subsequent life chances experienced by other children from less advantaged families who attend the low-SES schools which this action creates.

Final thoughts

Investigation of school mix highlights yet another way in which middle class families, wittingly or unwittingly, gain advantage in education at the expense of the poor. It provides further evidence for the market as a class strategy. At the same time a belief expressed by Dewey almost a century ago remains as salient at ever. '[W]hat the best and wisest parent wants for his [sic] own child', he suggested, 'that must the community want for all its children. Any other ideal for our schools is narrow and unlovely: acted upon, it destroys our democracy' (Dewey 1902: 3). The last part of this argument reminds us that the effects of school mix will have costs for our whole society, not just the poor. As Connell (1993: 15) puts it, 'If the school system is dealing unjustly with some of its pupils, they are not the only ones to suffer . . . An education which privileges one child over another is giving the privileged child a corrupted education, even as it gives him or her a social or economic advantage.'

Nevertheless the most pressing need is to reconsider the problems of low-SES schools like Tui College and the students they serve. Even if they are difficult to address, the problems of such schools will not simply disappear. If anything, they will become more widespread if school intakes become further polarized as a result of educational markets. Unless considered and addressed, the impact of school mix will also continue to undermine even our best attempts at school reform. The educational and social prospects are truly alarming. With such a lot at stake, more than ever, we need to be realistic.

Notes

Chapter 1   Introduction: the social limits of reform

1 See Levin 1997; Marginson 1997; Taylor *et al.* 1997; Ball 1998a; Whitty *et al.* 1998; Hughes *et al.* 1999.
2 See for instance Waslander *et al.* 1994; Robertson 1998.

Chapter 2   School effectiveness research and the enduring problem of school mix

1 Meyer 1970; Jencks *et al.* 1972; Nelson 1972; Bain and Anderson 1974; Alexander and Eckland 1975; Alwin and Otto 1977.
2 Bowles and Levin 1968; Smith 1972.
3 For the controversy stemming from Sewell and Armer's study see the October 1966 issue of *American Sociological Review,* and for Hauser see Barton (1970).
4 Numerous reviews of SER are available as they constitute much of the literature in this field. See for instance Murphy 1992; Reynolds 1992; Reynolds *et al.* 1996; Stoll and Fink 1996; Stringfield and Herman 1996.
5 With the rise of the school improvement movement notions of school ethos or climate have been overtaken by equally limited notions of 'school culture'. See Chapter 10.
6 See also Ralph and Fennessey 1983; Rowan *et al.* 1983.
7 E.g. Lee and Smith 1995. See also the discussion of Stringfield's school improvement claims in Chapter 10.
8 See for instance Summers and Wolfe 1977; Henderson *et al.* 1978; Shavit and Williams 1985; Lauder and Hughes 1990b.
9 This study is also reported in Brown 1994; Brown *et al.* 1996b and Riddell *et al.* 1998.
10 For example, one school variable that might influence school mix could be the calibre of the school principal. If good principals attract a disproportionate number of pupils from relatively privileged families we have an instance of the first case. If schools with a disproportionate number of pupils from relatively privileged families

attract good principals because of their school mix we have an example of the second case. If schools in certain parts of a city attract disproportionate numbers of good principals and pupils from relatively privileged families because of their geographic location (such as high-cost residential areas) we have an example of the third case.

Chapter 3   Possible mechanisms and a research strategy

1 For more detail see Thrupp 1996.
2 For example Lacey 1970; Ball 1981; Lightfoot 1983; Brantlinger 1992, 1993.
3 Alexander *et al.* 1978; Gamoran 1987; Van Fossen *et al.* 1987.
4 Alexander and Eckland 1975; Hauser *et al.* 1976; Alwin and Otto 1977; Alexander *et al.* 1979.
5 For the next section see Hargreaves 1967; Lacey 1970; Rosenbaum 1976; Metz 1978; Ball 1981; Schwartz 1981; Burgess 1983; Finley 1984; Oakes 1985; Jones 1991. See also Gamoran and Berends 1987; Oakes *et al.* 1992, and Orfield *et al.* 1996: 67–8.
6 The latter are not necessarily petit bourgeois as in the New Zealand labour force there is a lot of horizontal movement between self-employment and being an employee.
7 Pakeha is the Maori term for a New Zealander of European descent.
8 See Thrupp (1996) for more details.
9 No private schools were in the Smithfield sample. However, it should be noted that in New Zealand high-SES state schools probably have similar SES mixes and reputations to those of many private schools.
10 Years 9 to 12 only and rounded to prevent identification of the schools.
11 Figures have been changed to prevent identification of the schools, but remain relative to one another.
12 School Certificate is the first national examination that most New Zealand students sit, usually in their Year 11 year, aged 15 or 16. Traditionally it has been seen as almost a rite of passage.

Chapter 4   Setting the scene

1 Ihaka (1993) has provided an interesting discussion of the appeal of Afro-American youth culture to young Maori in New Zealand. Schaer (1993) also provides a guide to various New Zealand youth cultures around the time the research was being carried out.

Chapter 5   It's not what you know . . .

1 The 'self identified' measure examined the mean SES of students identified by the matched students in various relationships to themselves in questionnaires. The 'reciprocated' measure examined the mean SES of other students who listed the matched students as their contacts in the student questionnaires. The 'observed' measure looked at the mean SES of all the students I observed to be working alongside the matched students in terms one and two. By examining different groups of questions in the student questionnaires it was also possible to look at the mean SES of a number of types of informal reference groups here. One was students who were considered main 'friends'. Another was any students that the matched

students usually saw out of class – before or after school, or at intervals, including those in sports teams or other extracurricular groups – I refer to these as 'schoolmates'. A further group was the students that the matched students usually worked with in their core classes – these I call 'seatmates'. It should be noted that in the case of seatmates and schoolmates, the measures are based on counting the total number of mentions in any category rather than just counting once the specific students they represent. By counting mentions rather than individuals, the measures can give appropriate weight to the number of class or school contexts in which the matched students came into contact with particular students. See Thrupp (1996) for more details.

2 Arguably the formal reference group closest to the students and therefore, in most cases, that most likely to determine the nature of the students available for informal reference groups. However Terry, Wendy and Polly all had many friends outside their own class.

3 These cases have been put together because mostly the data were missing, yet it was not clear whether this was because of unemployment or the question was unanswered.

4 Wilson and Dupuis (1992) have pointed to working class New Zealand girls often having to undertake a lot more domestic duties than middle class girls.

5 This should not be confused with evidence discussed later, that in Tui College reports criticisms were muted. At the middle class schools there were many more students who got very good comments but when teachers were not pleased, concerns were expressed more vigorously.

6 McRobbie (1978,1991) suggests a culture of femininity (getting a boyfriend, getting married) among working class girls which might be expected to be stronger in working class schools.

7 However, whereas the possibility of (some) sexual experience seemed to provide status for boys and girls alike at the middle class schools, this was not always the case at Tui College. Here claims to virginity openly volunteered mainly by Pacific Islands girls suggested they considered this more a social asset than a liability.

8 Some ethnic differences amongst the matched students' experiences are noted in the next, instructional chapter. However, one possible ethnic reference group difference noted was that Terry's Samoan identity did open up a network of informal contacts that was considerably larger than any of the Pakeha kids in any of the schools. For instance, he identified 28 students as schoolmates in term three. Many of these were in his culture group and because of this, were all ages and in many classes. Others were boys he played touch rugby and volleyball with.

9 In this sense at times they took most of the orientations suggested by Lees (1993) except for the anti-school, anti-work orientation.

Chapter 6   The negotiated curriculum

1 Practical subjects inevitably appear less demanding in conventional academic terms (such as literacy and numeracy), yet there are other important types of knowledge and skills being covered (such as aesthetics, graphicacy and so on). In an attempt to avoid this problem as far as possible, I compared subjects with like curriculum areas. At the same time, there *are* differences in the way 'practical' subjects are approached by schools – for instance with a greater or lesser emphasis on understanding concepts or on literacy or numeracy. In terms of assessing academic difficulty

then, it was this dimension of practical subjects that is of interest. For instance, we can surely say that the treatment of music in a class where the students are being taught how to read music is more academically demanding than one where students learn by rote. It was on this basis that practical classes were assessed in this study, albeit relative to similar kinds of classes.

2 For instance 70 per cent of the Year 9 intake were thought to be reading two or more years behind their age.

3 Slee (1995) points to the multi-causal nature of classroom disruption. The complexity of the issue is accepted, nevertheless the apparently class-related trends noted here seemed very pervasive.

4 Oakes *et al.* (1992) suggest that evidence of the merits or otherwise of co-operative learning strategies at the secondary school level is not well researched. The present study has suggested that a key determinant of success with groupwork will be the nature of group tasks relative to group characteristics: challenging enough to maintain student interest but straightforward enough for students to cope without teacher help.

5 This was done by converting teachers assessments into a numerical score from 1–5 (or in the case of 'suitability for own school' from 1–4) corresponding to the teacher judgement categories. These were then added and converted to a score out of 100 based on the highest score possible.

6 Integrated Studies combined English and Social Studies under one teacher for seven hours a week.

7 See Thrupp (1996) for more details.

Chapter 7   The art of the possible

1 This school had a major theft problem. Rooms were kept locked, even staff toilets.

2 Boards of Trustees – mostly made up of parents – were set up in 1989 as part of the move to self-managing schools in New Zealand. Although they have considerable power and responsibility, in practice they probably mostly defer to principals. See Wylie (1997) for a recent evaluation of this development.

3 By having vertical form classes within a system of houses, students stayed with the same form teacher and House head throughout their school careers so there was seen to be a better chance for staff to get to know and respond more quickly to students' pastoral needs.

4 Gordon (1993) also found that poor schools were charging lower activity fees and were only able to collect in lower proportions of these fees. Some working class New Zealand schools have given up trying to collect school fees.

5 Wilson *et al.*'s (1995) study of 237 NZ schools also found that working class schools are generally less able to raise local funds.

Chapter 8   Understanding the impact of school mix

1 Summers and Woolfe 1977; Henderson *et al.* 1978; Oakes *et al.* 1997 argue that all students are advantaged in untracked schools.

2 A good example is Johnson *et al.*'s (1994) work used later in this chapter to illustrate the impact of school mix. Other examples are provided by the categorizations of school culture in the improvement literature discussed in Chapter 10, especially D. Hargreaves (1995).

3 It is also possible that Victoria and Wakefield colleges were forced to have (slightly) more structured policies because of their higher proportions of low-SES students.

Chapter 9 Social class segregation and the politics of polarization and blame

1 There are some studies which have suggested that SES is not important but their methodology or analysis is rarely convincing. For instance the study of Lee *et al.* (1996) used only a ranking of seven simple 'school quality statements' to come to the conclusion that the SES of the school and its academic qualities were less important than other factors in the school choices made by Detroit parents. In any case, safety (the study's first ranked item) could well be seen by many parents as linked to school SES.
2 In the context of residential segregation, school zoning as practised in New Zealand until 1989 supported a high level of between-school segregation. Even in the 1970s when New Zealand urban areas were becoming obviously less homogeneous, the stated philosophy underlying zoning was simply to foster 'neighbourhood' schools, a notion which ignored the effects of residential inequality.
3 See Ball 1993a; Carnoy 1993; OECD 1994b; Gewirtz *et al.* 1995; Waslander and Thrupp 1995; Elmore and Fuller 1996; Gordon 1997; Marginson 1997; Walford 1997; Whitty *et al.* 1998; Hughes *et al.* 1999.
4 The New Zealand Qualifications Authority is the government agency responsible for setting up and implementing a standards-based national qualifications 'framework'. The accreditation process involved schools documenting their systems for managing assessment quality.
5 ERO has recently combined these into 'accountability reviews'.
6 For more discussion and examples see also Robertson *et al.* 1997; Thrupp 1997.
7 While in New Zealand commissioners can also be bought into schools by the Minister of Education, there is nothing like the English special measures legislation there.
8 Other contributions in the same collection (Stoll and Myers 1998) tend to paint a more mixed picture of the success of special measures. See also Spooner (1998).
9 Connell (1993) uses this term to describe much research done for policy purposes.
10 In New Zealand lists of characteristics of quality or competent teachers have been recently produced in association with unit standards developed by the NZQA; the Teacher Registration Board's criteria for teacher certification; collective employment contracts for teachers; the Green Paper on Teacher Education (Ministry of Education 1997b); and ERO's report, *The Capable Teacher* (ERO 1998).
11 Cited in *Eduvac*, July 24 1995, p. 1.
12 At least one group of New Zealand teachers has argued that they should not be held accountable for 'those matters outside their bailiwick. Social, environmental and economic issues came into this category' (Ministry of Education 1993: 42).

Chapter 10 Improvement research: how realistic?

1 Instead of the *Success against the Odds* researchers being given a free hand to investigate what they thought was making the schools successful, they were asked to make 'particular reference to ten postulated features of success' which were specified. Most are typical SER correlates.
2 Newmann and associates note that 'Because authentic pedagogy builds on what

students already know and can do, there may be some tendency for teachers to use it more extensively with higher performing students' (pp. 67–8). It is possibly also telling that they could not find examples of schools which had 'turned themselves around' by a focus on intellectual quality and strong professional community. The most successful schools in their sample 'seem[ed] to have begun their innovative work with a higher level of cultural and structural resources . . .' (p. 294).

Chapter 11   Conclusion: Let's be realistic!

1 There was little to suggest that Maori staff at Tui College were more effective or had a greater affinity with Maori students than other staff. There was also evidence that immersion bilingual classes at Tui College had become a place to dump the school's most difficult and disruptive students. This created a tension for the Maori teachers there who were forced to take a strong pastoral focus despite also wanting to raise academic standards.

References

Abraham, J. (1995) *Divide and School*. London: Falmer Press.

Acton, T.A. (1980) Educational criteria of success: some problems in the work of Rutter, Maughan, Mortimore and Ouston, *Educational Research*, 22: 163–9.

Adler, M. (1993) *An Alternative Approach to Parental Choice*, Briefing no. 13. London: National Commission on Education.

Aitken, J. (1994) Evaluation and education: is there a positive relationship? Keynote address at AES International Conference, Canberra, Australia.

Alexander, K.L., Cook, M.A. and McDill, E.L. (1978) Curriculum tracking and educational stratification: some further evidence, *American Sociological Review*, 43: 47–66.

Alexander, K.L and Eckland, B.K. (1975) Contextual effects in the high school attainment process, *American Sociological Review*, 40: 402–16.

Alexander, K.L., McDill, E.L., Fennessy, J. and D'Amico, R.J. (1979) School SES influences: composition or context?, *Sociology of Education*, 50: 259–73.

Alton-Lee, A., Nuthall, G. and Patrick, J. (1993) Reframing classroom research: a lesson from the private world of children, *Harvard Educational Review*, 63: 50–84.

Alwin, D.F. and Otto, L.B. (1977) High school context effects on aspirations, *Sociology of Education*, 50: 259–73.

Angus, L. (1993) The sociology of school effectiveness, *British Journal of Sociology of Education*, 14: 333–45.

Angus, L. (1994) Sociological analysis and educational management: the social context of the self-managing school, *British Journal of Sociology of Education*, 15: 79–91.

Anyon, J. (1981) Social class and school knowledge, *Curriculum Inquiry*, 11: 3–42.

Anyon, J. (1995) Educational reform, theoretical categories and the urban context, *Access*, 14: 1–11.

Apple, M. (1996) Power, meaning and identity: critical sociology of education in the United States, *British Journal of Sociology of Education*, 17: 125–44.

Apple, M. (1997) What postmodernists forget: cultural capital and official knowledge, in A.H. Halsey, H. Lauder, P. Brown and A. Stuart Wells (eds) *Education, Culture, Economy and Society*. Oxford: Oxford University Press.

Apple, M. and Weiss, L. (eds) (1983) *Ideology and Practice in Schooling*. Philadelphia: Temple University Press.

Arcaro, J.S. (1995) *Quality in Education: An Implementation Handbook*. Delray Beach, FL: St Lucie Press.

Aronowitz, S. (1997) Between nationality and class, *Harvard Educational Review*, 67: 188–207.

Astin, A.W. (1992) Educational 'choice': its appeal may be illusory, *Sociology of Education*, 65: 255–9.

Bain, R.K. and Anderson, J.G. (1974) School context and peer influences on educational plans of adolescents, *Review of Educational Research*, 44: 429–45.

Ball, S.J. (1981) *Beachside Comprehensive*. Cambridge: Cambridge University Press.

Ball, S.J. (1988) Comprehensive schooling, effectiveness and control: an analysis of educational discourses, in R. Slee (ed.) *Discipline and Schools*. London: Macmillan.

Ball, S.J. (1990) Management as moral technology: a luddite analysis, in S.J. Ball (ed.) *Foucault and Education: Disciplines and Knowledge*. London and New York: Routledge.

Ball, S.J. (1993a) Education markets, choice and social class: the market as a class strategy in the UK and the US, *British Journal of Sociology of Education*, 14: 3–19.

Ball, S.J. (1993b) Culture, cost and control, self-management and entrepreneurial schooling in England and Wales, in J. Smyth (ed.) *A Socially Critical View of the Self-managing School*. London: Falmer Press.

Ball, S.J. (1997a) Markets, equity and values in education, in R. Pring and G. Walford, *Affirming the Comprehensive Ideal*. London and Washington, DC: Falmer.

Ball, S.J. (1997b) Good school, bad school: paradox and fabrication, *British Journal of Sociology of Education*, 18: 317–36.

Ball, S.J. (1998a) Big policies/small world: an introduction to international perspectives in education policy, *Comparative Education*, 34: 119–30.

Ball, S.J. (1998b) Educational studies, policy entrepreneurship and social theory, in R. Slee and S. Tomlinson with G. Weiner (eds) *School Effectiveness for Whom?* London and Bristol, PA: Falmer.

Barber, M. (1995) The dark side of the moon: imagining an end to failure in urban education. *TES*-Greenwich Education Lecture, Woolwich Town Hall, London, 11 May.

Barber, M. (1996a) *The Learning Game: Arguments for an Educational Revolution*. London: Victor Gollancz.

Barber, M. (1996b) Creating a framework for sucess in urban areas, in M. Barber and R. Dann, *Raising Educational Standards in the Inner Cities*. London and New York: Cassell.

Barber, M. (1998) The dark side of the moon: imagining an end to failure in urban education, in L. Stoll and K. Myers, *No Quick Fixes: Perspectives on Schools in Difficulty*. London and Washington, DC: Falmer Press.

Barr, R. and Dreeban, R. (1983) *How Schools Work*. Chicago: University of Chicago Press.

Barton, A. (1970) Comments on Hauser's 'Context and consex', *American Journal of Sociology*, 76: 514–17.

Beck, L.R. and St George, R. (1983) The alleged cultural bias of PAT: reading comprehension and reading vocabulary tests, *New Zealand Journal of Educational Studies*, 18: 32–47.

Becker, H. J. (1952) The career of the Chicago public school teacher, *Journal of Sociology*, 27: 470–7.

Benn, C. (1997) Effective comprehensive education, in R. Pring and G. Walford, *Affirming the Comprehensive Ideal*. London and Washington, DC: Falmer.

Bernstein, B. (1970) Education cannot compensate for society, *New Society*, 15: 344–7.

Bernstein, B. (1975) *Class Codes and Control, Vol 3: Towards a Theory of Educational Transmissions*. London: Routledge and Kegan Paul.

Bonstingl, J.J. (1992) *Schools of Quality: An Introduction to Total Quality Management in Education*. Alexandria, VA: Association for Supervision and Curriculum Development.

Boomer, G. and Lester, N. (eds) (1992) *Negotiating the Curriculum*. London and Washington, DC: Falmer Press.

Boothroyd, C., Fitz-Gibbon, C., McNicholas, J., Thompson, M., Stern, E. and Wragg, T. (1997) *A Better System of Inspection?* Hexham: Ofstin.

Bossert, S. (1979) *Tasks and Social Relationships in Classrooms*. Cambridge: Cambridge University Press.

Bourdieu, P. and Passeron, J.C. (1977) *Reproduction in Education, Society and Culture*. London: Sage Publications.

Bowe, R., Ball, S. and Gold, A. (1992) *Reforming Education and Changing Schools: Case Studies in Policy Sociology*. London: Routledge.

Bowles, S. and Gintis, H. (1976) *Schooling in Capitalist America*. London: Routledge and Kegan Paul.

Bowles, S. and Levin, H.M. (1968) The determinants of scholastic achievement: an appraisal of some recent evidence, *Journal of Human Resources*, 3: 3–24.

Boyd, W.L. (1996) The politics of choice and market oriented school reforms in Britain and the United States: explaining the difference, in J.D. Chapman, W.L. Boyd, R. Lander, and D. Reynolds (eds) *The Reconstruction of Education – Quality, Equality and Control*. London and New York: Cassell.

Brantlinger, E.A. (1992) Low-income adolescents' perceptions of social class related peer affiliations in school, *Sociology of Education*, 65: 9–27.

Brantlinger, E. (1993) *The Politics of Social Class in Secondary School*. New York and London: Teachers College Press.

Brett, C. (1998) Middle class education panic, *North and South*, 145: 34–47.

Brighouse, T. and Moon, B. (eds) (1995) *School Inspection*. London: Pitman.

Brookover, W., Beady, C., Flood, P., Schweitzer, J. and Wisenbaker, J. (1979) *School Social Systems and Student Achievement: Schools Can Make a Difference*. New York: Praeger.

Brown, P. (1987) *Schooling Ordinary Kids*. London: Tavistock Publications.

Brown, S. (1994) School effectiveness research and the evaluation of schools, *Evaluation and Research in Education*, 8: 55–68.

Brown, S., Riddell, S. and Duffield, J. (1996a) Possibilities and problems of small-scale studies to unpack the findings of large-scale studies of school effectiveness, in J. Gray, D. Reynolds, C. Fitz-Gibbon, and D. Jesson (eds) *Merging Traditions*. London and New York: Cassell.

Brown, S., Riddell, S. and Duffield, J. (1996b) Responding to pressure: a study of four secondary schools, in P. Woods (ed.) *Contemporary Issues in Teaching and Learning*. London and New York: Routledge.

Buchbinder, D. (1994) *Masculinities and Identities*. Melbourne: Melbourne University Press.

Burgess, R.G. (1983) *Experiencing Comprehensive Education*. London: Methuen.

Caldwell, B.J. and Spinks, J.M. (1988) *The Self Managing School*. Lewes and Philadelpia: Falmer.

Carnoy, M. (1993) School improvement: is privatisation the answer?, in J. Hannaway and M. Carnoy (eds) *Decentralisation and School Improvement: Can We Fulfill the Promise?*, San Francisco: Jossey-Bass.

Chapman, J., Dunstan, J. and Spicer, B. (1996) Systems restructuring, school-based management and the achievement of effectiveness in Australian education, in J.D. Chapman, W.L. Boyd, R. Lander and D. Reynolds (eds) *The Reconstruction of Education – Quality, Equality and Control*. London and New York: Cassell.

Chapman, J.W., St George, R. and Ibell, R. (1985) Error rate differences in teacher marking of the PATs: sex, ability, SES and ethnicity effects, *New Zealand Journal of Educational Studies*, 20: 165–9.

Chubb, J. and Moe, T. (1990) *Politics, Markets and America's Schools*. Washington, DC: The Brookings Institute.

Clarke, B. (1997) What comprehensive schools do better, in R. Pring, and G. Walford, *Affirming the Comprehensive Ideal*. London and Washington, DC: Falmer.

Clifton, J. (1995) Government plans school takeovers, *Sunday Star Times*, 29 January.

Coleman, J. S. (1973) Review of Jencks' 'Inequality', *American Journal of Sociology*, 78: 1523–7.

Coleman, J. S. (1990) *Equality and Achievement in Education*. London: Westview Press.

Coleman, J. S., Campbell, E., Hobson, C., McPartland, J., Mood, A., Weinfeld, F. and York, R. (1966) *Equality of Educational Opportunity*. Washington, DC: US Government Printing Office.

Connell, R.W. (1993) *Schools and Social Justice*. Philadelphia: Temple University Press.

Connell, R.W. (1994) Poverty and education, *Harvard Educational Review*, 64: 125–49.

Connell, R.W., Ashenden, D.J., Kessler, S. and Dowsett, G.W. (1982) *Making the Difference*. Sydney: Allen and Unwin.

Corbett, J. (1994) White flight – often seen, seldom talked about, *Metro*, July.

Creemers, B. (1994) *The Effective Classroom*. London and New York: Cassell.

Cuttance, P. (1997) Quality assurance for schools, in T. Townsend (ed.) *Restructuring and Quality: Issues for Tomorrow's Schools*. London and New York: Routledge.

Dale, R. (1992) Recovering from a pyrrhic victory? Quality, relevance and impact in the sociology of education, in M. Arnot and L. Barton (eds) *Voicing Concerns: Sociological Perspectives on Contemporary Educational Reforms*. Wallingford: Triangle Books.

Dale, R. (1997) Educational markets and school choice, *British Journal of Sociology of Education*, 18: 451–68.

Davies, B. (1983) The role pupils play in the social construction of classroom order, *British Journal of Sociology of Education*, 4: 55–69.

Davis, J.A. (1966) The campus as a frogpond, *American Journal of Sociology*, 72: 17–31.

Delamont, S. (1981) All too familiar, *Education Analysis*, 3: 69–83.

Delamont, S. (1983) *Interaction in the Classroom*. London: Routledge.

Delamont, S. (1992) *Fieldwork in Educational Settings*. London: Falmer Press.

Delamont, S. and Galton, T. (1986) *Inside the Secondary Classroom*. London: Routledge and Kegan Paul.

Delamont, S. and Hamilton, D. (1984) Revisiting classroom research: a continuing cautionary tale, in S. Delamont, *Readings on Interaction in the Classroom*. London: Methuen.

Department Of Statistics (1992) *Northland/Auckland regional report. 1991 census of population and dwellings, vol. 2*. Wellington: Government Printer.

Dewey, J. (1902) *The School and Society*. Chicago: University of Chicago Press.

DfEE (Department for Education and Employment) (1997) *Excellence in Schools*. London: HMSO.

Douglas, R. (1993) *Unfinished Business*. Auckland: Random House.

Doyle, W. (1992) Curriculum and pedagogy, in P. Jackson (ed.) *Handbook of Research on Curriculum*. New York: Macmillan.

Dreeban, R. and Barr, R. (1988) Classroom composition and the design of instruction, *Sociology of Education*, 61: 129–42.

Dunphy, A. (1996) Quality outcomes for all students and the issues for low decile schools in a climate of choice. Unpublished paper. Auckland: At Risk Committee.

Echols, F.H. and Willms, J.D. (1995) Reasons for school choice in Scotland, *Journal of Education Policy*, 10: 143–56.

Edmonds, R. (1979) Effective schools for the urban poor, *Educational Leadership*, 37: 15–27.

Edwards, T., Fitz, J. and Whitty, G. (1989) *The State and Private Education: An Evaluation of the Assisted Places Scheme*. Lewes: Falmer Press

Edwards, T. and Whitty, G. (1997) Marketing quality: traditional and modern versions of educational excellence, in R. Glatter, P. A. Woods and C. Bagley (eds) *Choice and Diversity in Education: Perspectives and Prospects*. London and New York: Routledge.

Elley, W.B. and Irving, J.C. (1985) The Elley–Irving socio-economic index 1981 census revision, *New Zealand Journal of Educational Studies*, 20: 115–28.

Elliott, J. (1996) School effectiveness research and its critics: alternative visisons of schooling, *Cambridge Journal of Education*, 26: 199–224.

Elmore, R.F. and Fuller, B. (1996) Empirical research on educational choice: what are the implications for policymakers? in B. Fuller, R.F. Elmore with G. Orfield (eds) *Who Chooses, Who Loses? Culture, Institutions and the Unequal Effects of School Choice*. New York and London: Teachers College Press.

Elmore, R.F, Peterson, P. and McCarthy, S. (1996) *Restructuring in the Classroom: Teaching, Learning and School Organisation*. San Francisco: Jossey-Bass.

ERO (Education Review Office) (1995) *Barriers To Learning*. Wellington: ERO.

ERO (1996a) *Addressing Barriers To Learning*. Wellington: ERO.

ERO (1996b) *Improving Schooling in Mangere and Otara*. Wellington: ERO.

ERO (1998) *The Capable Teacher*. Wellington: ERO.

Evans, L. and Teddlie, C. (1995) Facilitating change in schools: is there one best style? *School Effectiveness and School Improvement*, 6: 1–22.

Evans, R. (1996) *The Human Side of School Change: Reform, Resistance and the Real Life Problems of Innovation*. San Francisco: Jossey-Bass.

Fine, M., Weis, L. and Powell, L.C. (1997) Communities of difference: a critical look at desegregated spaces created for and by youth, *Harvard Educational Review*, 67: 247–84.

Finley, M.K. (1984) Teachers and tracking in a comprehensive high school, *Sociology of Education*, 57: 233–43.

Fitz-Gibbon, C.T. (1996) *Monitoring Education*. London and New York: Cassell.

Fitz-Gibbon, C.T. (1997) *The Value Added National Project Final Report*. London: School Curriculum and Assessment Authority.

Fitz-Gibbon, C.T. and Stephenson, N.J. (1996) Inspecting Her Majesty's Inspectors: should social science and social policy cohere? Paper presented at the European Conference on Educational Research, Seville, Spain, 25–8 September.

Flanagan, C. (1993) Gender and social class: intersecting issues in women's achievement, *Educational Psychologist*, 28: 35–7–78.

Ford, J. (1969) *Social Class and the Comprehensive School*. London: Routledge and Kegan Paul.

Foster, M. (1993) 'Savage Inequalities': where have we come from? Where are we going?, *Educational Theory*, 43: 23–32.

Fowler, M. (1993) *Factors Influencing Choice of Secondary School – A Case Study*. Christchurch: University of Canterbury.

Fullan, M.G. (1982) *The Meaning of Educational Change*. Toronto: OISE Press.

Fullan, M.G. (1991) *The New Meaning of Educational Change*. London: Cassell.

Fullan, M.G. (1992) *Successful School Improvement: The Implementation Perspective and Beyond*. Buckingham: Open University Press.

Fullan, M.G. (1993) *Change Forces: Probing the Depths of Educational Reform*. London: Falmer.

Fullan, M.G. (1997) Emotion and hope: constructive concepts for complex times, in A. Hargreaves (ed.) *Rethinking Educational Change with Heart and Mind*, ASCD Yearbook. Alexandria VA: Association for Supervision and Curriculum Development.

Fullan, M.G. and Hargreaves, A. (1992) *What's Worth Fighting For in Your School*. Buckingham: Open University Press.

Furlong, V.J. (1991) Disaffected pupils: reconstructing the sociological perspective, *British Journal of Sociology of Education*, 12: 293–307.

Gamoran, A. (1987) The stratification of high school learning opportunities, *Sociology of Education*, 60: 135–55.

Gamoran, A. and Berends, M. (1987) The effects of stratification in secondary schools: synthesis of survey and ethnographic research, *Review of Educational Research*, 4: 415–35.

Garet, M.S. and Delany, B. (1988) Students, courses and stratification, *Sociology of Education*, 61: 61–77.

Gewirtz, S., Ball, S.J. and Bowe, R. (1995) *Markets, Choice and Equity in Education*. Buckingham: Open University Press.

Gibson, A. and Asthana, S. (1998) School performance, school effectiveness and the 1997 White Paper, *Oxford Review of Education*, 24: 195–210.

Glasser, W. (1992) *The Quality School: Managing Students Without Coercion*. New York: Harper Perennial.

Glatter, R., Woods, P.A. and Bagley, C. (1997) Diversity, differentiation and hierarchy: school choice and parental preferences, in R. Glatter, P.A. Woods and C. Bagley (eds) *Choice and Diversity in Education: Perspectives and Prospects*. London and New York: Routledge.

Good, T. and Brophy, J. (1994) *Looking In Classrooms*. New York: Harper Collins.

Gordon, L. (1993) *A Study of Boards of Trustees in Canterbury Schools*. Christchurch, NZ: University of Canterbury.

Gordon, L. (1994) 'Rich' and 'poor' schools in Aotearoa, New Zealand, *New Zealand Journal of Educational Studies*, 29: 113–25.

Gordon, L. (1997) 'Tomorrow's Schools' today: school choice and the education quasi-market, in M. Olssen and K. Morris Matthews (eds) *New Zealand Education Policy in the 1990s*. Palmerston North: Dunmore Press.

Gordon, L. and Whitty, G. (1997) Giving the 'hidden hand' a helping hand? The rhetoric and reality of neo-liberal educational reform in England and New Zealand, *Comparative Education*, 33(3): 453–67.

Gouldner, A. (1971) *The Coming Crisis of Western Sociology*. New York: Avon Books.

Grace, G. (1995) *School Leadership: Beyond Educational Management*. London and Washington, DC: Falmer.

Grant, C.A. and Sleeter, C.E. (1996) *After the School Bell Rings*. London and Washington, DC: Falmer.

Gray, J. (1997) A bit of a curate's egg? Three decades of official thinking about the quality of schools, *British Journal of Educational Studies*, 45: 4–21.

Gray, J. and Hannon, V. (1986) HMI's interpretations of school's examination results, *Journal of Education Policy*, 1: 23–33.

Gray, J., Jesson, D. and Sime, N. (1990) Estimating differences in the examination performances of secondary schools in six LEAs: a multi-level approach to school effectiveness, *Oxford Review of Education*, 16: 137–56.

Gray, J., Reynolds, D., Fitz-Gibbon, C. and Jesson, D. (eds) (1996) *Merging Traditions*. London and New York: Cassell.

Gray, J. and Wilcox, B. (eds) (1995a) Inspection at the crossroads: time for review? *Cambridge Journal of Education*, Special Issue, 25(1).

Gray, J. and Wilcox, B. (1995b) *Good School, Bad School: Evaluating Performance and Encouraging Improvement*. Buckingham: Open University Press.

Gray, J. and Wilcox, B. (1995c) The methodologies of school inspection: issues and dilemmas, in T. Brighouse and B. Moon (eds) *School Inspection*. London: Pitman.

Greenwood, M.S. and Gaunt, H.J. (1994) *Total Quality Management for Schools*. London and New York: Cassell.

Hackett, G. (1996) Collaborating in assessment: the Ofsted experience, in J. Mills (ed.) *Partnership in the Primary School*. London and New York: Routledge.

Hallinan, M.T. (1988) School composition and learning: a critique of the Dreeban-Barr model, *Sociology of Education*, 61: 143–6.

Hallinan, M.T. (1994) Tracking from theory to practice, *Sociology of Education*, 67: 79–84.

Hallinger, P. and Murphy, J.F. (1986) The social context of effective schools, *American Journal of Education*, 94: 328–55.

Halsey, A.H., Heath, A.F. and Ridge, J.M. (1980) *Origins and Destinations*. New York: Oxford University Press.

Hamilton, D. (1998) The idols of the market-place, in Slee, R., Tomlinson, S. with Weiner, G. (eds) *School Effectiveness for Whom?* London and Bristol PA: Falmer.

Hannaway, J. (1995) School-based management: some theoretical considerations. Paper presented at the Conference on Improving the Performance of America's Schools: Economic Choices, Washington, DC, 12–13 October.

Hargreaves, A. (1994) *Changing Teachers, Changing Times: Teachers' Work and Culture in the Postmodern Age*. London: Cassell.

Hargreaves, A. (1997a) Introduction, in A. Hargreaves (ed.) *Rethinking Educational Change with Heart and Mind*, ASCD Yearbook. Alexandria VA: Association for Supervision and Curriculum Development.

Hargreaves, A. (1997b) From reform to renewal: a new deal for a new age, in A. Hargreaves and R. Evans (eds) *Beyond Educational Reform: Bringing Teachers Back*. Buckingham: Open University Press.

Hargreaves, D.H. (1967) *Social Relations in a Secondary School*. London: Routledge and Kegan Paul.

Hargreaves, D.H. (1995) School culture, school effectiveness and school improvement, *School Effectiveness and School Improvement*, 6: 23–46.

Hargreaves, D.H. and Hopkins, D. (1991) *The Empowered School*. London: Cassell.

Hargreaves, D.H. and Hopkins, D. (1994) Introduction, in D.H. Hargreaves and D. Hopkins, *Development Planning for School Improvement*. London and New York: Cassell.

Harker, R. and Nash, R. (1996) Academic outcomes and school effectiveness: type 'A' and type 'B' effects, *New Zealand Journal of Educational Studies*, 31: 143–70.

Hatcher, R. (1996) The limitations of the new social agendas: class, equality and agency, in R. Hatcher, K. Jones, B. Regan and C. Richards, *Education after the Conservatives*. Stoke-on-Trent: Trentham Books.

Hauser, R.M. (1970) Context and consex: a cautionary tale, *American Journal of Sociology*, 75: 645–64.

Hauser, R.M., Sewell, W.H. and Alwin, D.F. (1976) High school effects on achievement, in W.H. Sewell, R.M. Hauser and D.L. Featherman (eds) *Schooling and Achievement in American Society*. New York: Academic Press.

Hawk, K. and Hill, J. (1996) *Towards Making Achievement Cool – Achievement in Multicultural High Schools*. Auckland, NZ: ERDC Massey University, Albany.

Heath, A.F. and Blakey, L.S. (1992) Differences between comprehensive schools: some preliminary findings, in D. Reynolds and P. Cuttance (eds) *School Effectiveness: Research Policy and Practice*. London: Cassell.

Heath, S.B. (1983) *Ways with Words*. Cambridge: Cambridge University Press.

Henderson, V., Mieszkowski, P. and Sauvageau, Y. (1978) Peer group effects and educational production functions, *Journal of Public Economics*, 10: 97–106.

Hirsch, D. (1997) Polices for school choice: what can Britain learn from abroad? in R. Glatter, P.A. Woods and C. Bagley (eds) *Choice and Diversity in Education: Perspectives and Prospects*. London and New York: Routledge.

Hirsch, F. (1976) *The Social Limits to Growth*. Cambridge: Harvard University Press.

Hogan, D. (1992) School organisation and student achievement: a review essay, *Educational Theory*, 42: 83–105.

Hopkins, D. (1987) *Improving the Quality of Schooling*. Lewes: Falmer Press.

Hopkins, D. (1996) Towards a theory for school improvement, in Gray, J., Reynolds, D., Fitz-Gibbon, C. and Jesson, D. (eds) *Merging Traditions*. London and New York: Cassell.

Hopkins, D., Ainscow, M. and West, M. (1994) *School Improvement in an Era of Change*. London and New York: Cassell.

Hotere, A. (1998) Lifting strategy, *New Zealand Education Review*, 11 March.

Hubbard, A. (1995) Lessons in survival, *Listener*, New Zealand, 1 April.

Huberman, A.M. and Miles, M.B. (1984) *Innovation Up Close: How School Improvement Works*. New York: Plenum Press.

Hughes, D., Lauder, H., Watson, S., Hamlin, J. and Simiyu, I. (1996) *Markets in Education: Testing the Polarisation Thesis*. Wellington: Ministry of Education.

Hughes, D., Lauder, H., Watson, S., Strathdee, R., Simiyu, I. and Hamlin, J. (1997) *School Effectiveness: An Analysis of Differences Between Nineteen Schools on Four Outcome Measures using Hierarchical Linear Modelling*. Report to the Ministry of Education. Christchurch: University of Canterbury.

Hughes, D., Lauder, H., Watson S., Waslander, S., Thrupp, M., Strathdee, R. *et al.* (1999) *Trading in Futures: Why Markets in Education Don't Work*. Buckingham: Open University Press.

Ihaka, J. (1993) Why the kids wanna be black, *Mana: the Maori News Magazine for all New Zealanders*, 3: 10–17.

Jencks, C., Smith, M., Ackland, H., Bane, M.J., Cohen, D., Gintis, H. *et al.* (1972) *Inequality*. New York: Basic Books.

Jensen, A.R. (1969) How much can we boost IQ and scholastic achievement?, *Harvard Educational Review*, 39: 1–123.

Johnson, B., Whitington, V. and Oswald, M. (1994) Teachers' views on school discipline – a theoretical framework, *Cambridge Journal of Education*, 24: 261–76.

Jones, A. (1991) *At School I've got a Chance*. Palmerston North: Dunmore Press.

Karabel, J. and Halsey, A.H. (1977) *Power and Ideology in Education*. New York: Oxford University Press.

Kealey, M. (1984) Meats and veges: an ethnographic study of two grammar school classes, *Set*, 2: 10.

Kearns, D.T. and Anderson, J.L. (1996) Sharing the vision: creating new American schools, in S. Stringfield, S.M. Ross and L. Smith (eds) (1996) *Bold Plans for School Restructuring: The New American School Designs*. Mahwah, NJ: Lawrence Erlbaum.

Kelsey, J. (1995) *The New Zealand Experiment*. Auckland: AUP/Bridget Williams.

Kozol, J. (1991) *Savage Inequalities*. New York: Crown Publishing.

Kozol, J. (1993) 'Savage Inequalities': an interview with Johnathan Kozol, *Educational Theory*, 43: 55–70.

Lacey, C. (1970) *Hightown Grammar*. Manchester: Manchester University Press.

Lareau, A. (1989) *Home Advantage*. Philadelphia: Falmer Press.

Lareau, A. and Shumar, W. (1996) The problem of individualism in family–school policies, in P.W. Cookson, J.C. Conaty and H.S. Himmelforb (eds) *Sociology and Educational Practice: Bringing Scholarship and Practice Together. Sociology of Education*, Special Issue, 24–39.

Lauder, H. and Hughes, D. (1990a) Social origins, destinations and educational inequality, in J. Codd, R. Harker and R. Nash (eds) *Political Issues in New Zealand Education*. Palmerston North: Dunmore Press.

Lauder, H. and Hughes, D. (1990b) Social inequalities and differences in school outcomes, *New Zealand Journal of Educational Studies*, 25: 37–60.

Lauder, H., Hughes, D., Dupuis, A. and McGlinn, J. (1992) *To Be Somebody: Class, Gender and the Rationality of Educational Decision-making*. Christchurch: University of Canterbury.

Lauder, H., Jamieson, I. and Wikeley, F. (1997) Models of effective schools: limits and capabilities. Unpublished paper.

Lauder, H., Jamieson, I. and Wikeley, F. (1998) Models of effective schools: limits and capabilities, in Slee, R., Tomlinson, S. with Weiner, G. (eds) *School Effectiveness for Whom?* London and Bristol, PA: Falmer.

Lee, C. (1983) *The Ostrich Position: Sex, Schooling and Mystification*. Unwin: London.

Lee, V.E., Coninger, R.G. and Smith, J.B. (1996) Equity and choice in Detroit, in B. Fuller, R.F. Elmore with G. Orfield (eds) *Who Chooses, Who Loses?* New York and London: Teachers College Press.

Lee, V.E. and Smith, J.B (1995) Effects of high school restructuring and size on gains in the achievement and engagement for early secondary school students, *Sociology of Education*, 68: 241–70.

Lees, S. (1993) *Sugar and Spice: Sexuality and Adolescent Girls*. London: Penguin.

Levin, B. (1997) The lessons of international educational reform, *Journal of Education Policy*, 12: 253–66.

Lieberman, A. and Miller, L. (1992) *Teachers: Their World and Their Work: Implications for School Improvement*. New York and London: Teachers College Press.

Lightfoot, S.L. (1983) *The Good High School: Portraits of Character and Culture*. New York: Basic Books.

Lingard, B., Ladwig, J. and Luke, A. (1998) School effects in postmodern conditions, in R. Slee, S. Tomlinson with G. Weiner (eds) *School Effectiveness for Whom?* London and Bristol, PA: Falmer.

Lodge, C. (1998) What's wrong with our schools? Understanding 'ineffective' and 'failing' schools, in L. Stoll and K. Myers, *No Quick Fixes: Perspectives on Schools in Difficulty*. London and Washington, DC: Falmer Press.

Louis, K.S. and Miles, M.B. (1990) *Improving the Urban High School: What Works and Why*. New York and London: Teachers College Press.

Mac an Ghaill, M. (1994) *The Making of Men*. Buckingham: Open University Press.

Mac an Ghaill, M. (1996) Sociology of education, state schooling and social class: beyond critiques of New Right hegemony, *British Journal of Sociology of Education*, 17: 163–76.

McCullough, G. (1991) School zoning, equity and freedom: the case of New Zealand, *Journal of Education Policy*, 6: 155–68.

McLaughlin, M.W. and Talbot, J. (1993) How the world of students and teachers challenges policy coherence, in S.H. Fuhrman (ed.) *Designing Coherent Education Policy*. San Francisco: Jossey-Bass.

McPherson, A. and Willms, J. D. (1987) Equalisation and improvement: some effects of comprehensive reorganisation in Scotland *Sociology*, 21: 509–39.

McRobbie, A. (1978) Working class girls and the culture of femininity, in CCCS Women's Studies Group, *Women Take Issue*. London: Hutchinson.

McRobbie, A. (1991) *Feminism and Youth Culture: From Jackie to Just Seventeen*. London: Macmillan.

Marginson, S. (1997) *Markets in Education*. St Leonards, NSW: Allen and Unwin.

Maughan, B., Mortimore, P., Ouston, J. and Rutter, M. (1980) Fifteen thousand hours: a reply to Heath and Clifford, *Oxford Review of Education*, 6: 289–303.

Maughan, B. and Rutter, M. (1987) Pupils' progress in selective and non-selective schools, *School Organisation*, 7: 49–68.

Metz, M.H. (1978) *Classrooms and Corridors*. Berkley: University of California.

Metz, M.H. (1990) How social class differences shape teachers' work, in M.W. McLaughlin, J.E. Talbert and N. Bascia (eds) *The Contexts of Teaching in Secondary Schools*. New York: Teachers College Press.

Meyer, J.W. (1970) High school effects on college intentions. *American Journal of Sociology*, 76: 59–70.

Minister of Education (1995) *New Zealand Schools 1994: Statistical Annex*. Wellington: Ministry of Education.

Ministry of Education (1993) *The New Zealand Report on Teacher Quality Seminars*. Wellington: Ministry of Education.

Ministry of Education (1997a) Schooling in Mangere and Otara: a strategy for improvement. Unpublished briefing paper to the Minister of Education.

Ministry of Education (1997b) *Quality Teachers for Quality Learning*. Wellington: Ministry of Education.

Moe, T.M. (1995) Private Vouchers, in T.M. Moe (ed.) *Private Vouchers*. Stanford: Hoover Institution Press.

Moore, R. (1996) Back to the future: the problem of change and the possibilities of advance in the sociology of education, *British Journal of Sociology of Education*, 17: 145–61.

Mortimore, P. (1995) The balancing act, *Education Guardian*, 28 February.

Mortimore, P., Sammons, P., Stoll, L., Lewis, D. and Ecob, R. (1988) *School Matters*. Wells: Open Books.

Mortimore, P., Sammons, P. and Thomas, S. (1994) School effectiveness and value-added measures. Unpublished paper presented at the Desmond Nuttall Memorial Lecture, 10 June.

Murphy, J. (1991) *Restructuring Schools*. London: Cassell.

Murphy, J. (1992) Effective schools: legacy and future directions, in D. Reynolds and P. Cuttance (eds) *School Effectiveness: Research, Policy and Practice*. London: Cassell.

Myers, K. and Goldstein, H. (1998) Who's failing?, in L. Stoll and K. Myers, *No Quick Fixes: Perspectives on Schools in Difficulty*. London and Washington, DC: Falmer Press.

National Commission on Education (1996) *Success Against the Odds*. London and New York: Routledge.

Neave, G. (1988) On the cultivation of quality, efficiency and enterprise: an overview of recent trends in higher education in Western Europe 1968–1988, *European Journal of Education*, 23: 7–23.

Nelson, J.I. (1972) High school context and college plans: the impact of social structure on aspiration, *American Sociological Review*, 37: 143–8.

Newmann, F. and associates (1996) *Authentic Achievement: Restructuring Schools for Intellectual Quality*. San Francisco: Jossey-Bass.

Newmann, F. and Wehlage, G. (1995) *Successful School Restructuring*. Madison, WI: Centre on Organisation and Restructuring of Schools, University of Wisconsin.

New Zealand Herald (1996a) Office canes suburban schools, 9 September.

New Zealand Herald (1996b) Otara schools go public to counter image, 30 May.

Noddings, N. (1993) For all its children, *Education Theory*, 43: 15–22.

Oakes, J. (1985) *Keeping Track*. New York: Yale University Press.

Oakes, J., Gamoran, A. and Page, R. (1992) Curriculum differentiation, opportunities, outcomes, and meanings, in P. Jackson (ed.) *Handbook of Research on Curriculum*. New York: Macmillan.

Oakes, J., Wells, A.S., Yonezawa, S. and Ray, K. (1997) Equity lessons from detracking schools, in A. Hargreaves (ed.) *Rethinking Educational Change with Heart and Mind*, ASCD Yearbook. Alexandria, VA: Association for Supervision and Curriculum Development.

OECD (Organization for Economic Co-operation and Development) (1994a) *Quality in Teaching*. Paris: OECD.

OECD (1994b) *School: A Matter of Choice*. Paris: OECD.

OECD (1995) *Schools Under Scrutiny*. Paris: OECD.

Ofsted (Office for Standards in Education) (1994) *Improving Schools*. London: HMSO.

Ofsted (1995) *Guidance on the Inspection of Secondary Schools*. London: HMSO.

O'Neill, J. (1996) Teacher appraisal and the Education Review Office: back to the Medieval Inquisition?, *New Zealand Principal*, August, 21–2.

Orfield, G., Eaton, S.E. and the Harvard Project on School Desegregation (1996) *Dismantling Desegregation*. New York: New Press.

Ouston, J., Earley, P. and Fidler, B. (eds) (1996) *OFSTED Inspections: The Early Experience*. London: David Fulton Publishers.

Parsons, T. (1959) The school class as a social system, *Harvard Educational Review*, 29: 297–318.

Paterson, L. (1991) Socio-economic status and educational attainment: a multi-dimensional and multi-level study, *Evaluation and Research in Education*, 5: 97–121.

Petrie, S. (1984) Delinquency and the school. Unpublished PhD thesis, University of Queensland.

Powell, A., Farrar, E. and Cohen, D. (1985) *The Shopping Mall High School*. Boston: Houghton Mufflin.

Power, S. (1997) Not drowning but waving? Comprehensive education in the 1990s, *British Journal of Sociology of Education*, 18: 445–50.

Purkey, S.C. and Smith, M.S. (1983) Effective schools: a review, *Elementary School Journal*, 83: 427–52.

Ralph, J.H. and Fennessey, J. (1983) Science or reform: some questions about the effective schools model, *Phi Delta Kappan*, 64: 689–94.

Ramsay, P. and Oliver, D. (1995) Capacities and behaviours of quality classroom teachers, *School Effectiveness and School Improvement*, 6: 332–66.

Ramsay, P., Sneddon, D., Grenfell, J. and Ford, I. (1981) *Tomorrow May Be Too Late*. Hamilton: University of Waikato.

Raudenbush, S.W., Rowan, B. and Cheong, Y.F. (1992) Contextual effects on the self-perceived efficacy of high school teachers, *Sociology of Education*, 65: 150–67.

Raudenbush, S.W. and Willms, J.D. (1991) *Schools, Classrooms and Pupils: International Studies of Schooling from a Multi-level Perspective*. New York: Academic Press.

Rea, J. and Weiner, G. (1998) Cultures of blame and redemption – when empowerment becomes control: practitioners' views of the effective schools movement, in Slee, R., Tomlinson, S. with Weiner, G. (eds) *School Effectiveness for Whom?* London and Bristol, PA: Falmer.

Reay, D. and Ball, S. (1997) 'Spoilt for choice': the working classes and educational markets, in G. Walford (ed.) *Special Issue on Choice, Diversity and Equity in Secondary Education, Oxford Review of Education*, 23: 89–101.

Reynolds, D. (1992) School effectiveness and school improvement: an updated review of the British literature, in D. Reynolds and P. Cuttance (eds) *School Effectiveness: Research, Policy and Practice*. London: Cassell.

Reynolds, D. (1996) School effects from decentralisation, in J.D. Chapman, W.L. Boyd, R. Lander and D. Reynolds (eds) *The Reconstruction of Education – Quality, Equality and Control*. London and New York: Cassell.

Reynolds, D. and Farrell, S. (1996) *Worlds Apart: A Review of International Surveys of Educational Achievement Involving England*. London: HMSO.

Reynolds, D., Sammons, S., Stoll, L., Barber, M. and Hillman, J. (1996) School effectiveness and school improvement in the United Kingdom, *School Effectiveness and School Improvement*, 7: 133–58.

Reynolds, D. and Stringfield, S. (1996) Failure-free schooling is clear for take off, *Times Educational Supplement Management Update*, 19 January, 10.

Riddell, S., Brown, S. and Duffield, J. (1998) The utility of qualitative research for influencing policy and practice on school effectivness, in R. Slee, S. Tomlinson with G. Weiner (eds) *School Effectiveness for Whom?* London and Bristol, PA: Falmer.

Riley, K. and Rowles, D. (1997) Inspection and school improvement in England and Wales: national contexts and local realities, in T. Townsend (ed.) *Restructuring and Quality: Issues for Tomorrow's Schools*. London and New York: Routledge.

Robertson, S. (1998) *Changing Teachers' Work – The New Era of Fast Capitalism and Fast Schools*. Buckingham: Open University Press.

Robertson, S., Dale, R., Thrupp, M., Vaughan, K. and Jacka, S. (1997) *A Review of ERO – Final Report for the PPTA*. Auckland: University of Auckland.

Rosenbaum, J.E. (1976) *Making Inequality*. New York: Wiley.

Rosenholtz, S. (1989) *Teachers' Workplace: The Social Organization of Schools*. New York: Longman.

Rosenholtz, S.J. and Simpson, C. (1984) The formation of ability conceptions: developmental trend or social construction?, *Review of Educational Research*, 54: 131–63.

Rout, B. (1992) Being staunch: boys hassling girls, in S. Middleton and A. Jones (eds) *Women and Education in Aotearoa 2*. Wellington: Bridget Williams Press.

Rowan, B., Bossert, S.T. and Dwyer, D.C. (1983) Research on effective schools: a cautionary note, *Educational Researcher*, 12: 24–31.

Rudduck J., Chaplin, R. and Wallace, G. (1996) *School Improvement: What Can Students Tell Us?* London: David Fulton.

Rutter, M., Maughan, B., Mortimore, P. and Ouston, J. (1979) *Fifteen Thousand Hours*. London: Open Books.

Sammons, P., Hillman, J. and Mortimore, P. (1995) *Key Characteristics of Effective Schools: a Review of School Effectiveness Research*. London: Ofsted.

Sammons, P., Mortimore, P. and Thomas, S. (1996) Do schools perform consistently across outcomes and areas?, in J. Gray, D. Reynolds, C. Fitz-Gibbon and D. Jesson, *Merging Traditions*. London and New York: Cassell.

Sammons, P. and Reynolds, D. (1997) A partisan evaluation – John Elliot on school effectiveness, *Cambridge Journal of Education*, 27: 123–36.

Sammons, P., Thomas, S., Mortimore, P., Owen, C. and Pennell, H. (1994) *Assessing School Effectiveness: Developing Measures to Put School Performance in Context*. London: London University Institute of Education.

Sarason, S. B. (1995) *School Change: The Personal Development of a Point of View*. London and New York: Teachers College Press.

Schaer, C. (1993) Youth quake, *More*, 116: 32–41.

Scheerens, J. (1991) Process indicators of school functioning: a selection based on the research literature on school effectiveness, *Studies in Educational Evaluation*, 17: 371–403.

Scheerens, J. (1992) *Effective Schooling: Research, Theory and Practice*. London: Cassell.

Schein, E.H. (1985) *Organizational Culture and Leadership: A Dynamic View*. San Francisco: Jossey-Bass.

Schwartz, F. (1981) Supporting or subverting learning: peer group patterns in four tracked schools, *Anthropology and Education Quarterly*, 12: 99–121.

Selden, R. (1994) How indicators have been used in the USA, in K.A. Riley and D.A. Nuttall, *Measuring Quality*. London and Washington, DC: Falmer.

Sergiovanni, T.J. (1990) *Value-Added Leadership*. Orlando, FL: Harcourt Brace Jovano-vich.

Sergiovanni, T.J. (1994) *Building Community in Schools*. San Francisco: Jossey-Bass.

Sergiovanni, T.J. (1996) *Leadership for the Schoolhouse: How is it Different? Why is it Important?* San Francisco: Jossey-Bass.

Sewell, W.H. and Armer, J.M. (1966) Neighbourhood context and college plans, *American Sociological Review*, 31: 159–68.

Shavit, Y. and Williams, R. (1985) Ability grouping and contextual determinants of educational expectations in Israel, *American Sociological Review*, 50: 62–73.

Shaw, H. (1995) Quality Management in Education. Cambridge: Hobsons Publishing.

Slavin, R.E. (1987) Ability grouping and student achievement in elementary schools: a best-evidence synthesis, *Review of Educational Research*, 57: 347–50.

Slavin, R.E. (1990) Achievement effects of ability grouping in secondary school: a best-evidence synthesis, *Review of Educational Research*, 60: 471–99.

Slavin, R.E. (1996) *Education for All*. Lisse: Swets and Zeitlinger.

Slee, R. (1995) *Changing Theories and Practices of Discipline*. London: Falmer Press.

Slee, R. (1998) High reliability organisations and liability students – the politics of recognition, in R. Slee, S. Tomlinson with G. Weiner (eds) *School Effectiveness for Whom?* London and Bristol, PA: Falmer.

Slee, R., Tomlinson, S. with Weiner, G. (eds) (1998) *School Effectiveness for Whom?* London and Bristol, PA: Falmer.

Slee, R. and Weiner, G. (1998) Introduction: school effectiveness for whom?, in R. Slee, S. Tomlinson with G. Weiner (eds) *School Effectiveness for Whom?* London and Bristol, PA: Falmer.

Smith, L.J., Maxwell, S., Lowther, D., Hacker, D., Bol, L. and Nunnery, J. (1997) Activities in schools and programmes experiencing the most and least early implementation successes, *School Effectiveness and School Improvement*, 8: 125–50.

Smith, M. (1972) Equality of educational opportunity: the basic findings reconsidered, in F. Mosteller and D. Moynihan (eds) *On Equality of Educational Opportunity*. New York: Vintage Books.

Smyth, J. (ed.) (1993) *A Socially Critical View of the Self-Managing School*. London and Washington, DC: Falmer.

Spooner, B. (1998) A tale of two schools in one city: Foxwood and Cross Green, in R. Slee, S. Tomlinson with G. Weiner (eds) *School Effectiveness for Whom?* London and Bristol, PA: Falmer.

Stanley, J.R. (1986) Sex and the quiet schoolgirl, *British Journal of Sociology of Education*, 7: 275–86.

Stark, M. (1998) No slow fixes either, in L. Stoll and K. Myers, *No Quick Fixes: Perspectives on Schools in Difficulty*. London and Washington, DC: Falmer Press.

State Services Commission (1997) *Achieving Excellence*. Wellington: SSC.

Stoll, L. and Fink, D. (1996) *Changing Our Schools*. Buckingham and Philadelphia: Open University Press.

Stoll, L. and Fink, D. (1998) The cruising school: the unidentified ineffective school, in L. Stoll and K. Myers (eds) *No Quick Fixes: Perspectives on Schools in Difficulty*. London and Washington, DC: Falmer Press.

Stoll, L. and Myers, K. (eds) (1998) *No Quick Fixes: Perspectives on Schools in Difficulty*. London and Washington, DC: Falmer Press.

Stoll, L. and Reynolds, D. (1997) Connecting school effectiveness and school improvement, what have we learnt in the last ten years?, in T. Townsend (ed.) *Restructuring and Quality: Issues for Tomorrow's Schools*. London and New York: Routledge.

Stringfield, S. (1995) Attempting to enhance students' learning through innovative programs: the case for schools evolving into high reliability organisations, *School Effectiveness and School Improvement*, 6: 67–96.

Stringfield, S. (1997) Underlying the chaos: factors explaining exemplary US elementary schools and the case for high-reliability organisations, in T. Townsend (ed.) *Restructuring and Quality: Issues for Tomorrow's Schools*. London and New York: Routledge.

Stringfield, S. (1998) An anatomy of ineffectiveness, in L. Stoll and K. Myers, *No Quick Fixes: Perspectives on Schools in Difficulty*. London and Washington DC: Falmer Press.

Stringfield, S., Datnow, A., Herman, R. and Berkeley, C. (1997a) Introduction to the Memphis restructuring initiative, *School Effectiveness and School Improvement*, 8: 3–35.

Stringfield, S. and Herman, R. (1996) Assessment of the state of school effectiveness research in the United States of America, *School Effectiveness and School Improvement*, 7: 159–80.

Stringfield, S., Millsap, M., Herman, R., Yoder, N., Brigham, N., Nesselrodt, P. *et al.* (1997b) *Special Strategies Studies Final Report*. Washington, DC: US Department of Education.

Summers, A.A. and Wolfe, B.L. (1977) Do schools make a difference?, *American Economic Review*, 67: 639–52.

Taskforce to Review Education Administration (1988) *Administering for Excellence*. Wellington: Government Print.

Taylor, S., Rizvi, F., Lingard, B. and Henry, M. (1997) *Educational Policy and the Politics of Change*. London and New York: Routledge.

Teddlie, C. and Stringfield, S. (1993) *Schools Make a Difference: Lessons Learned from a Ten Year Study of School Effects*. New York: Teachers College Press.

Teddlie, C., Stringfield, S., Wimpleberg, R. and Kirby, P. (1989) Contextual differences

Rea

in models for effective schooling in the USA, in B. Creemers, T. Peters and D. Reynolds (eds) *School Effectiveness and School Improvement*. Amsterdam: Swets and Zeitlinger.

Thomas, S. and Mortimore, P. (1994) *Report on Value-Added Analysis of 1993 GCSE Examination Results in Lancashire*. London: Curriculum Studies Department, Institute of Education, University of London.

Thrupp, M. (1995) The school mix effect: the history of an enduring problem in educational research, policy and practice, *British Journal of Sociology of Education*, 16: 183–203.

Thrupp, M. (1996) The school mix effect: a study of the likely effect of school social class composition on school processes and student achievement in four New Zealand schools. Unpublished PhD thesis, Victoria University, Wellington.

Thrupp, M. (1997) ERO's reviews and audits: how seriously should we take them? Paper presented at the New Zealand Association for Research in Education Conference, Auckland, 4–7 December.

Thrupp, M. (1998) Exploring the politics of blame: school inspection and its contestation in New Zealand and England, *Comparative Education*, 34: 195–209.

Times Educational Supplement (1996a) Inspectors to take account of deprivation, 23 February.

Tomlinson, S. (1997) Sociological perspectives on failing schools. Paper presented at the International Sociology of Education Conference, Sheffield, UK, 3–5 January.

Tomlinson, S. (1998) A tale of one school in one city: Hackney Downs, in R. Slee, S. Tomlinson with G. Weiner (eds) *School Effectiveness for Whom?* London and Bristol, PA: Falmer.

Townsend, T. (1997) Afterword: problems and possibilities for tomorrow's schools, in T. Townsend (ed.) *Restructuring and Quality: Issues for Tomorrow's Schools*. London and New York: Routledge.

Tyack, D. and Cuban, L. (1995) *Tinkering Towards Utopia: A Century of Public School Reform*. Cambridge, MA and London: Harvard University Press.

United States National Commission on Excellence in Education (1983) *A Nation at Risk*. Washington, DC: Government Printing Office.

Van Fossen, B.E., Jones, J.D. and Spade, J.D. (1987) Curriculum tracking and status maintenance, *Sociology of Education*, 60: 104–22.

Walford, G. (1994) *Choice and Equity in Education*. London and New York: Cassell.

Walford, G. (1997) Privatisation and selection, in R. Pring and G. Walford, *Affirming the Comprehensive Ideal*. London and Washington, DC: Falmer.

Walford, G. and Pring, R. (1997) Introduction, in R. Pring and G. Walford, *Affirming the Comprehensive Ideal*. London and Washington, DC: Falmer.

Walker, J.C. (1985) Rebels with our applause? A critique of resistance theory in Paul Willis' ethnography of schooling, *Journal of Education*, 167: 63–83.

Walker, J.C. (1986) Romanticising resistance, romanticising culture: problems in Willis' theory of cultural production, *British Journal of Sociology of Education*, 7: 59–80.

Walker, J.C. (1988) *Louts and Legends*. Sydney: Allen and Unwin.

Waslander, S., Hughes, D., Lauder, H., McGlinn, J., Newton, S., Thrupp, M. and Dupuis, A. (1994) *The Smithfield Project Phase One: An Overview of Activities*. Wellington: Ministry of Education.

Waslander, S. and Thrupp, M. (1995) Choice, competition and segregation: an empirical analysis of a New Zealand secondary school market 1990–1993, *Journal of Education Policy*, 10: 1–26.

Wells, A.S. (1996) African American students' views of school choice, in B. Fuller, R.F.

Elmore with G. Orfield (eds) *Who Chooses, Who Loses?* New York and London: Teachers College Press.

Whatford, C. (1998) Rising from the ashes, in L. Stoll and K. Myers (eds) *No Quick Fixes: Perspectives on Schools in Difficulty*. London and Washington, DC: Falmer Press.

Whitty, G., Power, S. and Halpin, D. (1998) *Devolution and Choice in Education*. Buckingham: Open University Press.

Willis, P. (1977) *Learning to Labour*. Farnborough: Saxton House.

Willms, J.D. (1986) Social class segregation and its relationship to pupils' O grade examination results in Scotland, *American Sociological Review*, 51: 224–41.

Willms, J.D. (1992) *Monitoring School Performance*. London: Falmer Press.

Wilson, A., Houghton, R., Honigberg, V. and McAlvey, L. (1995) *School Operations Grant Review*. Dunedin: University of Otago Consulting Group.

Wilson, A.B. (1959) Residential segregation of social classes and aspirations of high school boys, *American Sociological Review*, 24: 836–45.

Wilson, C. and Dupuis, A. (1992) Poverty and performance, *Set*, 1: 15.

Wimpleberg, R.K., Teddlie, C. and Stringfield, S. (1989) Sensitivity to context: the past and future of effective schools research, *Educational Administration Quarterly*, 25: 82–107.

Woodhead, C. (1996) Letter, *Times Educational Supplement*, 1 March, p. 23.

Woods, P. (1979) *The Divided School*. London: Routledge and Kegan Paul.

Woods, P. (1990) *The Happiest Days?* Basingstoke: Falmer Press.

Wylie, C. (1997) *Self-managing Schools Seven Years On: What Have We Learnt?* Wellington: New Zealand Council for Educational Research.

Index

References in italic indicate figures or tables

DEVOLUTION AND CHOICE IN EDUCATION
THE SCHOOL, THE STATE AND THE MARKET

Geoff Whitty, Sally Power and David Halpin

- What is the background to, and significance of, policies of devolution and choice in education that are currently fashionable in many parts of the world?
- What has been the actual impact of these policies on school managers, teachers, students and local communities?
- How might equity be preserved in systems of education where increased responsibility is delegated to the level of the school?

This book examines recent school reforms in England and Wales, the USA, Australia, New Zealand and Sweden. It suggests that, at the same time as appearing to devolve power to individual schools and parents, governments have actually been increasing their own capacity to 'steer' the system at a distance. Focusing particularly on the 'quasi-markets' favoured by the New Right, the authors review the research evidence on the impact of the reforms to date. They conclude that there is no strong evidence to support the educational benefits claimed by the proponents of the reforms and considerable evidence that they are enabling advantaged schools and advantaged parents to maximize their advantages. They argue that, if these damaging equity effects are to be avoided, there is an urgent need to redress the balance between consumer rights and citizen rights in education.

Contents
Part I: Mapping education reform – Introduction – Restructuring public education in five countries – Devolution and choice: a global phenomenon? – Part II: The school, the state and the market – School managers, the state and the market – Changing teachers' work – Classrooms and the curriculum – The self-managing school and the community – Part III: Problems and prospects in the politics of education – Effectiveness, efficiency and equity – Beyond devolution and choice – References – Index.

176pp   0 335 19711 6 (Paperback)   0 335 19712 4 (Hardback)

MARKETS, CHOICE AND EQUITY IN EDUCATION

Sharon Gewirtz, Stephen J. Ball and Richard Bowe

- What has been the impact of parental choice and competition upon schools?
- How do parents choose schools for their children?
- Who are the winners and losers in the education market?

These important and fundamental questions are discussed in this book which draws upon a three year intensive study of market forces in education. The authors carefully examine the complexities of parental choice and school responses to the introduction of market forces in education. Particular attention is paid to issues of opportunity and equity, and patterns of access and involvement related to gender, ethnicity and social class are identified.

This is the first comprehensive study of market dynamics in education and it highlights the specificity and idiosyncrasies of local education markets. However, the book is not confined to descriptions of these markets but also offers a systematic theorization of the education market, its operation and consequences. It will be of particular interest to students on BEd and Masters courses in education, headteachers and senior managers in schools, and policy analysts.

Contents
Researching education markets – Choice and class: parents in the marketplace – An analysis of local market relations – Managers and markets: school organization in transition – Schooling in the marketplace: a semiological analysis – Internal practices: institutional responses to competition – Choice, equity and control – Glossary of terms – References – Index.

224pp   0 335 19369 2 (Paperback)   0 335 19370 6 (Hardback)